Welcome to

THE

EVERYTHING

Family Guides

THESE HANDY, PORTABLE BOOKS are designed to be the perfect traveling companions. Whether you're traveling within a tight family budget or feeling the urge to splurge, you will find all you need to create a memorable family vacation.

Use these books to plan your trips, and then take them along with you for easy reference. Does Jimmy want to go sailing? Or maybe Jane wants to go to the local hobby shop. *The Everything® Family Guides* offer many ways to entertain kids of all ages while also ensuring you get the most out of your time away from home.

Review this book cover to cover to give you great ideas before you travel, and stick it in your backpack or diaper bag to use as a quick reference guide for activities, attractions, and excursions you want to experience. Let *The Everything® Family Guides* help you travel the world, and you'll discover that vacationing with the whole family can be filled with fun and exciting adventures.

🧳 TRAVEL TIP

Quick, handy tips

🌐 HOT SPOT

Places not to be missed

≡ FAST FACT

Details to make your trip more enjoyable

THE EVERYTHING®
— Family Guides —

The Walt Disney World Resort, Universal Studios, and Greater Orlando,
5th Edition

Dear Reader,

Did you know that Orlando is the number one vacation spot in the world? If you are holding this book, rest assured that you will find tips and hints not found in any other Orlando guide.

I have lived in Orlando since 1989, worked at Walt Disney World, and am able to give you the inside scoop on many attractions, dining, accommodations, and entertainment for the entire Orlando area. Whatever your budget, you'll see that I provide plenty of information for you to make the right decisions for you and your family.

Vacations take planning, and my only hope is that this book makes this challenge much easier for you. Curl up with a highlighter in hand and start marking everything of interest to you. The key is to gravitate toward activities that you and your family find interesting so everyone has a great time.

Feel free to e-mail me with any questions or concerns you may have, at *cheryl@misscharming.com*. I'll be glad to help you connect the dots!

Cheryl Charming

THE

EVERYTHING®

FAMILY GUIDE TO THE

WALT DISNEY WORLD RESORT®, UNIVERSAL STUDIOS®, AND GREATER ORLANDO

5TH EDITION

A complete guide to the best hotels, restaurants, parks, and must-see attractions

Cheryl Charming

Avon, Massachusetts

To my mother, Babs

• • •

Innovation Director: Paula Munier
Editorial Director: Laura M. Daly
Associate Copy Chief: Sheila Zwiebel
Acquisitions Editor: Lisa Laing
Development Editor: Brett Palana Shanahan
Production Editor: Casey Ebert

Director of Manufacturing: Susan Beale
Production Project Manager:
Michelle Roy Kelly
Prepress: Erick DaCosta, Matt LeBlanc
Interior Layout: Heather Barrett,
Brewster Brownville, Colleen
Cunningham, Jennifer Oliveira

• • •

An Everything® Series Book.
Everything® and everything.com® are registered trademarks of F+W Media, Inc.

Published by Adams Media, a division of F+W Media, Inc
57 Littlefield Street, Avon, MA 02322 U.S.A.
www.adamsmedia.com

ISBN 10: 1-59869-390-5
ISBN 13: 978-1-59869-390-4

Printed in the United States of America.

10 9 8 7 6 5 4 3

Library of Congress Cataloging-in-Publication Data
Charming, Cheryl.
The everything family guide to the Walt Disney World Resort, Universal Studios, and greater Orlando / Cheryl Charming.
p. cm.
Includes index.
ISBN-13: 978-1-59869-390-4 (pbk.)
ISBN-10: 1-59869-390-5 (pbk.)
1. Walt Disney World (Fla.)—Guidebooks. 2. Universal Studios Florida (Orlando, Fla.
: Amusement park)—Guidebooks. 3. Orlando Region (Fla.)—Guidebooks. I. Title.
GV1853.3.F62W34315 2007
791'.06'875924—dc22
2007019138

This publication is designed to provide accurate and authoritative information with regard to the subject matter covered. It is sold with the understanding that the publisher is not engaged in rendering legal, accounting, or other professional advice. If legal advice or other expert assistance is required, the services of a competent professional person should be sought.
—From a *Declaration of Principles* jointly adopted by a Committee of the American Bar Association and a Committee of Publishers and Associations

Many of the designations used by manufacturers and sellers to distinguish their products are claimed as trademarks. Where those designations appear in this book and Adams Media was aware of a trademark claim, the designations have been printed with initial capital letters.

The following are registered trademarks of The Walt Disney Company: Adventureland, Audio-Animatronics, Disney's Animal Kingdom Park, Epcot, Fantasyland, Frontierland, Indiana Jones Epic Stunt Spectacular!, Magic Kingdom Park, Main Street U.S.A., Mickey Mouse, Tomorrowland, The Twilight Zone: Tower of-Terror, Walt Disney World. Universal Studios is a registered trademark of Universal Studios, Inc.

This book is available at quantity discounts for bulk purchases.
For information, please call 1-800-289-0963.

Visit the entire Everything® series at *www.everything.com*

Contents

Acknowledgments

A big O-Town thank-you full of mile-high fireworks to my agent, June Clark, for all of her hard work and a thrill ride of thanks to my editor, Lisa Laing, at Adams Media.

The Top Ten Family Attractions in Orlando

1. "Wishes" Fireworks Show (Magic Kingdom)

2. "Believe" Shamu Show (SeaWorld)

3. Cirque du Soleil: La Nouba (Downtown Disney)

4. IllumiNations: Reflections of Earth (Epcot)

5. Blue Man Group (Citywalk)

6. Fantasmic! (Disney-MGM Studios)

7. Kilimanjaro Safaris (Disney's Animal Kingdom)

8. Kennedy Space Center

9. The Festival of the Lion King (Disney's Animal Kingdom)

10. The Living Seas (Epcot)

Introduction

What you're about to read is the all-new fifth edition of *The Everything® Family Guide to the Walt Disney World Resort, Universal Studios, and Greater Orlando*. This travel guide was written to help you make the most of your vacation experience. Unless you're planning to spend several weeks and an absolute fortune, there's no possible way that you'll be able to experience everything the Greater Orlando area has to offer. Therefore, you'll have to make decisions about which theme parks you want to visit, which attractions within those theme parks you want to experience, what shows and parades you want to see, and which restaurants you want to patronize.

The WDW Resort is a city unto itself, but it's a 30,500-acre (47 square-mile) city unlike any other found on this planet. Yet, with everything that already exists in this ultimate vacation destination, less than one-quarter of the total acreage of the resort complex has been developed. Thus, in the years and decades to come, you can bet that the WDW Resort will continue to evolve and provide many future generations with a taste of Disney magic and the wholesome family vacation experience that Walt Disney himself (along with his brother Roy) intended for all who visit this unique resort.

Located less than a fifteen-minute drive from the WDW Resort is another fast-growing tourist destination, which is the second most popular theme park complex in the Greater Orlando area. Universal Studio Resort offers some of the most incredible rides, shows, and attractions found anywhere in the world, yet here you'll find a very different type of vacation experience.

Originally, when Universal Studios Florida opened, it was a single, medium-sized theme park that could be experienced within a day. Now, this park has expanded dramatically, and as you'll read later in this book, it continues to go through massive construction and development. As a result, vacationers can easily plan on spending two or three full days experiencing everything there is to see and do at Universal Studio Resort, which now comprises two theme parks, the City-Walk area, and three resort hotels.

Located in between WDW and Universal Studios is the third most popular theme park attraction in Orlando—SeaWorld. This marine park offers an up-close look at marine life, like dolphins and whales, plus it features an assortment of marine-related rides, shows, attractions, tours, and adventure camps.

Inside this book you'll find detailed descriptions of all the activities and things there are to see and do at the WDW Resort, Universal Studios Florida Resort, SeaWorld, and other popular tourist attractions. There are all sorts of tips and suggestions on how you can save money while making the most of your vacation.

To help you choose which rides, shows, and attractions are most worth experiencing while visiting the Magic Kingdom (and all of the theme parks at the WDW Resort), this book offers a star-based rating system. The ratings are based on the age group for which each attraction will hold the most appeal. For each ride, you'll see a chart listing several age groups, plus a one- to three-star rating for that attraction.

★	Rides and attractions that earned just one star aren't worth waiting for and could be skipped, especially if your time within the theme park is limited.
★★	Rides and attractions that earned two stars are good, but they don't fall into the "must-see" category.
★★★	The rides and attractions that earned three stars are definitely worth seeing and should not be missed.
N.S.	This denotes rides and attractions that are "not suitable" for a specific age group.

These ratings are only recommendations. If you have a mature nine-year-old, he or she may very well enjoy a ride, show, or attraction that's more suitable for an eleven- to fifteen-year-old. As a parent, that's a judgment call you'll need to make based on the information provided within this book and after seeing the ride, show, or attraction for yourself once you get to the theme park.

This book is "unofficial," which means that it is in no way authorized or sanctioned by the Walt Disney Company, Universal Studios, SeaWorld, or any other attraction, travel agency, hotel chain, restaurant, or airline. Thus, this book has the freedom to tell it like it is, and to offer you money- and time-saving advice that you won't find in any other travel guide or vacation-planning book.

As you read through this book, know that the various theme parks and resorts are constantly evolving. New rides, attractions, shows, parades, shops, restaurants, and activities are always being updated, changed, or canceled. Thus, when you actually visit Orlando, don't be surprised if you encounter something new and different that's not described in this book.

The Magic Kingdom

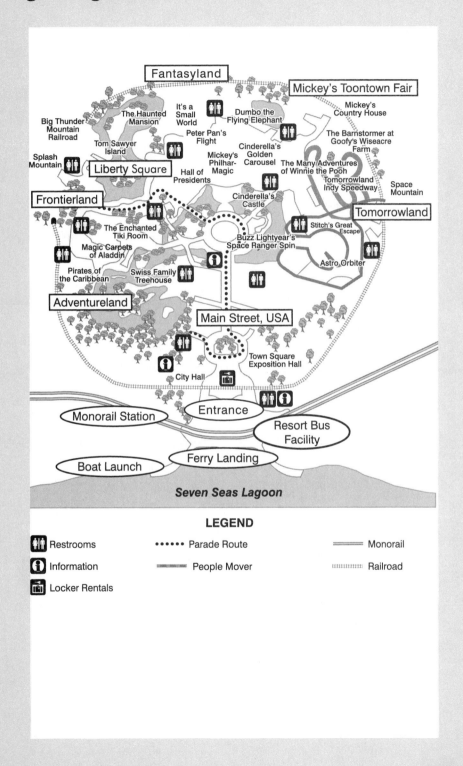

Fantasyland

Mickey's Toontown Fair

Big Thunder Mountain Railroad

The Haunted Mansion

It's a Small World

Dumbo the Flying Elephant

Mickey's Country House

Peter Pan's Flight

The Barnstormer at Goofy's Wiseacre Farm

Tom Sawyer Island

Cinderella's Golden Carousel

Splash Mountain

Mickey's Philhar-Magic

The Many Adventures of Winnie the Pooh

Liberty Square

Hall of Presidents

Tomorrowland Indy Speedway

Space Mountain

Frontierland

Cinderella's Castle

Tomorrowland

Stitch's Great Escape

The Enchanted Tiki Room

Buzz Lightyear's Space Ranger Spin

Magic Carpets of Aladdin

Astro Orbiter

Pirates of the Caribbean

Swiss Family Treehouse

Adventureland

Main Street, USA

Town Square Exposition Hall

City Hall

Entrance

Monorail Station

Resort Bus Facility

Boat Launch

Ferry Landing

Seven Seas Lagoon

LEGEND

- Restrooms
- Information
- Locker Rentals
- •••••• Parade Route
- People Mover
- Monorail
- Railroad

1

Germa

China

Norway

Mexico

Showcase Plaza

Test Track

Mission: SPACE

East Side
Innoventions

Future World

Universe of Energy

West Side
Innoventions

Imagination!

Space Ship
Earth

Leave a
Legacy

The Land

Entrance

The Living Seas

Monorail Station

Resort Bus
Facility

Italy

The American Adventure

Japan

Morocco

World Showcase

IllumiNations

World Showcase Lagoon

France

United Kingdom

International Gateway

Canada

World Showplace Events Pavilion

	Restrooms		Attractions
	Information	•••••	Parade Route
	Locker Rentals		Monorail

The Disney-MGM Studios

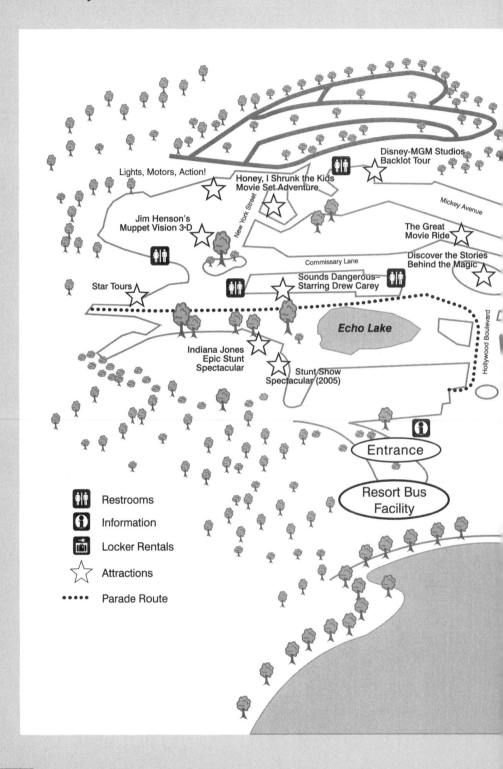

Lights, Motors, Action!

Honey, I Shrunk the Kids Movie Set Adventure

Disney-MGM Studios Backlot Tour

Jim Henson's Muppet Vision 3-D

Mickey Avenue

The Great Movie Ride

Discover the Stories Behind the Magic

Star Tours

Commissary Lane

Sounds Dangerous— Starring Drew Carey

New York Street

Echo Lake

Hollywood Boulevard

Indiana Jones Epic Stunt Spectacular

Stunt Show Spectacular (2005)

Entrance

Resort Bus Facility

Restrooms

Information

Locker Rentals

Attractions

Parade Route

ey Into Narnia

Walt Disney:
One Man's Dream

Voyage of The
Little Mermaid

Animation Courtyard

The Magic of
Disney Animation

Playhouse
Disney

Rock 'n' Roller Coaster
Starring Aerosmith

Sunset Boulevard

Beauty and
the Beast
Live on Stage

The Twilight Zone
Tower of Terror

Fantasmic!

Resort Boat
Facility

Disney's Animal Kingdom

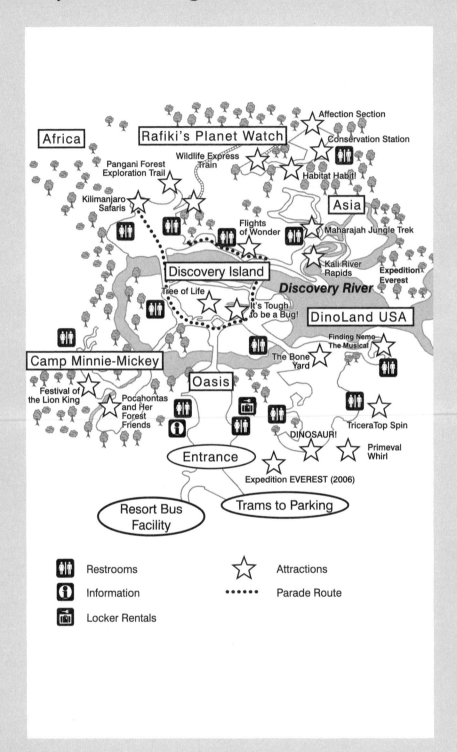

Affection Section

Africa

Rafiki's Planet Watch

Conservation Station

Wildlife Express Train

Pangani Forest Exploration Trail

Habitat Habit!

Asia

Kilimanjaro Safaris

Flights of Wonder

Maharajah Jungle Trek

Discovery Island

Kali River Rapids

Expedition Everest

Tree of Life

Discovery River

It's Tough to be a Bug!

DinoLand USA

Finding Nemo— The Musical

Camp Minnie-Mickey

The Bone Yard

Festival of the Lion King

Pocahontas and Her Forest Friends

Oasis

TriceraTop Spin

DINOSAUR!

Entrance

Primeval Whirl

Expedition EVEREST (2006)

Resort Bus Facility

Trams to Parking

Restrooms   ☆ **Attractions**

Information   •••••• **Parade Route**

Locker Rentals

Downtown Disney

Universal Studios Florida

New York

42nd St

Revenge
of the Mummy

The Blues Br

TWISTER...
Ride It Out

57th St

Delancey St

South St

Park Ave

Amblin Ave

7th Ave

Production Central

Stage 54

South St

Battery Park

8th Ave

Hollywood

Nickelodeon
Studios

Jimmy Neutron's
Nicktoon Blast

Shrek 4-D

Hollywood Blvd

Nickelodeon Way

Plaza Of The Stars

Rodeo Dr

Lucy—A Tribute ℠

Hard Rock
Cafe

TERMINATOR 2:
3-D BATTLE ACROSS TIME

Entrance

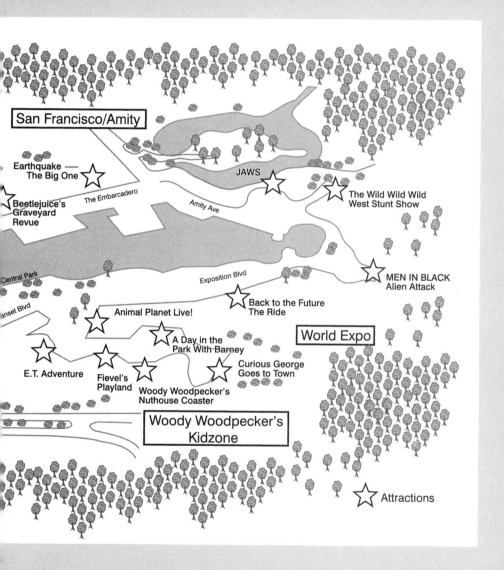

San Francisco/Amity

Earthquake —
The Big One

Beetlejuice's
Graveyard
Revue

The Embarcadero

Amity Ave

JAWS

The Wild Wild Wild
West Stunt Show

Central Park

Exposition Blvd

MEN IN BLACK
Alien Attack

Sunset Blvd

Animal Planet Live!

Back to the Future
The Ride

World Expo

E.T. Adventure

A Day in the
Park With Barney

Fievel's
Playland

Woody Woodpecker's
Nuthouse Coaster

Curious George
Goes to Town

Woody Woodpecker's
Kidzone

Attractions

Universal Escape's Islands of Adventure

Jurassic Park
River Adventure

Camp
Jurassic

Pteranodon
Flyers

Triceratops
Encounter

Popeye & Bluto's
Bilge Rat Barges

Toon Lagoon®

Dudley Do-Right's
Ripsaw Falls

Toon Trolley
Beach Bash

Me Ship, The Olive

The Amazing
Adventures of
Spider–Man

Port of Entry

Doctor Doom's
Fearfall

Marvel Super Hero Island

Incredible Hulk
Coaster

Storm Force
Accelatron

Greater Orlando Metro Area

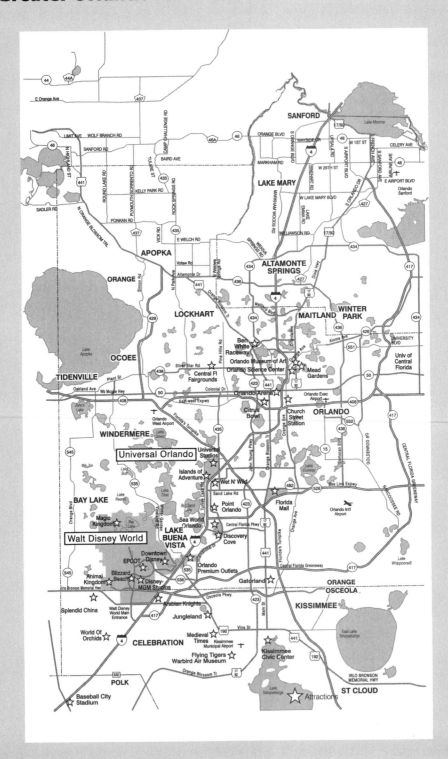

CHAPTER 1

Preparing for Your Vacation

ORLANDO IS THE NUMBER ONE vacation destination in the world. More than 50 million people visit this city every year. Know that you will not be able to see everything O-Town has to offer in one visit, but that's alright because you can return many times. Your first step in planning an Orlando vacation is to determine how long your vacation is going to last and how much money you have in your travel budget. Next, you'll need to book your airfare and hotel accommodations, and possibly reserve a rental car. This chapter will help you save money and time as you take care of these initial vacation-planning steps.

Flying to Orlando

All of the airlines listed in this section (and possibly a few others) offer competitive rates and travel packages to the Orlando International Airport, so be sure to shop around for the best airfares and flights. Keep in mind that not all of the airlines will offer service from your home city.

As a general rule, you want to book your airfare as far in advance as possible. Many airlines offer the best prices if you book and pay for your tickets twenty-one days in advance You can, however, also obtain good fares if you make your reservations (and pay for your airline tickets) fourteen or seven days early. When making your travel plans, try to have the most flexible schedule possible. If your schedule permits, you'll almost always get a better airfare if your stay includes a Saturday night.

Keep in mind, with "discounted" or "special" airfares, the tickets will not be refundable, and there will be a fee to change the ticket's booked travel dates. The change fee is usually between $100 and $150, plus the price difference in the airfare itself. To avoid this change fee, most airlines will allow you to fly standby; however, this does not guarantee you a seat on a specific flight, and if you're traveling with a family and the flight you're trying to get on is close to capacity, your chances of all getting on the same flight are slim, especially during peak travel periods.

TRAVEL TIP

To make your vacation the best it can possibly be, you'll want to invest some time before you depart to properly plan your trip. Especially if you're traveling with children or a group of people, the more preplanning you do now, the more organized and relaxing your trip will be when it actually begins.

If you choose to use your frequent-flier miles to book your airline ticket to Orlando, keep in mind that seats may be difficult to reserve during peak travel periods, so make your reservations early. The advantages of using a frequent-flier ticket are that it's free and most airlines allow you to change your travel plans at the last minute with no penalties or fees.

Always ask the airline reservation representative you speak with for the lowest airfare available. After an airfare is quoted to you, ask again if it is the best deal. Next, ask if there are flights to and from Orlando at around the same times as the ones quoted to you that would make the airfare less expensive. You won't often be quoted the absolute lowest prices the first time you ask. Sometimes, airlines will offer discounted "online-only" fares exclusively from their Web site. For example, US Airways' Web site is at *www.usairways.com.*

Also, check the travel section of your local newspaper for advertised special fares and promotions. You can make a reservation that will be held for twenty-four hours without having to pay for the ticket, so make an unpaid reservation and then shop around by calling additional airlines.

═FAST FACT

If you're traveling cross-country, red-eye (overnight) flights that leave the West Coast between 10:00 P.M. and midnight and arrive in Orlando the following morning are almost always the cheapest flights available. While most people hate flying all night, you can sometimes save up to several hundred dollars when traveling between the West Coast and the East Coast via a red-eye flight on any airline.

Strategies for the Best Airfare

There are several alternatives available to you when it comes to shopping around for the best airfares. You can go to the airport and visit a ticket counter, or book your travel directly with the airline via telephone or its Web site.

You can also surf the Internet and visit the various travel-related Web sites such as Travelocity.com, Hotwire.com, Priceline.com, Last-MinuteTravel.com, or Orbitz.com (described later in this chapter).

Another alternative is to call a travel agent and have her or him do the busywork for you. Travel agents have computer systems that allow them to search for flight availability on all airlines at once. Most travel agents will be happy to work with you over the telephone, so it's not necessary to take time out of your busy schedule during business hours to visit a travel agent's office in person.

When choosing a travel agent, find someone who comes highly recommended by someone you trust. Travel agents can be extremely helpful and save you money, but some will purposely quote you higher-priced airfares since they're receiving a commission from the airline based on the price of the ticket they sell. If you're a member of AAA or have an American Express card, both of these companies offer highly reputable travel agencies that offer their services either in person or by telephone to members.

Finally, you might want to look into package deals offered by the various airlines. Many packages include airfare, hotel, rental car, and perhaps meals or show tickets. Most airlines have a separate "Vacation Package" reservation department that's different from the regular airline reservation department. The Walt Disney Travel Company also offers a handful of discounted packages to the WDW Resort (407) 939-7675.

 TRAVEL TIP

To save money, consider using public transportation to get to the airport in your home city. It'll almost always be cheaper than parking your own car at the airport. The cheapest option is to have a friend or family member drop you off at the airport and pick you up when you return. Another option is to use a door-to-door shuttle bus service, which is usually cheaper than a taxi, limo, or town car service.

The Orlando International Airport

The Orlando International Airport is the closest major airport to all of the theme parks, resorts, and attractions within the Greater Orlando area. If you'll be flying to Orlando, chances are this is the airport you'll be flying into. While this list is subject to change, the major airlines that service this airport include:

AeroMexico: ☎(800) 237-6639

Air Canada: ☎(800) 247-2262

AirJamaica: ☎(800) 523-5585

AirTran Airways: ☎(800) AIR-TRAN

AirTransat: ☎(877) 872-6728

Alaska Airlines: ☎(800) 252-7522

American Airlines: ☎(800) 433-7300

American Eagle: ☎(800) 422-7300

AmericaWest Airlines: ☎(800) 235-9292

ANA: ☎(800) 235-9262

ATA: ☎(800) 225-2995

Bahamasair: ☎(800) 222-4262

British Airways: ☎(800) AIR-WAYS

Champion Air: ☎(800) 225-5658

ConJet: ☎(800) 809-7777

Continental: ☎(800) 523-3273

Copa Airlines: ☎(800) 359-2672

Delta Airlines/Delta Express: ☎(800) 221-1212

El Al: ☎(800) 223-6700

Frontier: ☎(800) 432-1359

Iberia: ☎(800) 772-4642

Icelander: ☎(800) 223-5500

JetBlue: ☎(800) 538-2583

LTU: ☎(800) 888-0200

Martinair: ☎(800) 627-8462

Mexicana: ☎(800) 531-7921

Midwest Airlines: ☎(800) 452-2022

Northwest Airlines/KLM: ☎(800) 225-2525

Saudia: ☎(800) 472-8342

Song: ☎(800) 359-7664

Southwest Airlines: ☎(800) 435-9792

Spirit Airlines: ☎(800) 772-7117

United: ☎(800) 241-6522

US Airways: ☎(800) 428-4322; Vacation Packages ☎(800) 455-0123

Vanguard Airlines: ☎(800) 826-4827

Varig Brazil: ☎(800) 468-2744

Virgin Atlantic: ☎(800) 862-8621

Zoom: ☎(866) 359-9666

Note: A handful of other airlines also operate charter flights to and from Orlando and other major U.S. cities and foreign countries. For more information about the Orlando International Airport, you can call ☎(407) 825-2001 or visit the airport's Web site at ✎www.orlandoairports.net.

TRAVEL TIP

If you're planning to meet people in Orlando, be sure they're provided with the appropriate airline, flight number, and departure time/date. With this information, anyone can contact your airline for arrival information or use one of these Web sites: *✎http://flighttracker.lycos.com*, *✎www.travelocity.com*, or *✎www.flightarrivals.com.*

If you're driving from the airport to the Walt Disney World (WDW) Resort, there are multiple routes that'll get you there. One direct route is to take the north exit from the airport to the Beeline Expressway West (Route 528). Get onto I-4 West and then follow signs to the WDW Resort. You'll want to exit I-4 at either Exit 26B or Exit 25, depending on your final destination within the huge resort complex. Another is to take 417 straight to WDW. The trip is less than twenty-five miles and should take about thirty minutes (without traffic).

Mears Motor Shuttles offers van service to the various hotels at the WDW Resort (as well as nearby areas) from the Orlando airport (and back). The cost is around $20 each way or $40 round trip for adults, $15 one way or $30 round trip for kids (ages four to eleven), and free to kids under age four. These shuttles leave the airport every fifteen minutes or so and can be picked up right outside of the airport terminals. For reservations, call (407) 423-5566 (*www.mearstransportation.com*).

Taxi service is available outside of the airport's main terminals, but this is one of the more expensive ways to reach the WDW Resort. Check with the Ground Transportation Information Desk located inside the airport for various other transportation options to get you from the airport to your hotel in the Orlando area. You can also call the Yellow Cab Company (a fleet of bright orange cars and vans) at (407) 699-9999.

Orlando/Sanford International Airport

The Orlando/Sanford International Airport is a smaller airport located only thirty-five miles east of Walt Disney World (between Orlando and Daytona Beach). It's a straight shot on no-toll I-4 and some say that the airfare is half the price of what it costs to fly into the Orlando International airport. Most flights are European, but for America, Allegiant Air offers roundtrip flights from Allentown, PA; Boston/Portsmouth, NH; Boston/Worcester, MA; Cedar Rapids, IA; Chicago/Rockford, IL; Des Moines, IA; Lansing, MI; McAllen, TX (seasonal); Newburgh, NY (New York City area); Roanoke, VA; Sioux Falls, SD; South Bend, IN; Springfield, MO; St. Louis/MidAmerica (Belleville, IL); Toledo, OH (Detroit area); and Youngstown/Warren, OH. It's worth checking into if you plan to rent a car while in Orlando. Every little bit helps. You can contact them at *www.AllegiantAir.com* or (702) 505-8888.

Airport Security Information

Security is extremely tight at all U.S. airports. Be sure to arrive at the airport at least one hour prior to your scheduled departure time and have your driver's license, military ID, or passport ready to show multiple times at various security checkpoints, including the airline ticket counter.

A wide range of items, such as pocket knives, golf clubs, and scissors, cannot be taken aboard any flight as part of a carry-on. For additional security information, point your Web browser to: *www .orlandoairports.net/goaa/security.htm*.

TRAVEL TIP

If you live in a city with multiple airports, or you live between two cities that both have airports, price your airline tickets going to and from each of the airports closest to you. Airlines often offer special deals and promotions from specific airports.

Taking the Train

Located extremely close to the WDW Resort, there's an Amtrak station in Kissimmee, Florida (Amtrak Station Code: KIS). Information about taking an Amtrak train from anywhere in the country to WDW can be obtained by calling (800) USA-RAIL or by visiting the Web site *www.amtrak.com.*

Amtrak offers travel discounts to all students and veterans, as well as to AAA and AARP members who present their membership card when purchasing a train ticket. Amtrak train tickets can be purchased from many travel agents, by visiting any Amtrak ticket office, or by calling Amtrak directly and using a major credit card.

Busing It to Orlando

Greyhound ((800) 229-9424; *www.greyhound.com*) has two bus terminals close to the WDW Resort: one in Orlando (555 North John Young Parkway, Orlando) and the other in Kissimmee (located at 103 East Dakin Avenue, Kissimmee). From these bus terminals, taxi service is available to the WDW Resort, Universal Studios, or any other nearby hotel or destination.

Renting a Car

Just like when making airline reservations, there are several tricks to use when reserving a rental car that will help ensure that you get the lowest rate possible. For starters, reserve your rental car as far in advance as possible (seven days in advance, minimum), and if you can, try to get the weekly rate instead of the daily rate offered by the car rental company. Most rental car companies will apply their weekly rates to five-, six-, or seven-day rentals.

Finding the Best Rate

Especially in tourist areas, like Orlando, the various rental car companies are always running special promotions, so be sure to ask about them, and keep your eyes open for ads from the rental car companies in your local newspaper and in your favorite magazines. In addition, many of the rental car companies provide a discount to AAA members, so after getting the rental car company's best rate, ask for the AAA member discount. The Entertainment Book (described later in this book) also has discount coupons and special offers that apply to many of the popular rental car companies. Finally, visit the various travel-related Web sites (such as *www.travelocity.com*, *www .priceline.com*, or *www.hotwire.com*) for great deals on rental cars.

Some popular credit cards have special promotional deals with the major rental car companies, so call the customer service phone number listed on your credit card and inquire about what deals they offer for renting a car. While you're on the phone with the credit card company, also ask if your credit card automatically provides rental car insurance if you use that credit card to pay for the rental. American Express, Diner's Club, and virtually all Visa and MasterCards (issued as part of an airline's frequent-flier program) automatically offer rental car insurance.

If you think you've found an awesome rental car rate, reserve the car, but continue to shop around. Call three or four other rental car companies and see if they'll beat the deal you've been offered. Many travelers believe that the best-known rental car companies are always the most expensive, but this isn't always the case. You'll often be pleasantly surprised to discover that companies like Hertz, Avis, and National offer highly competitive rates once you take advantage of their special promotional deals, airline frequent-flier discounts, and/ or the AAA (or any auto club) member discount.

◼ TRAVEL TIP

If you're a member of any airline's frequent-flier program, you can often receive a rental car discount from promotional partners of that airline. Check your monthly frequent-flier statement from the airline for information about special rental car offers.

When making a rental car reservation, make sure unlimited mileage is included in the rental price. Some rental car companies charge by the mile, in addition to the daily rental fee, so make sure you understand what's included in the price you're being quoted. Extremely low daily or weekly rental rates often do not include unlimited mileage, and once you travel above the allowed miles, you're charged a hefty fee per mile.

Insurance

No matter what hourly, daily, or weekly rate you're quoted by the rental car companies you call, these rates do not include the various types of optional insurance choices that are offered, nor is tax included in the quoted rate. If you choose to pay for all of the different insurance options, the quoted rate for the rental car often more than doubles. What most travelers don't know, however, is that they do not need all of the optional insurance, because their own regular insurance policies, as well as the travel insurance provided free of charge by some credit card companies, offer more than adequate protection.

Prior to renting a car, call the customer service number for your auto insurance company as well as your homeowner's insurance company. Ask if rental car insurance is automatically offered under your existing policy. If so, you probably don't need any of the insurance offered by the rental car companies. If you rely on your existing insurance, however, and you're forced to make a claim due to an accident in the rental car, your regular insurance rates could go up in the future.

≡ FAST FACT

One benefit of purchasing the optional insurance from the rental car companies is that your existing policies won't be affected if a claim has to be made (assuming any damage or injury claims are under the limit of the insurance you purchase).

Rental Car Companies

The following are rental car companies in the Orlando area:

Alamo: ☎(800) 327-9633
Avis: ☎(800) 831-2847
Budget: ☎(800) 527-0700
Dollar: ☎(800) 800-4000
Econo Car: ☎(800) 665-9001
Enterprise: ☎(800) RENT-A-CAR
E-Z: ☎(407) 352-3131
Hertz: ☎(800) 654-3131
Hertz Gold Club Reservations: ☎(800) CAR-GOLD
National: ☎(800) 227-7368
Payless Car Rental: ☎(800) PAY-LESS
Thrifty: ☎(800) 367-2277

When reserving your vehicle, make sure the rental car company offers airport service (either a pickup at the airport or a free shuttle to their nearby pickup location). All of the nationally known car rental companies including Hertz, Avis, National, Alamo, and Budget are located within a five-minute free shuttle-bus ride from the Orlando airport.

Renters must be at least twenty-five years of age, have proof of insurance coverage, and have a major credit card in their name.

Special Services

Most of the rental car companies will provide child safety seats, either free of charge or for a small daily fee. These seats must be reserved in advance. This will save you the hassle of having to bring your own child safety seats with you on your trip. However, you must bring your own if you want your child to sit in one on the airplane.

If you're a nonsmoker, be sure to ask for a nonsmoking vehicle when you make your reservation. Otherwise, you could get stuck with a car that reeks of smoke.

When you pick up your rental car at the airport, computer-generated driving directions and maps are often provided free of charge from the airport to virtually any location in Florida, including all of the popular hotels and attractions.

 TRAVEL TIP

If you're worried about getting lost, Hertz offers an optional feature in some of its rental cars, called NeverLost. The NeverLost unit identifies exactly where you are at any time, and shows and tells you how to get wherever you want to go. The additional daily cost is about $8 per day. NeverLost must be ordered in advance when making your reservation.

When you pick up the rental car, ask about the rental car company's policy for additional drivers. Typically, when you rent a car, only the person whose name appears on the rental agreement is legally permitted to drive the car, unless additional paperwork is completed. Some rental car companies charge to add additional names to the rental contract, allowing for multiple drivers. The following are often exempt from additional driver charges (but check with the rental car company): the renter's employer or regular fellow employee when on company business; the renter's spouse; the renter's mate, life companion, significant other, or live-in; and disabled renters who have completed a special form.

Final Suggestions

Before leaving the rental agency, ask if you're required to return the car with a full tank of gas, or if you're paying for the gas in advance. If you're required to return the car with a full tank of gas and you fail to do so (which many people do), you'll be billed up to three times the going rate per gallon of gas needed to fill the tank. Before returning the car, find a low-priced gas station and fill the tank with basic unleaded gasoline (the cheapest stuff you can find). This will fulfill your obligation to return the car with a full tank of gas.

When you pick up the car, ask what time the car must be returned to ensure that you won't be billed overtime hours, and ask what the overtime rate is. For example, the policy may state that if you pick up the car at 3:00 P.M., you must return the car before 3:00 P.M. on the day your rental agreement ends or you'll automatically be billed for additional hours at a high rate.

As soon as you pick up your car, before leaving the rental car company's parking lot, make sure there is nothing obviously wrong with the vehicle. If there's a problem, report it immediately. Once you leave the rental car company's parking lot, if you notice a problem, call the rental car company and report it. Likewise, if you get stuck on the road, call the rental car company and report your situation. Free assistance, often including towing services, will be provided, and you'll often be given a replacement rental car.

When returning your car, plan on arriving at the airport about ninety minutes (or even two hours) prior to your scheduled flight time. You will most likely be returning your car several miles from the actual airport, and you'll need to allow ample time to return the car, take the complimentary shuttle bus to your airline terminal, check in at the airline terminal, check your bags, and get to the actual gate. It's a common problem for travelers to miss their flight because they didn't allow enough time to return their rental car, so plan accordingly.

TRAVEL TIP

Before getting behind the wheel, make sure you're totally awake and alert and that you have detailed driving directions. If you're too tired to be driving, take a taxi or shuttle bus to your hotel and pick up your rental car later in the day or the following day. Be sure to call the rental car company and mention your change of plans to avoid being charged.

Your Travel Budget

As you begin to plan your trip, it's important to establish a basic travel budget for yourself and to stick to that budget. Once you reach your destination, you'll no doubt be tempted to dine at fancy restaurants, buy extravagant souvenirs, and participate in costly activities. When creating your budget, you'll want to make allowances for these unplanned splurges, but you'll want to maintain control over your spending at all times. Otherwise, you could easily end up with massive credit card bills after your vacation.

The first step in planning a budget is to figure out how much money you have to spend on your upcoming vacation. Next, determine how many people you'll be traveling with (and paying for), how many days you'll be away, and what you want your travel itinerary to be.

Based on this information, start pricing out airfares, hotel/motel accommodations, rental cars, and the cost of various activities (such as admission to the theme parks and dining). The checklist in this chapter will help you predict some of the costs.

Saving Money

Hopefully, once you've priced out everything, the total price of your planned vacation will be within your proposed budget. Before making your reservations, however, invest some time in shopping around for money-saving deals and/or packages. Finding a coupon or utilizing a deal that'll save you $50 on a hotel, for example, is money that can be used for souvenirs or kept in your bank account.

≡FAST FACT

Unless your budget is unlimited, chances are, once you get to Orlando, you will not be able to afford to do absolutely everything you'd like to during a single trip. Thus, you'll want to use this book (and your firsthand experience) to determine which activities you'd most enjoy, and focus on those to start off with.

Also, you can save money by eating outside of the theme parks. Instead of having the fancy (and sometimes costly) breakfast at your resort every morning during your trip, consider experiencing that breakfast once, then eating off-property on the rest of the mornings to save some money. Obviously, there's something very special (especially for kids) about eating Mickey Mouse–shaped waffles with the Disney characters roaming the dining room and meeting guests. However, this is something that doesn't need to be experienced every morning.

TRAVEL TIP

WDW and Universal resorts (as well as many Orlando-area resorts) have small refrigerators in their rooms, so it's recommended to stop at a grocery store and buy groceries before checking in to the hotel. You are allowed to bring as many cases of water, soda, or alcohol on property that you desire. It also makes it easier to have a bellman take these things to your room instead of hauling them yourself.

If this isn't your first trip to Orlando, you can save a lot of money by staying at a non-Disney or Universal-owned hotel/motel that's close to the theme parks. While you won't experience the legendary service, ambiance, or perks associated with staying at a Disney or Universal-owned hotel, the financial savings will add up quickly.

Budget Checklist

Use this form to help you approximate the cost of your trip to the WDW Resort/Greater Orlando area in advance. Planning your schedule/itinerary before you leave and setting budgetary spending limits will help you enjoy your vacation without going into unexpected debt or spending outside of your budget.

BUDGET CHECKLIST

Expense	Calculation	Totals
Adult airfare	$_____ per ticket × _____ (# of adults)	$_____
Child airfare	$_____ per ticket × _____ (# of children)	$_____
Rental car	$_____ per day/week × _____ (# of days/weeks)	$_____
Insurance/gas	$_____ per day × _____ (# of days)	$_____
Transportation	$_____ per trip × _____ (# of people) × _____ (# of trips)	$_____
Hotel/motel	$_____ per night × _____ (# of rooms) × _____ (# of nights)	$_____
Adult Disney ticket	$_____ per ticket × _____ (# of people) × _____ (# of days)	$_____
Child Disney ticket	$_____ per ticket × _____ (# of people) × _____ (# of days)	$_____

Expense	Calculation	Totals
Adult Universal Studios ticket	$_____ per ticket × _____ (# of people) × _____ (# of days)	$_____
Child Universal Studios ticket	$_____ per ticket × _____ (# of people) × _____ (# of days)	$_____
Other attraction	$_____ per ticket × _____ (# of people) × _____ (# of days)	$_____
Other attraction	$_____ per ticket × _____ (# of people) × _____ (# of days)	$_____
Adult nighttime entertainment	$_____ per person × _____ (# of nights)	$_____
Child nighttime entertainment	$_____ per person × _____ (# of nights)	$_____
Show/movie tickets	$_____ per person × _____ (# of shows)	$_____
Total meal budget	$_____ per person × _____ (# of meals) × _____ (# of days)	$_____
Snack/drink budget	$_____ per person × _____ (# of days)	$_____
Souvenir budget	$_____ per person	$_____
Child care	$_____ per hour × _____ (# of hours) × _____ (# of children)	$_____
Kennel costs	$_____ per day × _____ (# of days) × _____ (# of pets)	$_____

Expense	Calculation	Totals
Airport parking	$_____ per day × _____ (# of days)	$_____
Other	_____	$_____
Other	_____	$_____
Other	_____	$_____
Approximate Vaca-tion Expenses Total:	$_____	

Using a Travel Agent

Utilizing a full-service travel agency to plan your trip and make your travel reservations will typically save you a lot of time, but not necessarily a lot of money. Most travel agents these days specialize in corporate travel or high-priced vacations and earn their income by taking a commission of the total price of the trip they coordinate for you. Thus, unless you have an established relationship with a travel agent, they're not always apt to find you the lowest possible rates. Of course, there are plenty of exceptions.

If you don't already have a reliable travel agent that you use, consider seeking out a favorable recommendation from a friend or relative as opposed to opening the telephone book. When choosing a travel agent, make sure he or she specializes in planning family vacations and is familiar with Orlando.

Hotel room brokers, discount travel agents, and hotel reservation services in the Orlando area include:

Central Reservation Service: ✆(800) 548-3311

Check-in Reservation Services: ✆(800) 237-1033

Destinations Travel Service: ✆(407) 859-3501

Eventures Unlimited, Inc.: ✆(800) 356-7891
(This service offers special package deals designed specifically for senior citizens interested in vacationing at the WDW Resort.)

Booking Your Vacation Online

If you have some time to invest when planning your vacation, and you have access to the Internet, you can save an absolute fortune by planning and booking your travel arrangements online. Airfares, hotels, and rental cars can all be reserved and paid for using the Web and a major credit card.

When using the Internet to plan and book your own travel, you have three primary options:

1. **Visit the Web site of the specific airline, hotel chain, and/or rental car company.** For example, if you're booking your airfare on US Airways, you'd visit *www.usairways.com*. Often, each individual airline offers discounted online-only fares and specials that cannot be obtained anywhere else. The drawback to using an airline's Web site is that to shop around for the best fares, you'll need to visit the Web sites of multiple airlines.

2. **Utilize the services of an online travel-related Web site,** such as Travelocity (*www.travelocity.com*), Hotwire.com (*www.hotwire.com*), Expedia (*www.expedia.com*), Orbitz (*www.orbitz.com*), or Yahoo! Travel (*http://travel.yahoo.com*). These services allow you to quickly search all of the major airlines for the best flights and fares. You'll also find great deals on hotels, rental cars, and travel packages. When using one of these services, the more time you spend exploring them, the better your chances of saving a lot of money will be. Once you know when you want to travel, try searching for better fares by altering your travel dates slightly. Sometimes, leaving a day earlier or later, for example, can save you money. You can also try looking up various airport combinations. For example, if you're flying from New York's LaGuardia Airport to Orlando International Airport, you can also look up departing flights from Newark Airport and New York's Kennedy Airport. Checking each variable takes only seconds using one of these online travel services.

3. **If you have a somewhat flexible travel schedule, you can save between 30 and 70 percent on airfares, hotels, and rental cars** using a service such as Priceline.com (*www.priceline.com*), Last Minute Travel (*www.lastminutetravel.com*), or TravelHub (*www.travelhub.com/airfares*). Many of these online services now offer even greater package deal savings if you book your airfare along with your hotel and/or rental car.

Vacation Packages and When to Visit

There are a variety of organizations that offer various types of discounts and travel packages to the WDW Resort, Universal Studios, and other Orlando-area destinations. A travel package might consist of any or all of the following: airfare, hotel accommodations, meals, rental car, and admission to one or more theme parks. Using the budget checklist in this chapter, calculate what it will cost you to plan your own vacation, then compare those rates with those offered by comparable travel packages from an airline or one of the following travel organizations.

≡FAST FACT

The Hotel Reservations Network in Orlando advertises up to 60 percent off hotel rates at more than 300 hotels and motels in the Orlando area. This company will also help you find available hotel rooms during peak travel periods. For more information, call ✆(800) 511-5321. Also, be sure to check out the Web site Hotels.com (✉*www.hotels.com*) for discounts of up to 60 percent on hotels, motels, and resorts.

In addition to contacting the various airlines directly about individual airfares or travel packages, contact organizations such as the AAA, which has a travel department ((800) 222-7448, *www.aaa.com*), or the AARP ((800) 424-3410, *www.aarp.org*).

Two travel agencies that offer an assortment of different travel packages for people interested in the WDW Resort include:

American Express Travel: ☎(800) 346-3607, ✍*www.itn.net*

Walt Disney Travel Company: ☎(800) 225-2024

The Entertainment Book

Entertainment Books ((800) 933-2605, *www.entertainment.com*) offer 50 percent off and two-for-one discounts at your favorite places for dining and shopping, at attractions, for sports, and for services like dry cleaning and movie rentals. Entertainment Books also include discounts for hotels and other travel services.

TRAVEL TIP

The 2007 Entertainment Book for the Orlando area offers discounts and money-saving coupons for 276 local area restaurants, more than 5,000 hotels (nationwide), and special deals from rental car companies and various retail stores and tourist attractions. The Orlando edition of the Entertainment Book is priced at $25.

The Entertainment Book is an extremely useful resource for finding restaurants in the Orlando area that are not located on Disney property. The book typically offers sample menus as well as money-saving offers. People with access to a rental car who can travel freely around the Orlando area will get the most out of this discount book.

The Best Times to Visit

During the WDW Resort's peak summer season, spring break, and major holidays you could be sharing your vacation with 40,000 to 65,000 other visitors in each theme park. Throughout the year, Saturday is each theme park's busiest day of the week. Around noon, the park is usually the most crowded. On Sundays and during the week, the park is less crowded. The drawback to visiting the WDW Resort on a weekday is that the parades and shows happen less frequently.

When you arrive at the theme park of your choice pick up a copy of the free guide-maps at the main entrances of each park. These maps offer a detailed map of the park that lists all of the major attractions, restaurants, and amenities (restrooms, public phones, ATM machines, etc.) in many languages.

There will also be a one-sheet flyer the same size as the maps containing the times for all parades and shows. Anytime during the year, if it's raining, you can count on much smaller crowds than usual. Bring along rain gear (avoid umbrellas), or pick up one of the plastic rain ponchos sold throughout the park on rainy days. Expect all parades, outdoor shows, and a few outdoor rides to be canceled or closed on rainy days. Much of the park (including most of the attractions) will, however, be open, and the lines will be far shorter.

For the shortest lines, visit the theme parks during any weekday in the off-season. If you happen to visit on a busy day, go against the crowds. For example, you'll notice that in the morning, most people race toward the most popular rides and attractions, and these same people stake out a prime viewing spot for a parade up to two or three hours before showtime. Most of the park's most popular parades happen twice each afternoon or evening. During the first parade presentation is the best time to visit all of the most popular attractions. You can catch the second showing of the parade when the crowds are greatly reduced. Likewise, when most people break for lunch or dinner, many of the lines for attractions are shorter.

⊕ HOT SPOT

One of the best places to view the fireworks at Magic Kingdom is at the California Grill on the top floor of the Contemporary Resort. You'll need reservations for at least three months in advance for this award-winning restaurant, so plan accordingly.

The very best times of year to visit the parks in Orlando, due to lack of crowds, are:

- The first two weeks of September
- The first two weeks of December

The first two weeks of September and December you'll be able to walk on every ride at every theme park without a wait. The best week out of the four is the first week of December because hurricane season is over, the weather is 75 degrees, and all the holiday decorations are up, making everything seem very magical.

Attendance is considered "average" during the following times of year. If you're planning to travel during one of these times, expect to wait in line for thirty to ninety minutes for the most popular WDW theme park attractions.

- Mid-January until mid- February
- Late April until early June
- Mid-September through November

Busiest Times of Year

All of the Orlando-area theme parks are the busiest during the following times of year. These times are considered "peak" travel periods. The good news is that the theme parks are open longer hours and more parades and shows are held per day, but you can expect long waits for the major theme park attractions, and you'll have to deal with relatively large crowds, even if the weather is bad. These "peak" travel periods are:

- First week of January
- Late February until late April (spring break)
- Mid-June until late August (the summer season)
- Mid-December through New Year's Day

≡FAST FACT

During peak season, each night a different WDW park stays open extra late for resort guests only. It's called "Extra Magic Hours." The best are the Magic Kingdom nights, when the park stays open from 11:00 P.M. until as late as 3:00 A.M. Since most children are asleep, adults can visit the Magic Kingdom without kids and strollers everywhere.

Packed Like Sardines

The following holidays are extremely crowded to the point where you'll feel that you are packed in like sardines: Easter Day, the Fourth of July, Christmas, and New Year's Eve. The Fourth of July will get so busy that the parks are to capacity by 3:00 P.M. At this point they shut the entrance gates to nonresort guests. If you leave a park, you will not be able to return unless you are a resort guest.

The summer season is extremely hot and humid. Summer is the rainy season for Florida and it will rain a couple of times a day. However, it never lasts long because the coastal winds from the east and west keep the clouds moving. Pools, boats, water parks, and fireworks will shut down or be canceled mostly due to lightning.

Hours of Operation

Prior to choosing the exact dates for your trip (if you have flexibility), call your resort and inquire about hours of operation during the dates of your visit. During the "off peak" times, the parks tend to close around 7:00 P.M. or 9:00 P.M. as opposed to 11:00 P.M. or midnight during "peak" periods. The hours of operation for each theme park are also posted at the official Disney World Web site (*www.disneyworld.com*).

Even if the parks will be closing early during off-peak times, you probably won't have to wait in any really long lines to experience attractions, so you'll get to experience a lot more each day. You will, however, have to plan evening and nighttime activities that don't include the theme parks. If you want to stay on Disney property, spending evenings and nights at Downtown Disney and/or Disney's BoardWalk will provide plenty of dining and entertainment options until as late as 2:00 A.M. (throughout the year). If you stay near Universal Studios, CityWalk provides nightly entertainment until 2:00 A.M. as well.

TRAVEL TIP

When making a hotel reservation, if your first choice is already booked solid, make alternate reservations, but keep checking back with your first-choice hotel. Even during the busy times of year, last-minute cancellations are common. This goes for popular restaurants as well.

If you're planning your vacation during one of the busy periods, book your reservations as early as possible, especially if you hope to stay at one of the more popular Disney-owned hotels.

Packing for Your Vacation

In addition to carefully planning out an itinerary and prebooking all of your travel arrangements, you'll also want to ensure that you pack all the belongings and wardrobe items you'll need while traveling. This section will help you actually put together the ultimate packing list.

The Orlando Climate

To find out the current weather in Orlando, be sure to watch the Weather Channel, check the weather map in *USA Today*, or visit the WDW Web site at *www.disneyworld.com*. You can also call (407) 824-4104 for Walt Disney Resort weather or visit one of these Web sites:

MSNBC Weather: *www.msnbc.com*

USA Today: *www.usatoday.com/weather*

Weather Channel Online: *www.weather.com*

Yahoo! Weather: *http://weather.yahoo.com*

Average Temperatures at the WDW Resort

Month	Average High Temperature (°F)	Average Low Temperature (°F)	Average Rainfall
January	70	50	2.2"
February	72	51	2.9"
March	77	56	3.3"
April	82	61	2.2"
May	88	66	4.0"
June	90	71	7.4"
July	92	73	7.8"
August	92	73	6.3"
September	90	73	5.6"
October	84	65	2.8"
November	78	57	1.8"
December	71	54	1.8"

Theme Park Attire

The trick to dressing appropriately at any theme park is not to wear the trendiest or most stylish outfits. Comfort and protection from the sun are the keys! On hot days, wear light and comfortable clothing. On cooler days, wear layers that can be removed and that aren't too bulky. (You can always store clothing items in the lockers available at the theme parks.)

Finally, comfortable shoes should round out your theme park attire. Do not buy yourself or your children new shoes for your vacation. Always pack broken-in shoes for the most comfort because long-distance walking will be part of your daily lifestyle. You'll want to keep your hands as free as possible, so try to avoid heavy purses, several backpacks, and shoulder bags. Waist packs are a good solution for carrying smaller items such as wallets, glasses, keys, and small cameras. Consolidating everything into one backpack per group is the way to go. Make sure to leave a little room for those souvenirs you will be acquiring. Lots of pockets on clothing are lifesavers as well. Light jackets tied around the waist with secured zippered pockets will work too.

On rainy days, many people are inclined to bring an umbrella to the theme parks. This is a bad idea. Navigating around within the theme parks (among the crowds) is difficult with an open umbrella. You're better off wearing a waterproof hat, raincoat, or one of the plastic rain ponchos sold at the theme parks for about $6 each.

Before getting dressed in the morning, find out what the weather will be like and dress accordingly. Keep in mind that at night the temperature may drop.

≡FAST FACT

Due to heightened security measures, all bags you carry into a theme park will be hand-searched by security personnel at the park, so plan accordingly. Clear backpacks are highly welcomed by security and will get you through the line faster.

Rain or Shine: Always Wear a Hat

You'll want to protect your head and neck area from Florida's intense sun while you're exploring the various theme parks or spending time by the pool. Even on overcast days, the Florida sun can cause a serious burn relatively quickly if you're not protected, so make sure that you use powerful sunblock on all exposed skin. This is particularly important with kids.

A hat and sunglasses are virtually always a must. Wearing a hat will protect you from the sun (or the rain), and help keep you comfortable throughout the day. You can pack your own hat or cap, or purchase a park-themed hat at almost any souvenir or gift shop.

Carry-On Luggage

All of the airlines have changed their policies regarding carry-on luggage—the bags you physically carry onto the airplane with you and store either under the seat or in the overhead compartment. Virtually all airlines are now strict about allowing only one or two carry-on bags (including a purse or laptop case) per passenger, and the size requirements for each bag continue to change. Be sure to bring along a book or magazine to keep you entertained, as well as a snack or meal. Many airlines have discontinued in-flight meals and video entertainment. Also, within your carry-on, pack any electronics (cameras, video equipment, etc.), jewelry, prescription medications, and valuables that you wouldn't want lost or stolen.

Leaving Home

Due to the increased security within airports, arrive at the airport at least one hour (or even ninety minutes) prior to your flight's scheduled departure. For international flights, arrive at the airport at least two hours early. As you get ready to depart on your vacation, here's a quick checklist of things you might want to do prior to leaving.

- ✔ Arrange for someone to care for your pets and plants.
- ✔ Ask a friend, relative, or neighbor to check on your home or apartment while you're gone.
- ✔ Have the post office hold your mail.
- ✔ Close and lock all windows and close the blinds/curtains.
- ✔ Contact your child's teacher if he/she will be missing classes.
- ✔ Empty your refrigerator of perishable items.
- ✔ Empty your trash.
- ✔ Get a haircut, manicure, etc.
- ✔ Give a copy of your house keys to a nearby friend or relative.
- ✔ Leave your contact information with coworkers, friends, relatives, or anyone who might need to call you in an emergency.
- ✔ Pay your mortgage, rent, credit card bills, and other bills.
- ✔ Refill all prescription medications.
- ✔ Stop daily newspaper delivery or arrange for newspapers to be placed out of sight.
- ✔ Turn down the heat or air conditioning.
- ✔ Unplug electrical appliances.
- ✔ Visit a bank to get cash and traveler's checks.

CHAPTER 2

Choosing Your Accommodations

WHETHER YOU WISH TO stay at a theme resort, pitch a tent, or indulge in luxury, Orlando has it all covered. You'll find several options to fit your budget. Orlando has more rooms and hotels than Las Vegas, baby, and this chapter will help you select the accommodations that are most suited to your needs.

The WDW Resort Hotels

There are twenty-four places to stay at WDW and they are split into five price-based categories. Disney is all about storytelling, so it's no surprise to anyone that they have extended their imaginative tales to their resorts through themes. Staying at a WDW resort helps you escape your everyday routine life and makes you feel like you're getting away to a fantasyland. All that's left is to choose which fantasy appeals to you and your budget. The five categories of places to stay at WDW are:

1. Campground facilities and cabins range from $35 to $250 per night.
2. Value hotel rooms range from $80 to $150 per night.
3. Moderate hotel rooms range from $150 to $250 per night.
4. Deluxe hotels range from $250 to $920 (and up) per night.

5. Home Away From Home/Disney Club Vacation hotel rooms range from $250 to over $1,800 per night.

Besides creating memories for a lifetime by staying at a Disney-owned and -operated resort, you may be asking yourself what are the real perks for digging so deep into your pockets? Well, for one, when you stay at one of the Disney resorts, you'll be treated to the world-class service and hospitality that Disney is known for. Listed below are the other perks:

- **Complimentary transportation to and from the airport.** Disney's Magical Express air-conditioned motor coach will pick you up at the Orlando International Airport and take you to your WDW resort. They even carry your bags to your room. Make sure you make reservations for the bus at least six weeks in advance.
- **Complimentary access to the WDW Transportation.** Disney offers guests free bus service, water taxis, and monorail.
- **Complimentary parking.** Resort guests simply show their resort ID cards to receive free parking in the parks and free valet parking at Downtown Disney.
- **Advance dining reservations.** Resort guests can make advance dining reservations for priority seating up to sixty days before their arrival at many of the more than 200 restaurants throughout the WDW Resort. Call (407) WDW-DINE to make reservations.
- **Child care services.** Enjoy a break away from your kids! Resort guests can drop off their kids at a resort Kid's Club, or arrange in-room baby-sitting services.
- **Guaranteed entry into the theme parks.** Even on the busiest days, when the parking lots are full and gates have been shut to the public, resort guests using Disney transportation are guaranteed entry to all WDW theme parks and water parks.
- **Lifeguards.** WDW overstaffs pools and water parks at the WDW resorts. The security of having lifeguards watching your children is comforting and results in a more relaxing time for you.

- **Complimentary package delivery.** When you purchase items in the parks that you'd prefer not to carry around, simply have it sent to your resort.
- **Preferred tee times.** You'll receive preferred tee times at Disney's five courses.
- **Schedule updates.** You are in-the-know for all times for every show at every resort or park on WDW property.
- **Central billing.** The one WDW Resort identification card/room key/park ticket is used to charge food and merchandise, open the door to your room, get you entrance into the parks, and is used for the FASTPASS machines. You can choose to have as many active or nonactive charging ability cards (for merchandise and food) for the rest of your family. The resort ID cards are issued upon check-in, and all purchases are charged to guests' resort hotel accounts.
- **Extra Magic Hours.** Each day, one of the four WDW theme parks opens for Disney resort guests one hour early, providing exclusive time in the parks to experience select attractions and meet and greet Disney characters. During this hour, the parks are less crowded, allowing people to experience the most popular attractions in less time. During peak seasons there are also late-night Extra Magic Hours.
- **Security.** Staying on WDW property gives you and your family an overall sense of security because every inch of WDW is security controlled. Of course, you don't see this tight but invisible security force, but just know that it's there.
- **Information.** Cast members are trained to provide you with all the information that you need about practically anything. If the cast member gets busy with other guests, simply ask for a manger and he or she will accommodate you.
- **Satisfaction.** Cast members are trained to overexceed your expectations. If you have any complaint whatsoever about anything small or large, simply ask for a manager and your problem will be resolved.

- **Mickey wakes you up.** When you stay at WDW Resort and arrange a wake-up call for the morning it's the big cheese himself, Mickey Mouse, who calls you.

To make reservations to stay within "the heart of the magic" or to request color brochures for WDW Resort properties, a free Disney vacation video, or other information about any of the WDW Resort hotels, call (407) W-DISNEY or visit *www.disneyworld.com*.

BREAKDOWN OF THE FIVE WDW RESORT CATEGORIES

WDW Campground: Fort Wilderness Resort & Campground

WDW Value Resorts: All-Star Movies, All-Star Music, All-Star Sports, and Pop Century

WDW Moderate Resorts: Caribbean Beach, Coronado Springs, Port Orleans French Quarter, and Port Orleans Riverside

WDW Deluxe Resorts: Animal Kingdom Lodge, Beach Club, Yacht Club, Grand Floridian Resort & Spa, BoardWalk Inn, Contemporary, Polynesian, Wilderness Lodge

WDW Home Away from Home /Disney Vacation Club

Hotel Rooms: Beach Club Villas, BoardWalk Villas, Old Key West, Saratoga Springs, and the Villas at Wilderness Lodge

WDW Campground Facilities

Fort Wilderness Resort & Campground can be the least expensive place to stay on WDW property. In addition to providing 784 campsites (between 25 and 65 feet in length), Fort Wilderness offers 408 Wilderness Homes and Cabins (which have air conditioning and full amenities). Many of the sites offer cable TV connections (for RVs), electricity and water hookups, and sanitary disposal. The sites also feature a picnic table, a paved driveway pad, and a charcoal grill. Restrooms, showers, ice machines, telephones, and a laundry room are available at the campsites.

The Wilderness Homes are designed to hold up to six people (four adults and two children). The log cabins are more rustic in design than other Disney Resort hotel accommodations, but each has a private deck.

⊕ HOT SPOT

The campsites at Fort Wilderness offer the cheapest way to stay on Disney property. You can pitch a tent or pull in a pop-up on a campsite with partial hookups for around $35 per night!

Transportation to and from the other theme parks is available via the WDW Transportation bus system. Transportation to Magic Kingdom and the Wilderness Lodge is available by water taxi. Golf carts can also be rented for use around the campground facility and other activities include an arcade, carriage rides, bike rentals, horseback riding, pony rides, petting farm, wagon rides, and haunted wagon rides in October.

Fort Wilderness also has free outdoor movies every night (weather permitting). It also showcases the number one dinner show on WDW property, The Hoop Dee Doo Musical Revue.

To reach guests staying at this hotel, call (407) 824-2900 or ask the Disney operator to connect you if you're calling from a courtesy phone or WDW Resort hotel room phone.

WDW Value Resorts

The All-Star Music Resort, All-Star Sports Resort, All-Star Movies Resort, and Pop Century Resort have thousands of rooms starting around $79 per night. Each of these complexes has at least 1,920 nice but no-frills rooms, consisting of two double beds, a color TV, a small amount of furniture, and a bathroom. The rooms aren't large (260 square feet), but if you're looking to stay on Disney property and don't want to spend a fortune, these no-frills hotels are your best bet. The All-Star resorts also have family suites available, so make sure you inquire about them if you like. The décor of the resorts includes oversized icons of each one's theme. These resorts have in-room pizza delivery, baby-sitting and child care services, laundry facilities, arcades, playgrounds, and their pools, pool bars, and food courts stay open until midnight.

You can also purchase a refillable mug at the food courts to use throughout your stay.

Transportation is limited to the WDW Transportation buses (unless you drive or take a taxi). Expect to spend between thirty and forty-five minutes (each way) traveling from these WDW hotels to most of the Disney attractions.

To reach guests staying at the All-Star Music Resort, call (407) 939-6000. Guests staying at the All-Star Sports Resort can be reached by calling (407) 939-5000. To reach guests at the Pop Century Resort, call (407) 938-4000. You can reach people at the All-Star Movies Resort by calling (407) 939-7000, or ask the Disney operator to connect you if you're calling from a courtesy phone or WDW Resort hotel room phone.

≡FAST FACT

All WDW resorts close at midnight with the exception of the front desk services. The only areas of WDW that stay open later are Downtown Disney and the nightlife at BoardWalk, which are open until 2:00 A.M.

Moderate WDW Resorts

The moderate resorts at WDW have pools with slides, full-service dining, pizza delivery, marinas with watercraft rentals, whirlpools, laundry facilities, arcades, jogging trails, volleyball, and bike rentals.

Caribbean Beach

The Caribbean Beach Resort is a 200-acre resort consisting of many two-story buildings that are divided into clusters named after islands in the Caribbean. Everything has a tropical island feel. It has six heated pools throughout the resort and one large pirate-themed pool with waterfalls and water slides at Old Port Royale. To be near the large pool and facilities try to book a room in Martinique or Trinidad North. Caribbean Beach also has the only resort pool bar that stays open until midnight. There is one full-service restaurant named Shutter's and one quick-service food court. The 2,000-plus rooms offered here are pretty basic. Most rooms contain two double beds and are designed to sleep four people. Transportation is limited to the WDW Transportation buses (unless you drive or take a taxi). Expect to spend between thirty and forty-five minutes (each way) traveling from these WDW hotels to most of the Disney attractions.

TRAVEL TIP

One of the biggest challenges with the Caribbean Beach Resort is that all of the buildings look identical, so it's easy to get lost. If you're staying here, make sure you don't forget what Island you're staying at as well as your room number.

To reach guests staying at this hotel, call (407) 934-3400 or ask the Disney operator to connect you if you're calling from a courtesy phone or WDW Resort hotel room phone.

Coronado Springs Resort

The Coronado Springs Resort celebrates the Spanish culture. It features 1,967 guest rooms that encircle a 15-acre lagoon. It was built to accommodate guests visiting large conferences, as they have 95,000 square feet of meeting, function, and ballroom space. This resort is divided into three two-story guest buildings, each with its own pool. The hotel also features a food court area, a full-service restaurant, a lounge, a salon, a business center, wireless Internet, and a health club. Transportation is limited via the WDW Transportation buses (unless you drive or take a taxi). Expect to spend between thirty and forty-five minutes (each way) traveling to the Magic Kingdom. The other parks are a bit closer and require less time.

To reach guests staying at this hotel, call (407) 939-1000 or ask the Disney operator to connect you if you're calling from a courtesy phone or WDW Resort hotel room phone.

≡ FAST FACT

The biggest challenge with the Coronado is the extreme distance from the main building and your room. You'll get plenty of exercise here.

Port Orleans Resort—French Quarter

Modeled after the historic French Quarter of New Orleans, the Port Orleans resort offers 1,008 rooms located in seven three-story buildings complete with black wrought-iron trim, making you feel that you're staying on Bourbon Street. The French Quarter pool is fun and whimsical, with saxophone-playing alligators and a Mardi Gras sea serpent water slide. The sea serpent's tongue is the slide into the pool.

⊕ HOT SPOT

The lounges on both sides of Port Orleans have live free family entertainment Wednesday through Saturday, 8:00 to midnight. Bob Jackson, the Piano Guy, should not be missed in River Roost Lounge at Riverside, and Elliot Dyson heats up the night in Scat Cats at the French Quarter. (You can also catch Elliot Dyson at the Blues Brothers show at Universal Studios.)

The French Quarter does have a quick-service food court and a lounge (Scat Cats) that is open until midnight, but it does not have a full-service restaurant. However, you can eat at Port Orleans Riverside's full-service restaurant, Boatwright's Dining Hall (a half-mile walk along the river or water taxi ride). You can also take a water taxi (weather permitting) to Downtown Disney until 11:00 P.M., which lets you off at Rainforest Café. Overall, it's very easy to get around this resort. The Mardi Grogs pool bar closes at sunset, but the pool stays open until midnight. Transportation buses take guests to and from all of the Disney theme parks. To reach guests staying at this hotel, call (407) 934-5000 or ask the Disney operator to connect you if you're calling from a courtesy phone or WDW Resort hotel room phone.

Port Orleans Riverside

Disney's Port Orleans Riverside is divided into two primary sections, the Mansion area and the Bayou. The resort has a very Tom Sawyer feel about it. There are 2,048 spread-out rooms within this property. There is a main pool, which stays open until midnight, and smaller pools around each group of buildings, which are open twenty-four hours. Muddy Rivers pool bar stays open until sunset. A water taxi will take you to the French Quarter and to Downtown Disney. Fishing, watercraft rentals, and horse-drawn carriage rides are available too. Transportation buses take guests to and from all of the Disney theme parks.

To reach guests staying at this hotel, call (407) 934-6000 or ask the Disney operator to connect you if you're calling from a courtesy phone or WDW Resort hotel room phone.

WDW Deluxe Resorts

Deluxe resorts at WDW offer elaborate pools, several world-class restaurants, character restaurants, dinner shows, easy access to theme parks, room service, Kids' Clubs, valet parking, concierge services, fitness centers, spa services, baby-sitting, laundry facilities, tennis, marinas, and so much more.

Animal Kingdom Lodge

This is a 1,307-room, African-themed resort featuring deluxe guest rooms and luxury suites. The atmosphere alone makes these accommodations worth every penny. What makes this resort so special are the wild animals that coexist with the guests. Animal Kingdom Lodge has two full-service restaurants and one casual-dining food court. It features a zero-depth entry pool and a 67-foot-long water slide. It's located next to the Animal Kingdom Park for easy access.

⊕ HOT SPOT

Over 1,000 exotic animals live at Disney's Animal Kingdom, and guests of this resort will find themselves overlooking a 33-acre African savanna. So, instead of looking out the window or off the balcony and seeing a parking lot, swimming pool, or golf course, what guests see are incredible views of real-life giraffes, zebras, antelopes, and other wild animals.

Transportation buses take guests to and from all of the Disney theme parks. To reach guests staying at this unique hotel, call (407) 934-7639.

Beach Club and Yacht Club

Located along a lovely 25-acre lake, these are two of the nicest WDW Resort hotels, both inside and out. The Beach Club and the Yacht Club are modeled after New England seashore hotels from the 1880s. Both are full-service hotels that are within walking distance to and from the back entrance of Epcot. Both have water taxis to Epcot and Disney-MGM Studios. Transportation buses take guests to and from all other Disney attractions (unless you drive or take a taxi).

The Beach Club offers 583 guest rooms, while the Yacht Club offers 630 guest rooms. Both have a nautical theme and absolutely fabulous outdoor pool/beach areas. Whether or not you're staying at one of these two hotels, checking out these hotels' joint 750,000-gallon pool area is worthwhile; however, to use the pool requires that you show your Y&B resort ID card, so be prepared. Both hotels also offer a variety of indoor and outdoor activities, a full-service health club, business center, wireless Internet, full-service restaurants, and character dining at Cape May Café.

The Beach Club resort's phone number is (407) 934-8000. The phone number for the Yacht Club is (407) 934-7000. To reach a guest at one of these hotels, call the number directly or ask the Disney operator to connect you if you're calling from a courtesy phone or another WDW Resort hotel room phone.

BoardWalk Inn

This hotel is modeled after the boardwalk in Atlantic City. It offers only 378 rooms and room rates are based on the view offered. The hotel offers everything you'd expect a WDW deluxe resort to offer. There are several restaurants, including ESPN, Spoodles, Flying Fish Café, and Big River Grille & Brewing Works. There's even a dueling piano bar named Jellyrolls and a huge nightclub named Atlantic Dance. You can walk to Epcot and Disney-MGM Studios or take a water taxi. Transportation buses take guests to and from all other Disney attractions (unless you drive or take a taxi).

≡FAST FACT

The BoardWalk Inn, Yacht & Beach Club, and the Swan and Dolphin are all connected around a lake. All three are considered Epcot and Disney-MGM Studios Resorts. Feel free to walk around and enjoy what each has to offer.

To reach guests staying at this resort, call (407) 939-5100 or ask the Disney operator to connect you if you're calling from a courtesy phone or WDW Resort hotel room phone.

Walt Disney Dolphin and Swan Resorts

Unlike many of the other official WDW Resort hotels that are owned and operated by Disney, the Swan is operated by Westin Hotels, while the Dolphin is operated by ITT Sheraton. Between them they have seventeen restaurants and bars. Shula's an award-winning steak house and Todd English's bluezoo rank among the top. Blue-zoo also has a cocktail lounge that happens to be the only lounge on WDW property where you can get a handmade, fresh-squeezed cocktail. The Swan also has a fun sushi bar, Kiminos, which has nightly karaoke. You can walk to Epcot and Disney-MGM Studios or take a water taxi. Transportation buses take guests to and from all other Disney attractions (unless you drive or take a taxi). These hotels also have a special Web site: *www.swandolphin.com.*

To reach guests staying at the Swan or Dolphin, call (407) 934-4000, or ask the Disney operator to connect you if you're calling from a courtesy phone or WDW Resort hotel room phone.

Contemporary Resort

This was the very first WDW Resort hotel and is the only resort that the Disney monorail system passes directly through. The best thing about the Contemporary is that it's close to Magic Kingdom. So close in fact that there is an award-winning restaurant on the top floor, California Grill, that takes reservations up to four months in advance. Perfect for a spectacular view of the Magic Kingdom fireworks. For adults to get a sneak peek of this sought-after glass room in the sky, go to the second floor of the Contemporary at the California Grill check-in desk and tell the elevator operator that you are simply going up to have a cocktail at the bar. They will escort you up. The other big attraction at the Contemporary is Chef Mickey's. This restaurant offers the most popular character meal for kids of all ages.

The monorail will take guests to Magic Kingdom and Epcot. You can also walk to Magic Kingdom or take a water taxi. Transportation buses are available to take guests to and from all other Disney attractions (or you can drive or take a taxi).

To reach guests staying at this hotel, call (407) 824-1000 or ask the Disney operator to connect you if you're calling from a courtesy phone or WDW Resort hotel room phone.

TRAVEL TIP

There are thirteen restaurants at WDW that offer character meals. Most are buffet-style, but the big attraction is that Disney characters come around to each and every table for photo opportunities and autographs. Kids of all ages love this guaranteed experience to be near a character. Always make reservations as soon as you can.

Polynesian Resort

This hotel is paradise in the tropics. The Polynesian has the best Kids Club on WDW property. It's called Never Never Land and is filled to the brim with activities. You'll want to experience dining at O'hana's, but make sure that you make a reservation. There's also a character meal called O'hana's Best Friends Breakfast with Lilo and Stitch. And don't miss the best Luau show in Disney's Spirit of Aloha Show.

You can take the monorail to Magic Kingdom and Epcot. You can also take a water taxi to Magic Kingdom. Transportation buses are available to take guests to and from all other Disney attractions (or you can drive or take a taxi).

FAST FACT

The Polynesian and the Grand Floridian have connecting beaches, so take a walk on the beach and explore. In between the two is the wedding pavilion so you may just be lucky enough to glimpse Cinderella's glass pumpkin carriage. At night you can view the water light parade and the Magic Kingdom fireworks from these beaches.

To reach guests staying at this hotel, call (407) 824-2000 or ask the Disney operator to connect you if you're calling from a courtesy phone or WDW Resort hotel room phone.

Grand Floridian Resort and Spa

This is the most expensive place to stay at WDW. Located along the Seven Seas Lagoon, the Grand Floridian is a 900-room resort with a Victorian theme that truly defines the word "elegance." In addition to offering elegant décor, full-service restaurants, and top-quality Disney service, this resort also offers business services for guests, a health club, a luxurious full-service day spa, wedding pavilion, and plenty of on-site activities for adults and children. There are two character meals: Buffet Breakfast with Mary Poppins and Cinderella's Gala Feast. Other wonderful events for children include a tea party with Alice and the Mad Hatter, a Pirate Adventure, Grand Adventures in Cooking, and My Disney Girl's Perfectly Princess Tea Party.

⊕ HOT SPOT

An orchestra plays on the mezzanine level of the Grand Floridian lobby between 5:00 and 8:00 P.M. daily. You can sit in the comfy chairs on the lower level of the lobby and be served refreshments. This is the only free live entertainment at the WDW resorts other than the entertainment at Port Orleans.

During the holidays you'll find gentlemen wearing top hats, roasting chestnuts on an open fire, and a life-size gingerbread house. Year round, it's quite common to see a bride riding in Cinderella's glass pumpkin carriage complete with gold adorned white horses and footmen. Nightly you can view a water light show and the Magic Kingdom fireworks. Also know that 80 percent of the famous people that visit WDW stay at the Grand Floridian, so please be discreet and respect their visit by not behaving like a fanatical fan (the other 20 percent usually stay at the Yacht & Beach Club Resort). The Grand Floridian is located along the Disney monorail system, so getting to and from the Magic Kingdom, Epcot, and the Ticket and Transportation Center is easy and fun. Transportation buses take guests to and from all other Disney attractions (or you can drive or take a taxi).

To reach guests staying at this hotel, call (407) 824-3000 or ask the Disney operator to connect you if you're calling from a courtesy phone or WDW Resort hotel room phone.

Disney's Wilderness Lodge

This resort looks like a giant log cabin from the Northwest. It's a deluxe extension of the Fort Wilderness Campground and even offers a water taxi back and forth to the campground (as well as to the Magic Kingdom). It offers 728 rooms, many of which are equipped with queen-size beds and bunk beds, or two sets of bunk beds, which are a favorite among kids and teens. The lobby is very grand and sure to grab your attention with its huge totem poles and fireplace. The swimming area has a rock cliff pool and a beach. You can take a water taxi to Magic Kingdom and transportation buses take guests to and from all other Disney attractions (or you can drive or take a taxi).

Shades of Green on Walt Disney World Resort

Formally known as the Disney Inn, this 288-room complex is located along one of Disney's popular PGA championship eighteen-hole golf courses and right next to the grand Floridian.

This resort is operated as an Armed Forces Recreation Center for the exclusive use of military members and their families. For reservations, call (407) 824-3600 (reservations for this property cannot be booked through (407) W-DISNEY).

WDW Home Away from Home /Disney Club Vacation Resorts

These accommodations are Disney's Vacation Club/time-share program and are typically available only to members; however, when vacancies exist (especially during off-peak times), they are offered as hotel rooms to the general public.

Disney's Beach Club Villas

These villas feature an ambiance of casual elegance. This 205-room property is situated next to Disney's Beach Club Resort. It offers studio, and one- or two-bedroom vacation villas. To reach guests staying here, call the Beach Club Resort at (407) 934-8000 or ask the Disney operator to connect you if you're calling from a courtesy phone or WDW Resort hotel room phone.

BoardWalk Villas

Studio, one-, two-, and three-bedroom villas include kitchenettes or kitchens are available, with amenities that typical hotel rooms don't offer. The BoardWalk Grand Villas offer the ultimate in comfort and luxury for families (up to twelve people). These Grand Villas are also among the most expensive accommodations you'll find anywhere within The WDW Resort complex.

To reach guests staying at this hotel, call (407) 939-6200 or ask the Disney operator to connect you if you're calling from a courtesy phone or WDW Resort hotel room phone.

Old Key West Resort

Modeled to look like Key West, Florida, these villas have studios as well as one-, two-, and three-bedrooms. All offer a kitchenette, a living room, and a bathroom in addition to the bedroom(s). Guests also enjoy the villas' whirlpool tubs and oversize showers.

If you're not a member of Disney's Vacation Club, call the regular reservation number (407-W-Disney) for room availability. To reach guests staying at this hotel, call (407) 827-7700 or ask the Disney operator to connect you if you're calling from a courtesy phone or WDW Resort hotel room phone.

Disney's Saratoga Springs Resort & Spa

Designed after Saratoga Springs, New York, the new resort occupies a 65-acre site overlooking the lakefront district of Downtown Disney and the Lake Buena Vista Golf Course. This is the largest Disney Vacation Club resort to date, complete with 552 units, including studios, one- or two-bedroom villas, and Grand Villa units that sleep up to twelve guests. For information or to make a reservation, call (407) W-DISNEY.

The Villas at Disney's Wilderness Lodge

The Villas at Disney's Wilderness Lodge offer more family-oriented Home Away from Home accommodations. To reach guests staying at this hotel, call (407) 824-3200 or ask the Disney operator to connect you if you're calling from a courtesy phone or WDW Resort hotel room phone.

WDW Resorts with Kids' Clubs

Disney's Kids' Clubs offer activities galore for resort guests. The resorts that offer this service are Animal Kingdom Lodge, Beach Club, Grand Floridian, Polynesian, Wilderness Lodge, Yacht Club, Dolphin, Swan, Beach Club Villas, and Wilderness Lodge Villas.

If you're not staying at a WDW resort that provides a Kids' Club and would like to treat yourself to a night out, you can always contact Kid's Nite Out, Inc., at (407) 828-0920 from 8:00 A.M. to 9:00 P.M.

Universal Orlando Accommodations

If you choose to stay near Universal Orlando Resort (where you'll find Universal Studios Florida, Islands of Adventure, and CityWalk), this area contains three conveniently located, on-property hotels. In conjunction with your stay at any of these properties, special theme park admission deals and travel packages are available. To make reservations for any of the following hotels on Universal Orlando Resort's property, call (888) 322-5541 or visit *www.uescape.com*.

The Portofino Bay Hotel

The Portofino Bay Hotel (owned and operated by Loews Hotels) is within walking distance from the theme parks and CityWalk (however, complimentary transportation is provided). This resort offers Mediterranean architecture and landscaping. The buildings surround a beautiful man-made bay.

In addition to offering all of the amenities you'd expect from a prestigious resort, the Portofino Bay Hotel offers several advantages to Universal Orlando Resort guests. For example, guests of the hotel are invited to enter the theme parks one hour before the general public. This means that for the first hour, there are virtually no lines for the most popular rides and attractions offered within either theme park.

≡FAST FACT

A wide range of room rates are available at Portofino Bay, based on season, type of guest room (or suite), and the room's view. Room rates begin around $250 per night and go up to over $2,500 per night for a multibedroom suite.

The Portofino Bay Hotel is an upscale, family-oriented resort with eight restaurants (with many more dining options available at City-Walk). There's also a 10,600-square-foot, fully equipped spa (offering Swedish massage, wraps, aromatherapy tubs, and a full-service salon). Outdoor activities include a Roman aqueduct–style pool with a water slide, a private villa pool, three whirlpools, and a children's pool. On Saturday nights there is a dive-in movie at the pool. In addition, you'll find an outdoor jogging, walking, and bicycle path, and two bocce ball courts. There are also child care services for $12 per hour per child, and a meal is available for $12 at Campo Portofino.

The Hard Rock Hotel

Rock legends and families alike will receive superstar treatment at the Hard Rock Hotel. Designed in the architectural style of a California mission, this resort caters to a hip crowd, offering 654 guest rooms, suites, and bungalows. The resort also offers two restaurants and bars, a music-filled pool area, a fitness center, retail shops, and a children's activity center called Kids' Crib.

Guests of this resort receive early admission to the theme parks, priority seating at certain restaurants, plus the option of purchasing length-of-stay theme park tickets. This is definitely a more adult-oriented hotel and will appeal to guests looking for an upbeat party atmosphere. It's ideal for spring breakers, young business travelers, honeymooners, and adults traveling alone. There are also child care services at Camp Lil' Rock.

Royal Pacific Resort

This 1,000-guest room property offers elaborate landscaping, waterfalls, and lagoons, plus it provides a unique design that will make guests feel as if they've been transported to the enchanted isles of the South Pacific. A variety of dining options includes a restaurant, a pool snack bar, and the Village Bazaar featuring a medley of fast-food options. Every Saturday night the pool has a dive-in movie and every night there is a dinner show called the Wantilan Luau. The luau is $49 for adults and $29 for children under twelve. The price includes gratuity, tax, food and unlimited beer, wine, and Mai Tais. There is also a nightly Torch Lighting Ceremony poolside every night at 6:30 P.M. There are retail shops, a business center, fitness and children's activity centers, plus meeting and function facilities, including a 28,000-square-foot ballroom. There are also child care services at the Mariner's Club. The cost is $12 an hour per child and a meal for $12 is available.

Orlando-Area Accommodations

In the Orlando area, there are literally more than 1,000 motels, resorts, and hotels, as well as luxury suites where you can stay. These facilities are located outside of Disney and Universal property, but many offer free shuttle service to and from Disney and Universal as well as many nearby attractions.

For about the same price as a "value" or "moderate" room at a WDW Resort hotel, you could enjoy a stay at a top-rated and often luxury hotel or resort that's located outside of Disney property but only a few minutes' drive away via a complimentary shuttle bus that's provided by the hotel or via rental car.

≡FAST FACT

The Orlando/Orange County Convention and Visitors Bureau (☎(407) 363-5871, ✎*www.orlandoinfo.com*) reports that in the Orlando area, there are more than 110,784 hotel rooms available. In 2006, the average per-night rate for a hotel in the Orlando area was $89.16. Call this visitors bureau for a complete listing of area hotels.

Many non-Disney hotels are often substantially cheaper than the Disney resort hotels, or at the very least offer a better value. If you're a AAA member, be sure to check out the TourBook for Florida (available free of charge at any AAA office or by calling ((800) AAA-HELP). The TourBook lists Orlando-area hotels rated by AAA, many of which offer discounts to members. Be sure to inquire about additional AAA discounts when renting a car or visiting any Orlando-area attraction.

The independent hotels located outside of Disney property are so competitive that basic rooms are available for as little as $50 per night. A deluxe two-bedroom suite that's complete with a kitchen, living room, and plenty of amenities and hotel services can be found starting as low as $150 per night (less if you receive a discount using the Entertainment Book or another discount hotel program).

Apartment-Style Accommodations

If you're looking for multibedroom, apartment-style accommodations (complete with kitchen and living room), several top-notch properties include: the Sheraton Safari Hotel ((407) 239-0444, (888) 625-4988, *www.sheraton.com*), the Caribe Royale All-Suites Resort and Convention Center ((800) 823-8300, *www.cariberoyale.com*), and the Staybridge Suites ((407) 238-0777, *www.ichotelsgroup.com*). These resort properties are mid-priced and ideal for families traveling with kids or teens. They're also very close to the WDW Resort and offer free shuttle transportation to and from Orlando's major attractions.

Kid-Favorite Resorts in Orlando

Some resorts are doing everything they can to attract families. Many have learned that providing a more kid-friendly atmosphere with themed suites, activities, perks, and just general attention to the little ones is the key. Following are the best kid-approved resorts around the Orlando area.

The Nick Hotel

Without a doubt, the number one favorite place that kids want to stay is at the Nick Hotel ((407) 387-5437) (*www.nickhotel.com*) It's a Holiday Inn hotel located only a mile from WDW property and is advertised on the Nickelodeon TV channel, so that's how kids know about it. It's a dream hotel for them. Rates start around $160 and the themed kid room/suites are brightly painted with Nickelodeon characters. There are so many activities for kids here that you'll have a hard time talking your kids into leaving—especially the pool! Visit the Web site to see all this fun hotel has to offer.

Ramada Maingate West

This hotel wins for the best kid-friendly budget hotel. The Ramada Maingate West ((407) 396-6000) is located on HWY 192 in Kissimmee, Florida. Room rates start around $67, and there is a kids check-in, which includes a goodie bag when they sign in. Some rooms have themed kid suites with bunk beds and a sign that says "no adults allowed." The biggest thrill for kids is the waterfall in the indoor pool, which happens to be the only indoor resort/hotel pool in all of Orlando. Their first glimpse of the pool is while they ascend to their room in the glass elevator. Adults like the option of having an indoor and outdoor pool. This hotel also has an all-you-care-to-eat buffet with a kids dining area that has a TV playing cartoons, a food court, game room, fitness center, free wireless Internet, and nightly karaoke until 11:00 P.M. Many other dining options are within walking distance. The lounge overlooking the indoor pool closes at midnight. This hotel is one mile from the WDW entrance and provides WDW and Universal Studios shuttles.

Holiday Inn Sunspree Resort

Rates at the Holiday Inn Sunspree Resort ((407) 238-7276) start around $95, but the rooms include kitchenettes. Their kid suites have bunk beds with themes like igloos, outer space, and a tree house. Kids eat free and have free movie screenings. Camp Holiday is a supervised kids' program for ages four to twelve.

The Enclave

The Enclave ((800) 457-0077) is located right across from Universal Studios on International Drive. As a matter of fact, from many rooms you can watch Universal's nightly fireworks. Rates start around $120 per night. The kid suites have themes like Scooby Doo and Woody Woodpecker, and include bunk beds and their own bathroom. Wet 'n Wild water park is within walking distance, and SeaWorld is only three miles away, not to mention all the activities on International Drive. They also have two outdoor pools, two kiddy pools, one indoor heated pool, a Jacuzzi, fitness center, game room, food court, and more!

Five-Star Resorts in Orlando

The Orlando area offers several five-star resorts close to WDW that provide the ultimate in comfort, luxury, and fun. Located less than two minutes from the Downtown Disney area at WDW is the Hyatt Regency Grand Cypress ((800) 835-7377, *www.hyattgrandcypress.com*), one of the nicest resorts you'll find in Orlando. This resort offers so much in the way of activities and amenities, you could easily enjoy a multiday vacation without ever leaving the property. This is a 1,500-acre property with more than 750 rooms and 74 suites that are all ultramodern, clean, spacious, and well equipped. Rates start around $250 per night. Adjoining rooms and multibedroom suites are available to families. Child care and kid activities are available.

A similar, family-oriented resort, located about one mile from the WDW Resort, is the new Gaylord Palms Resort ((407) 586-2000, *www.gaylordhotels.com/gaylordpalms*). It, too, offers a wide range of amenities and activities you can experience without ever leaving the property. This resort is also the home of the Canyon Ranch Spa, an award-winning world-class day spa. For kids, the La Petite Kids' Academy Kids' Station offers a camplike experience, complete with supervised activities every day of the year. If you visit during the holidays, Gaylord Palms puts on a spectacular indoor walk-through spectacle called ICE! Nearly 2 million tons of ice is carved into a different breathtaking theme each year.

One mile from SeaWorld sits the elegant yet vibrant Ritz Carlton Grande Lakes (407-206-2400). Rates start around $450 for connecting rooms and features a 40,000-square-foot spa, an eighteen-hole Greg Norman–designed championship golf course, a Ritz Kids' Club, and six dining options.

For a more complete listing of hotels, motels, and resorts, visit *www.switchboard.com* and do a search for "hotel and motel reservations" in Orlando and surrounding areas.

Orlando-Area Hotels

There are more than 1,000 hotels, resorts, and motels located in the Orlando, Lake Buena Vista, or Kissimmee areas that are close to the WDW Resort, Universal Orlando Resort, SeaWorld, Universal, and/ or other popular attractions. Here is a sampling of what's available.

The rates for these hotels vary based on season and room availability, so contact each hotel directly for exact rates and availability for the dates you plan on visiting. All rates listed are approximations (subject to change) and are based on double occupancy.

Orlando-Area Hotels

Hotel Name	Distance to WDW by Car	Phone Number	Price Range per Night
Adam's Mark of Orlando	25 minutes	☎(407) 859-1500	$90–$150
Arnold Palmer's Bay Hill Club & Lodge	15 minutes	☎(407) 876-2429 or ☎(800) 523-5999	$90–$150
Baymont Inn	5 minutes	☎(407) 240-0500 or ☎(800) 428-3438	$50–$100
Best Western Lake Buena Vista Hotel	On WDW Resort property	☎(407) 828-2424 or ☎(800) 348-3765	$100–$300
Best Western Orlando West	25 minutes	☎(407) 841-8600 or ☎(800) 645-6386	Under $50
Best Western Plaza International	10 minutes	☎(407) 345-8195	$50–$100
Buena Vista Suites	5 minutes	☎(407) 239-8588 or ☎(800) 537-7737	$100–$150
Caribe Royale Resort Suites	5 minutes	☎(407) 238-8000 or ☎(800) 823-8300	$100–$150
The Castle Double-tree Hotel	10 minutes	☎(800) 952-2785	$110 and up
Clarion Maingate	3 minutes	☎(407) 396-4000 or ☎(800) 568-3352	$60–$110
The Clarion Universal of Orlando	15 minutes	☎(407) 351-5009 or ☎(800) 445-7299	$50–$100
Comfort Inn – Universal Studios	10 minutes	☎(407) 363-7886	$50–$100

Hotel Name	Distance to WDW by Car	Phone Number	Price Range per Night
Comfort Suites Orlando	10 minutes	✆(407) 351-5050	$50–$100
Courtyard By Marriott	On WDW Resort property	✆(800) 223-9930	$110–$175
Courtyard By Marriott	10 minutes	✆(407) 239-6900 or ✆(800) 635-8684	$75–$150
Crowne Plaza Universal	10 minutes	✆(407) 355-0550	$100–$200
Days Inn Convention Center/SeaWorld	15 minutes	✆(407) 352-8700	$50–$100
Days Inn East of Universal Studios	20 minutes	✆(407) 351-3800	$50–$100
Days Inn Lake Buena Vista	3 minutes	✆(407) 239-4441 or ✆(800) 224-5058	$50–$100
Doubletree Guest Suites	On WDW Resort property	✆(407) 934-1000 or ✆(800) 222-8733	$130–$250
Doubletree Hotel	3 minutes	✆(407) 239-4646 or ✆(800) 521-3297	$100–$150
Econo Lodge Main-gate Hawaiian Resort	3 minutes	✆(407) 396-2000 or ✆(800) 365-6935	$50–$100
Embassy Suites International Drive/ Jamaican Court	10 minutes	✆(407) 345-8250 or ✆(800) 327-9797	$100–$150
Embassy Suites International Drive South	20 minutes	✆(407) 352-1400 or ✆(800) 433-7275	$120–$180
Embassy Suites Lake Buena Vista Resort	5 minutes	✆(800) 257-8483	$100–$150
The Enclave	15 minutes	✆(800) 457-0077	$120–$170
Fairfield Inn By Marriott	10 minutes	✆(407) 363-1944	$50–$100

Hotel Name	Distance to WDW by Car	Phone Number	Price Range per Night
Gaylord Palms Resort	5 minutes	☎(407) 586-2000	$250–$500
Grosvenor Resort	On WDW Resort property	☎(407) 828-4444 or ☎(800) 624-4109	$115–$500
Hampton Inn at Universal Studios	15 minutes	☎(407) 351-6716 or ☎(800) 231-8395	$50–$100
Hampton Inn Maingate Hotel	5 minutes	☎(407) 396-8484	$50–$100
Hampton Inn South of Universal Studios	15 minutes	☎(407) 345-1112 or ☎(800) 763-1100	$50–$100
Hilton	On WDW Resort property	☎(407) 827-4000 or ☎(800) 782-4414	$200–$800
Holiday Inn Express International Drive	15 minutes	☎(800) 365-6935	$50–$100
Holiday Inn Family Suites	10 minutes	☎(407) 387-5437	$129–$300
Holiday Inn International Drive Resort	15 minutes	☎(407) 351-3500 or ☎(800) 206-2747	$50–$100
Holiday Inn Main Gate East	5 minutes	☎(407) 396-4488 or ☎(800) 366-5437	$65–$130
Holiday Inn Sunspree	5 minutes	☎(407) 239-4500 or ☎(800) 366-6299	$90–$130
Holiday Inn Universal Studios	15 minutes	☎(407) 351-3333 or ☎(800) 327-1364	$50–$100
Homewood Suites Maingate at the Parkway	5 minutes	☎(407) 396-2229	$100–$150
Howard Johnson Inn Maingate East	5 minutes	☎(407) 396-1748 or ☎(800) 288-4678	$50–$100
Howard Johnson's Plaza Resort	20 minutes	☎(407) 351-2000 or ☎(800) 327-3808	$50–$150

Hotel Name	Distance to WDW by Car	Phone Number	Price Range per Night
Hyatt Regency Grand Cypress Hotel	3 minutes	☎(407) 239-1234 or ☎(800) 233-1234	$195–$850
Knights Inn Maingate	5 minutes	☎(407) 396-4200 or ☎(800) 944-0062	$35–$70
LaQuinta Inn Lakeside	5 minutes	☎(407) 396-2222 or ☎(800) 848-0801	$50–$100
Leisure Resorts at Orlando	10 minutes	☎(407) 239-0707 or ☎(800) 633-1405	$100–$150
Magic Castle Inn	10 minutes	☎(407) 396-1212 or ☎(800) 446-5669	$50–$100
Nick Hotel	1 minute	☎(407) 387-5437 or 1-866-GO2-NICK	$170+
Rosen Centre Hotel	15 minutes	☎(407) 354-9840 or ☎(800) 204-7234	$150 and up
Parc Corniche Resort	6 minutes	☎(407) 239-7100 or ☎(800) 446-2721	$69 and up
Peabody Orlando	20 minutes	☎(407) 352-4000 or ☎(800) 732-2639	$240–$1,400
Quality Inn Plaza	15 minutes	☎(407) 345-8585 or ☎(800) 999-8585	$50–$100
Radisson Barcelo Hotel Orlando	15 minutes	☎(407) 345-0505 or ☎(800) 333-3333	$100–$150
Radisson Inn Lake Buena Vista	5 minutes	☎(407) 239-8400 or ☎(800) 333-3333	$100–$150
Ramada Main-gate West	1 minute	☎(407) 396-6000	$67+
Ramada Plaza Gateway	3 minutes	☎(407) 396-4400 or ☎(800) 327-9170	$60–$300+
Ritz Carlton Orlando, Grande Lakes	15 minutes	☎(407)206-2400	$450+

Hotel Name	Distance to WDW by Car	Phone Number	Price Range per Night
Rosenplaza Hotel	15 minutes	☎(407) 352-9700 or ☎(800) 627-8258	$135–$700
Royal Plaza Hotel	On WDW Resort property	☎(407) 828-2828 or ☎(800) 248-7890	$110–$300
Sheraton Universal Resort Hotel	20 minutes	☎(407) 351-2100 or ☎(800) 327-1366	$100–$150
Sheraton Vistana Resort	15 minutes	☎(407) 239-3100 or☎(877) 668-9330	$160–$350
Sheraton World Resort	12 minutes	☎(407) 352-1100 or ☎(800) 325-3535	$100–$150
Summerfield Suites Hotel	20 minutes	☎(407) 352-2400 or ☎(800) 830-4964	$150 and up
Summerfield Suites Lake Buena Vista	6 minutes	☎(407) 238-0777 or ☎(800) 830-4964	$170–$275
Travelodge Main-gate Hotel	5 minutes	☎(407) 396-0100 or ☎(800) 327-9151	Under $50
Travelodge Orlando Convention Center	20 minutes	☎(407) 345-8000 or ☎(800) 346-1551	$70–$100

Travel times, as reported by each hotel, motel, or resort, are approximate and will vary based on traffic and weather conditions.

CHAPTER 3

Admission to the Theme Parks

FIRST REALIZE THAT YOU WILL NEVER get to see everything that every theme park in Orlando has to offer. Once you develop a preliminary itinerary for your trip, decide how many days you'll spend exploring the various theme parks, then be realistic about what is possible. Guests that have been visiting Orlando for many years always factor in a relaxing chill-out day for every busy park day. There are one-park/one-day tickets that provide unlimited admission to the theme parks for a single day, and other options include multiday/multipark passes (called "Park Hopper" or "Park Hopper Plus" passes), and annual passes.

Admission to WDW

Admission to the various theme parks can be purchased per park, by the day. If you're staying at WDW for multiple days, however, you'll save a tremendous amount of money by purchasing multiday Park Hopper passes that give you full access to all of the WDW theme parks. For example, compare the price of a $71 one-day WDW admission ticket to a $223 seven-day Park Hopper WDW admission ticket. That's almost a 50 percent savings! Like everything in life, buying in bulk is always cheaper. Keep in mind that you probably won't be hitting the parks hard every day, but you can take advantage of a night-time show, special events, activities, and themed restaurants in the WDW parks anytime you wish.

An alternative to purchasing single-day/single-park passes or multiday Park Hopper passes is to purchase a complete vacation package from the Walt Disney Travel Company or any travel agent. There are many packages and package prices to choose from that can include the water parks, meals, Pleasure Island, and more.

The following are some of the admission prices for the WDW theme parks. (All prices are subject to change.) For more information about park admission prices or to prepurchase your passes, call (407) W-DISNEY, visit Disney World's Web site (*www.disneyworld.com*), or visit any Disney Store.

Single-Day/Single-Park Ticket

These tickets are good for one day's admission to any one of the primary WDW theme parks.

ANY PRIMARY WDW THEME PARK		
Duration	Adult Pass	Child Pass
		(Ages 3 to 9)
1 day	$71	$59

Water Park One-Day Admission

Admission to Typhoon Lagoon or Blizzard Beach is included with this ticket. To avoid standing in line to enter a Disney water park, you can now purchase your admission tickets from automated ticket vending machines located at the front gates. All major credit cards and your Disney Resort room key (with charge privileges activated) are accepted.

TYPHOON LAGOON OR BLIZZARD BEACH		
Duration	Adult Pass	Child Pass
		(Ages 3 to 9)
1 day	$37	$30
Annual Pass (both water parks)	$106.45	$85.74

Pleasure Island Admission

During the day, Pleasure Island, which is located between the Downtown Disney shopping area and Disney's West Side, is open to the public. There is no admission fee. In the evenings and at night, however, when the Pleasure Island clubs open, there is a separate admission fee that includes admission to all of the clubs and attractions within this area. (Drinks and food, however, are sold separately.)

Note that for special events at Pleasure Island, an additional admission fee and advance reservations may be required.

PLEASURE ISLAND		
Duration	**Adult Pass ($18+ Only)**	**Child Pass**
1 night	$22	Not available
Annual Pass	$22	Not available

TRAVEL TIP

When you purchase a one-night admission ticket to Pleasure Island, you can upgrade to a six-consecutive-night ticket for just $5 more. This offer is subject to end at any time, however.

Disney's Wide World of Sports

For sports fans of all ages who wish to explore Disney's Wide World of Sports complex, there is a separate admission fee.

DISNEY'S WIDE WORLD OF SPORTS		
Duration	**Adult Pass**	**Child Pass (Ages 3 to 9)**
1 day	$10.81	$8.24

DisneyQuest

Within Disney's West Side area is an indoor, high-tech interactive attraction called DisneyQuest, which combines video arcade games with state-of-the-art virtual reality rides and attractions. While DisneyQuest will appeal especially to ages between ten and twenty-one, there is plenty to do here for everyone. The all-inclusive, one-day pass includes unlimited use of all rides and attractions within DisneyQuest.

DISNEYQUEST		
Duration	Adult Pass	Child Pass (Ages 3 to 9)
1 day	$37	$30
Annual Pass	$94.14	$75.10

Four-Day Park Hopper Pass

This pass allows you to visit the Magic Kingdom, Epcot, the Disney-MGM Studios, and Disney's Animal Kingdom only. You enter and exit these parks as often as you like during any four days. In most cases, unused days do not expire and the days do not have to be consecutive. Five-day Park Hopper passes are also available; however, you'll probably want the benefits of a Park Hopper Plus Pass if you'll be staying at the WDW Resort for more than four days.

PARK HOPPER PASS		
Duration	Adult Pass	Child Pass (Ages 3 to 9)
4 days	$257	$221
4 days (advance purchase)	$202	$202

Five-Day Park Hopper Plus Pass

This pass allows you to visit the Magic Kingdom, Epcot, the Disney-MGM Studios, and Disney's Animal Kingdom, and enter and exit these parks as often as you like during any five days. In addition to the primary theme parks, this type of ticket also grants the holder the choice of admission to two of the following: Blizzard Beach, Typhoon Lagoon, or Pleasure Island. Unused days do not expire. Six- and seven-day Park Hopper Plus passes are also available, as are Length-of-Stay passes with these benefits.

PARK HOPPER PLUS PASS		
Duration	Adult Pass	Child Pass (Ages 3 to 9)
5 days	$282	$238
5 days (advance purchase)	$259	$208

Length-of-Stay Pass

If you're staying at the WDW Resort for a number of days that isn't included in one of the pass options, you can purchase a special Length-of-Stay Pass that offers you unlimited access to all of the theme parks during your entire stay. These passes are good from the moment you check in at your WDW Resort hotel until midnight of the day you check out of the hotel. These passes give guests total freedom to go from park to park at will and use all WDW transportation. The price for this type of pass varies based on the length of your stay. For more information, call (407) W-DISNEY.

Annual Pass

If you plan on visiting the WDW Resort multiple times in any twelve-month period, consider purchasing an annual pass. These passes provide unlimited admission to the Magic Kingdom, Epcot, the Disney-MGM Studios, and Disney's Animal Kingdom during normal operating hours. Parking and unlimited use of WDW transportation is included. Special discounts are also offered for food and merchandise. The twelve-month period begins on the first day the pass is used to enter a theme park (not when it's issued).

ANNUAL PASS		
Duration	Adult Pass	Child Pass (Ages 3 to 9)
Annual Pass	$441	$388
Florida resident	$341	$288

Premium Annual Pass

These twelve-month passes offer unlimited admission to the Magic Kingdom, Epcot, the Disney-MGM Studios, and Disney's Animal Kingdom, plus Pleasure Island, Typhoon Lagoon, Blizzard Beach, Disney's Wide World of Sports complex, and DisneyQuest during normal operating hours. Parking and unlimited use of WDW transportation is included. Special discounts are also offered for food and merchandise.

PREMIUM ANNUAL PASS		
Duration	Adult Pass	Child Pass (Ages 3 to 9)
Premium Annual Pass	$499	$424
Florida resident	$399	$339

Beware of Counterfeit Passes and Scams

Up until recently, non-Disney tourist centers made a lot of money buying and selling unused passes for the WDW Resort. If a family purchased Five-Day Park Hopper passes, but used only three of the days on each pass, independent ticket agencies would purchase the unused days at a fraction of the true value, and then resell those passes to other tourists to earn a profit.

Recently, however, the Walt Disney Company began using new technology to print and issue passes for the Disney theme parks that prevents counterfeiting, unauthorized ticket brokering, or illegal ticket scalping. As a result, to protect yourself, do not purchase any admission passes to any Disney theme park (for any price) from any unauthorized ticket agent.

The safest places to purchase your admission passes for the Disney theme parks are from your own travel agent, directly from any WDW Resort ticket counter (on Disney property), from a Disney Store, or from Disney Online.

Avoid Long Lines with FASTPASS

It's everyone's dream to visit one of the Disney World theme parks and discover the place is absolutely empty—with none of those dreaded lines, even for the most popular rides. Well, the chances of that dream coming true, no matter how much pixie dust you use, are slim (unless you visit the first two weeks of September and the first two weeks in December). Thanks to WDW's FASTPASS, however, visitors don't have to wait hours at a time to experience the most popular rides within the various Disney theme parks.

Combine careful planning with the FASTPASS system, and you'll be able to enjoy most or all of each park's most popular rides without having to wait for hours at a time in line to experience each of them. FASTPASS use is free of charge to all theme park visitors.

⊕ HOT SPOT

Soarin', Mission: SPACE, and Test Track are three of the most popular attractions at Epcot; therefore, there's almost always a long wait, so a FASTPASS is highly recommended.

When you approach a ride that supports FASTPASS, you'll see two clocks located near the ride's entrance. One clock displays the estimated wait time in the regular line. The second clock displays the current return time for people using FASTPASS.

If you choose to use FASTPASS, simply insert your theme park admission ticket (resort ID or annual pass) into the special kiosk located near the ride's entrance. A special pass will be printed explaining what time to return to the ride. For example, if it's 1:00 P.M. when you approach the ride for the first time, and you insert your ticket into the FASTPASS turnstile, you may be told to return to the ride between 2:30 and 3:30 P.M., at which time you can proceed directly to the ride's preshow or boarding area. There will then be little or no wait.

TRAVEL TIP

Guests are given a one-hour window during which they can return to experience the ride once they take advantage of FASTPASS. So if the printed FASTPASS ticket you receive indicates you should return at 2:00 P.M., for example, you can arrive at the ride's entrance any-where between 2:00 and 3:00 P.M.

Using FASTPASS is like making a reservation to experience a ride, without having to wait in line. While guests can't specify a specific time they'd like to experience a ride, it is possible to save consider-able time and avoid waiting in long lines. While you're waiting for your designated FASTPASS time, you're free to experience other rides, shows, and attractions within the theme park.

Guests are only allowed one FASTPASS for one ride at a time. So, if you're waiting to experience Splash Mountain, for example, and you have ninety minutes until your designated boarding time, you can't race over to Space Mountain and also take advantage of FASTPASS there until after you've experienced Splash Mountain.

Since FASTPASS works with many of the most popular rides within each of Disney's theme parks, you can use this free feature to help plan your day and ensure that you're able to experience everything you'd like to during your visit to each park. FASTPASS is particularly useful if you're traveling with young kids, who are typically impatient and hate waiting in lines, especially on a hot day.

If used correctly, FASTPASS can save you up to two hours each day. This gives you up to 25 percent more time to experience rides and attractions, as opposed to waiting in long lines for the popular attractions.

Admission to Universal Studios

If you'll be in the Orlando area for multiple days (and you plan to visit Universal Studios Florida and Islands of Adventure), you can save money by purchasing a multiday/multipark pass.

After purchasing your admission ticket, if you decide you want to stay longer or upgrade your admission for additional days, special discounts are offered at the Customer Service counter near the entrance of the park. You must upgrade your ticket the day it's purchased, however.

Four-Park Orlando FlexTicket

The Orlando FlexTicket offers a way to see multiple Orlando-based attractions and theme parks and save money. If you're planning to visit Universal Studios Florida, Islands of Adventure, CityWalk, SeaWorld, and Wet 'n Wild, you'll save a fortune with this type of multiday, multipark pass. It's valid for fourteen consecutive days and offers unlimited admission to each of the following theme parks:

- Busch Gardens (Tampa Bay, Florida—ticket includes free bus transportation)
- SeaWorld Orlando
- Universal Studios Florida
- Universal Studios Islands of Adventure
- Wet 'n Wild
- CityWalk

While the Orlando FlexTicket does not include admission to any of the Disney-owned theme parks, it offers great savings to other popular Orlando-area attractions. If you're planning to visit the Universal theme parks, SeaWorld, and Busch Gardens, this type of ticket is worthwhile.

Universal Orlando Resort Theme Park Admission Prices

The following are the admission prices for Universal Studios Florida, Islands of Adventure, and CityWalk.

Type of Ticket	Adult Pass	Child Pass (ages 3 to 9)
1-day/1-park	$63	$52
1-day/2-park unlimited	$85	
4-Park FlexTicket	$175.95	$142.95
5-Park FlexTicket	$214.95	$179.95
2-Park Preferred Annual Pass	$179.95	$179.95
2-Park Annual Power Pass	$119.95	$119.95
Universal Orlando Bonus Pass	$99.95	$99.95
CityWalk Party Pass	$9.95	N/A
CityWalk Party Pass + movie	$13	N/A

The Two-Park Preferred Annual Pass and Annual Power Pass

The Two-Park Preferred Annual Pass gives you unlimited admission to both Universal Studios Florida and Islands of Adventure for one full year. There are no blackout dates and self-parking is free. The Two-Park Annual Power Pass also offers admission to both theme parks for a full year; however, there are blackout dates during peak periods and you still pay for parking.

TRAVEL TIP

Show your AAA membership card when purchasing tickets or making a purchase at gift shops or restaurants within the Universal Orlando Resort and receive up to a 10 percent discount. Being an annual pass holder offers a handful of privileges, such as a 10, 15, or 20 percent discount off food and merchandise throughout the theme parks and CityWalk.

The Universal Orlando Bonus Pass

This type of admission ticket offers five consecutive days at Universal Studios Florida, Islands of Adventure, and CityWalk. You're allowed unlimited park-hopping. This type of ticket is only available online from *www.usf.com*.

CityWalk Party Pass

Enjoy unlimited admission for one night to the various clubs located within CityWalk with this pass. For a few dollars more, you can also see a movie at the twenty-screen Universal Cineplex. For movie listings, call (407) 354-5998.

Same-Day Theme Park Re-entry

As you leave either of the Universal Orlando Resort theme parks, be sure to have your hand stamped as you exit in order to be granted readmission into that park later in the day or evening. In addition to the hand stamp, be sure to retain your ticket stub. The hand stamps are designed to be water-resistant, so don't worry if your hands get wet if you choose to return to your hotel in the middle of the day to go swimming and then want to return to Universal Studios Florida later that evening. Try to refrain, however, from scrubbing your hands clean with soap until your day's visit to the theme park is complete.

Admission to SeaWorld

SeaWorld has two parks and there is a separate admission fee for both SeaWorld and Discovery Cove.

Type of Ticket	Adult Pass	Child Pass (ages 3 to 9)
1 Day/1 Park	$62	$49
4-Park FlexTicket	$175.95	$142.95
5-Park FlexTicket	$214.95	$179.95
Annual Pass	$95	$85

Other annual passports that offer admission to SeaWorld as well as Busch Gardens are available, as are discounted two-year passports.

≡FAST FACT

SeaWorld charges a daily parking fee of $8 per car or $9 per RV or camper. If you're staying at a non-Disney hotel, consider utilizing shuttle bus service to the SeaWorld theme park. Ask your hotel's front desk attendant or concierge for details

Discounts are available to senior citizens, military personnel, AAA members, Florida residents, and guests with disabilities. You can also save 10 percent off the ticket prices by prepurchasing your tickets online at *www.seaworld.com.*

Admission to Discovery Cove

It costs around $250 per person for one-day admission to Discovery Cove and includes admission to SeaWorld or Busch Gardens for seven consecutive days. Or for $30 more you can purchase a combination pass with admission to both parks for fourteen days.

There are various discounted package deals available if you're also interested in participating in the programs at Discovery Cove.

There is a Dolphin Lover's Family Sleepover program priced around $330 per person, Trainer for a Day program priced around $450 per person, and a Twilight Discovery evening program priced around $250 per person. Call (877) 4-DISCOVERY for additional information.

Travel Tips

As you read this book and start thinking about how you want to spend your time, be sure to take notes and keep track of which rides, shows, attractions, parades, and activities are of interest to you and the people with whom you'll be traveling. Once you think you know what you want to experience, start planning out the actual days of your trip.

Make sure everyone you're traveling with gets to experience activities that he or she is most excited about. This may mean making compromises or separating at various times. There's no reason why every family member should be dragged to activities that don't interest others. While you'll definitely want to plan some "quality family time," that time together will be more thoroughly enjoyed if everyone you're traveling with is happy and excited about the activities he or she has experienced during the vacation.

TRAVEL TIP

To save yourself a considerable amount of time traveling between theme parks and activities, plan out your itinerary in half-day chunks. Also, try to schedule eating near an area where you will be that day instead of traveling to another area of a property.

Tips for Traveling with Small Kids

The theme parks offer plenty to do for people of all ages, including young children. When traveling with young kids, however, it's important to plan your day to accommodate their needs. For example, plan on arriving at any of the theme parks early in the day, then take a break in the middle of the day for lunch and a nap. Head back to the theme park again later in the day when everyone is rested. Also, be sure to take advantage of stroller rentals at each of the parks. Visiting a theme park requires a lot of walking and kids tire easily.

For two adults who are traveling with younger kids, take advantage of the "Kid Switch" program to save time waiting in lines for rides (For more details on this program see Chapter 5).

Tips for Seniors

Senior citizens should consider pacing themselves when visiting any of the theme parks, since a lot of walking is required. Anyone who tires easily or doesn't enjoy a lot of walking should seriously consider renting a wheelchair. Electronic wheelchairs can also be rented for around $35, and $5 is refundable. Also, wheelchairs have a special line for all attractions. You might also consider arriving at a park early in the morning, exploring for three or four hours, taking several hours to relax in the afternoon, and then venturing back out in the late afternoon or evening for several more hours. Epcot offers the most attractions designed for older guests.

 TRAVEL TIP

Freezing a few bottles of water the night before and carrying them around in your backpack throughout the day is a smart idea. It keeps the water cold and saves you money. Bottled water prices in the parks can be as high as $3 each.

In addition to a lot of walking, one of the biggest concerns older people should have when visiting the WDW Resort is dealing with the heat and sun. Overexposure to the sun can cause health problems. Be sure to wear plenty of sunblock, a hat, sunglasses, and light clothing that covers your entire body. Also, drink plenty of fluids and rest often. During the afternoon hours (when the weather is the hottest), plan to visit the indoor, air-conditioned attractions.

Guest Services

Within the theme parks you'll find the following guest services designed to make your visit more comfortable and enjoyable.

Automated Teller Machines

Ask any employee or cast member for directions to the closest machine, or check the map located within the souvenir guide map and daily schedule brochures. Your bank may charge a transaction/ withdrawal fee for using an ATM that's outside of your bank's own network.

The parks accept most forms of U.S. currency: cash, traveler's checks, Visa, MasterCard, Discover, and American Express. Credit cards are not accepted at the various food and merchandise kiosks located throughout the parks. If you're staying within a Disney hotel/ resort, your room key can also be used as a charge card within the parks. Your purchases will be billed directly to your hotel room.

Within the WDW Resort, there's a full-service SunTrust bank that's located across the street from Downtown Disney. The branch is open on weekdays between 9:00 A.M. and 4:00 P.M. (6:00 P.M. on Thursdays). Call (407) 237-4141 or (800) 432-4760 for details. At this branch, you can obtain a cash advance from a major credit card, receive a wire transfer, and perform many other banking functions. There are many banks to choose from near SeaWorld and Universal Studios as well.

Child Care

WDW has ten Kids' Clubs and baby-sitting/child care services at these ten resorts: Animal Kingdom Lodge, Beach Club Resort. Grand Floridian Resort & Spa, Polynesian Resort, Wilderness Lodge, Yacht Club Resort, Dolphin Resort, Swan Resort, Beach Club Villas, and Wilderness Lodge Villas.

TRAVEL TIP

The Polynesian Resort offers the biggest Kids' Club, called Never Never Land. WDW also offers a service called Kid's Nite Out. You get to treat yourself to a night out while your child enjoys one-on-one child care in the comfort of your hotel or resort room. To contact Kid's Nite Out, Inc., call ☎(407) 828-0920 from 8:00 A.M. to 9:00 P.M., seven days a week.

All three Universal Studios resorts offer child care. The Hard Rock Hotel has Camp Lil' Rock that costs $12 per hour per child. Call (407) 503-2236 for more information. They also have a Kids' Crib where kids can hang out. The Portofino Hotel offers Campo Portofino, where you can drop off the kids to enjoy movies and activities. The cost is $12 per hour per child. Call (407) 503-1200 for more information. And the Royal Pacific offers the Mariner's Club, which costs $12 per hour per child. Call (407) 503-3235 for more information. Baby Service areas can be found within all theme parks. Private rooms are available for nursing and feeding. Highchairs, bibs, plastic spoons, and diaper-changing rooms are provided. Additional baby care products (disposable diapers, formula, etc.) can be purchased. Baby-changing tables are available in all public restrooms throughout the theme parks.

FAST FACT

Even though SeaWorld does not provide a Kids' Club or baby-sitting service, they do offer around twenty fun and educational sleepover experiences, which makes them the only provider of overnight service. Call ☎(866) 4SW-CAMP for more information or check online.

For outside professional child care to come to you, call All about Kids and More at (407) 812-9300. You can visit their Web site at *www .all-about-kids.com*. They have been in business since 1991 and are bonded, insured, and licensed.

Emergency Services

No matter what type of emergency you experience, medical or otherwise, contact the nearest cast member or employee immediately. The people who work at the WDW resorts are highly trained to deal with virtually any type of emergency, such as lost children, medical-related problems, and lost or stolen items.

Within all of the theme parks, you'll find fully equipped first-aid stations. Various amenities such as pain relievers, sunblock, and bandages can be purchased at many gift shops. When adults get separated, messages can be left at a Guest Relations desk (typically located near the entrance to each park). It's highly recommended, however, that you predetermine a location and time to meet if you get separated within the theme parks. Many travelers also resort to cell phones and/or walkie-talkies to stay in contact with one another.

Health-Related Services

Aside from the first-aid stations located within each of the theme parks, there are walk-in medical facilities (operated by Florida Hospital) located between the WDW and Universal area. For information about these medical facilities, call (407) 238-2000 or (407) 239-6463. Complimentary transportation to these walk-in medical centers is available.

To receive an in-room visit from a doctor (at your Disney hotel), call the Doctors-on-Call service at (407) 399-3627. This service is available twenty-four hours per day. Two of the closest hospitals to the WDW Resort are Sandlake Hospital (407) 351-8500 and Celebration Health (407) 303-4000.

To arrange to have a prescription delivered to your hotel room, call Centra Care at (407) 239-7777. There are also three Walgreens pharmacies (800) 289-2273 located near the WDW Resort (near the Downtown Disney area).

Refrigeration facilities for prescription medications (such as insulin or antibiotics) are available, free of charge, within the theme parks and Disney hotels. Contact the First Aid office or Guest Relations for more information.

 TRAVEL TIP

Before leaving on your vacation, make sure to obtain a copy of your prescription to take with you, along with contact information for your doctor and medical insurance company. Thus, if you need to have your prescription refilled, it will be much less of a hassle.

Religious Services

To find a house of worship or nearby religious services, check any local Orlando-area telephone book or ask the front desk (or concierge) at your hotel. In many cases, free shuttle service is available from the WDW Resort to the house of worship of your choice.

Lockers

Lockers are available for rent within all of the theme parks. These are excellent for storing an extra change of clothing, jackets, or camera equipment during the day until they're needed. While visiting the parks, you'll want to keep your hands as free as possible. Storing items you bring into the park or that you purchase (souvenirs) is an excellent strategy. Renting a locker is a lot more convenient than running back and forth to your parked car or hotel room, which will typically require a long walk and/or a tram ride. The daily charge for unlimited use of a locker within each of the Disney theme parks is $7 (plus a $1 refundable deposit).

Lost and Found

There's a Lost and Found office located within each theme park. If you lose an item, report it missing as quickly as possible. If someone returns the item quickly, you can pick it up at the Lost and Found office. If the item is found after your departure from the park, you will be mailed the item to you at whatever address you provide.

If you find someone else's lost item, bring it to one of the park's Lost and Found offices. If the item is not claimed within sixty days, you have the option of keeping it.

Package Express Service

If you're staying at one of the Disney or Universal resorts, one of the perks is that whenever you make a purchase (of a souvenir, for example), you can have the purchased item delivered directly to your hotel room, free of charge. This means you won't have to carry around your purchases or store them in lockers.

For those who aren't staying at one of the Disney or Universal resorts, you can arrange to have your purchases delivered and held at the Package Express Pickup Window, located just outside the main entrance to the theme parks. You can pick up your items at the end of the day. This is a complimentary service provided by SeaWorld as well.

TRAVEL TIP

Looking for extra-special VIP treatment when you visit the various Disney theme parks? For guests who'd like the ultimate customized experience, there's a private guided tour service that can plan and lead a personalized itinerary. This service isn't cheap, but it's certainly memorable. To plan a custom guided tour, call Disney Special Activities at ✆(407) 560-4033.

Pet Care

The WDW Kennels can be found adjacent to the Transportation and Ticket Center, at the entrance to Epcot, at the entrances to the Disney-MGM Studios and Disney's Animal Kingdom Park, and near the entrance to Disney's Fort Wilderness Resort & Campground.

The daily fee is $6 per day (per pet) and/or $11 per night (per pet). When you leave your pet within the kennels, you will be required to drop in for a visit at least once per day. Dog owners, for example, are required to walk their own dogs at least twice daily (or three times daily for puppies). The Epcot location offers an extra dog-walking service for $2.50 per walk.

Kennel space is somewhat limited, especially during peak travel times, so be sure to reserve space in advance. Making a hotel reservation is separate from reserving space for your pet within one of the kennels. In addition to housing dogs, the kennels will also accept cats, birds, ferrets, small rodents, and nonvenomous snakes (if in their own carriers).

Universal Studios provides complimentary kennel service for park guests. Visit the Guest Services window at the park entrance, and your pet will be escorted by one of the Guest Service Representatives to the pet facility.

Keep in mind that all dogs and cats are required to have a certificate of vaccination signed by a licensed veterinarian (rabies, parvo, DHLP, Bordetella for dogs; rabies, FPRC for cats).

Public Telephones

Throughout every theme park and resorts you'll find an abundance of public telephones. The majority of the pay telephones accept coins, credit cards, or prepaid phone cards.

You'll find that virtually all of the nationwide cellular services work within the Orlando area; however, depending on your cellular service or digital PCS contract, you may be charged per-minute roaming fees.

Long-distance rates vary. If you can find a good deal on a calling card (with no per-call surcharge and only a per-minute rate), this will probably be the least expensive option when using a pay phone or making calls from a hotel room.

Before making calls from your hotel room, determine what the surcharges will be. Some hotels charge $1 or more every time you pick up the phone to make an outgoing call, even if you're calling locally or using a toll-free phone number. Note that when you call an Orlando number that you will need to include the area code 407.

Restaurant Priority Seating/Reservations

Many of the sit-down restaurants within the theme parks, the hotels, Downtown Disney, and CityWalk area accept reservations and many recommend it. You can call (407) WDW-DINE to make a restaurant reservation, drop into the restaurant in person, visit the Guest Relations desk within the theme parks, or ask the concierge at your hotel to make the reservation for you.

TRAVEL TIP

The WDW dining reservation service ☎(407) WDW-DINE is only allotted a certain amount of reservations, so a sneaky way to bypass them is to call a WDW operator by dialing "0" on any WDW phone or call ☎(407) 824-2222 and ask to be connected to the podium of the restaurant where you want to make a reservation.

For those restaurants that do accept lunch and dinner reservations (especially those within the parks), space fills up quickly, so make your reservations early. Group reservations (or plans for a special event or private party) should be made well in advance.

Services for the Disabled

All parks offer a wide range of services for physically disabled guests. Manually operated wheelchairs and electric convenience vehicles both can be rented near the entrance of each theme park. If you're staying at a Disney hotel, complimentary wheelchairs are available from the hotel. See the front desk for details. The buses that transport guests throughout the WDW Resort are all wheelchair accessible.

For guests with visual disabilities, a special Braille guidebook is available, free of charge, from Guest Relations at any of the theme parks. For those with hearing impairments, closed captioning is available on many of the movie/video-based attractions, written story lines are available for virtually all of the rides and attractions, and some of the rides and attractions utilize Assistive Listening Systems. (The receiver is available from Guest Relations within the theme parks.)

For additional information about all of the various services available for disabled guests, call Guest Relations at (407) 824-4321. A free publication, called "the Guidebook for Guests with Disabilities," offers information about accessibility to the various rides, shows, attractions, shops, and restaurants within the theme parks. This guide is available from Guest Relations.

If you have special dietary needs, speak with the chef at any of the sit-down (full-service) restaurants. Whenever possible, your special needs will be met.

All of the resort hotels also offer special accommodations for the disabled. These accommodations must be reserved in advance, when making your actual reservation.

Stroller Rentals

Within the theme parks, stroller rentals are available for around $8 per day (plus a $1 refundable deposit). A two-passenger stroller can be rented for $15 per day (plus a $1 refundable deposit). When renting a stroller, be sure to keep the receipt with you at all times. If you park your stroller in order to experience an attraction, and your stroller is gone when you return, simply go to a stroller replacement center or the main rental area for a replacement.

Because you'll be leaving the stroller unattended (parked outside of each attraction you experience), it's an excellent idea to rent a stroller when you get to one of the theme parks. Do not plan on bringing your own. Also, never leave anything valuable in the storage compartments of the stroller.

CHAPTER 4

Introduction to the Walt Disney World Resort

THE WDW RESORT IS SO BIG that it can be hard to wrap your head around it, much less see it all in one vacation. WDW spans 47 square miles, a distance as large as the city of Boston. This chapter will help give you an overview of this vast and intricate world, including places to eat, where to see characters, shows to see, activities not to be missed, and special experiences just for you.

WDW Overview

Glance at what WDW has to offer and you will soon have a better grasp of why there are almost 60,000 people that work for WDW. Also, click over to *www.google.com* and download the free version of Google Earth to see a bird's-eye view of this enormous resort. Here is a quick overview of the Walt Disney World Resort:

23 Resorts
1 Campground
1 Ranch and farm
4 Theme parks
2 Water parks
14 Monorails
240 Buses
140+ Places to dine

50+ Bars/lounges
2 Nightlife areas
13 Character meal experiences
4 Dinner/Meal shows
22 Tours
10 Kids' clubs
3 Spas
5 Championship golf courses (3 on the PGA Tour)
2 Miniature golf courses
1 Sports complex
1 Race track/speedway
9 Fitness gyms
10 Marinas
1 Yacht
19 Playgrounds
1 Kennel
9 Tennis courts (6 hard and 3 clay)
6 Volleyball courts
22 Arcades
8 Jogging trails
3 Horse-drawn carriage rides
1 Movie theater with 24 screens

As you see, the WDW Resort has become much more than just another theme park. Within the WDW Resort there are activities galore. So, no matter where your interests lie, you'll be able to spend your vacation participating in exciting activities or, if you choose, kicking back at your hotel's swimming pool, relaxing, and getting a tan.

TRAVEL TIP

Planning a family reunion? The WDW Resort makes planning a family get-together (with eight guests or more) fast, fun, and easy, allowing you to create the most memorable vacation experience possible for everyone in your extended family. The program is called "Magical Gatherings." To learn more about this online-based, free downloadable tool, point your Web browser to: ✎*www.disneyworld.com/magicalgatherings*.

The Top Things to Know about WDW

Whenever you travel anywhere there is always bits of informative tips that make your vacation easier. These top things to know about WDW are based on the top questions Disney guests ask several times a day:

- You don't have to keep track of, record, or remember several phone numbers. Simply program the number (407) 824-2222 into your cell phone and whenever you need to contact any-place anywhere on WDW property a WDW operator will connect you. While on property simply dial "0" on any WDW phone.
- All four theme parks have 3-D shows and all are excellent.
- Magic Kingdom, Epcot, and Disney's MGM have a big nightly show. Animal Kingdom and Downtown Disney do not.
- Buses do not run from resort to resort. You must take a bus to Magic Kingdom, Epcot, Disney's MGM, Animal Kingdom, Downtown Disney, or the Ticket and Transportation Station, and then wait for another bus for your desired resort. Also, to catch a bus to a park, you must be at a resort or at the Ticket and Transportation Station.
- The restaurant inside Cinderella's Castle at Magic Kingdom takes reservations four to six months in advance, so plan accordingly.

- California Grill, the top-floor restaurant at the Contemporary overlooking Magic Kingdom, takes reservations two to four months in advance, so plan accordingly.
- Soarin' is Epcot's most popular attraction, so as soon as you walk through the morning gates you must walk straight to the Land Pavilion and obtain a FASTPASS for this popular attraction, or they will be gone by noon.
- If you like the idea of never having to wait in line for an attraction, visit WDW during the first two weeks of September or the first two weeks of December.
- Cast members and managers are trained to meet and overexceed your expectations at WDW, so if you're dissatisfied with anything, always ask to speak to a manager and you will see results.
- No gum whatsoever is sold on WDW property and they discourage guests bringing gum onto the property.
- Pal Mickey is a talking 12-inch plush Mickey Mouse toy that uses wireless technology. As you explore the various theme parks, Pal Mickey shares over 700 up-to-date real-time tidbits of information. He also tells jokes, and interacts with your child based on where you are within the parks. Pal Mickey is priced at $65. The toy can be bought by searching online or at WDW gift shops at every park and resort.
- Smoking is allowed outside only. Theme parks have designated outside smoking areas. There are no cigarette machines at WDW. You may, however, purchase tobacco products at the gift shops. You'll have to ask, because these products are kept hidden behind the counter.
- Alcohol is sold everywhere on WDW except at Magic Kingdom. You can also travel with drinks in plastic cups everywhere except the WDW buses. Beer, wine, and liquor are sold in the resort gift shops. The liquor is behind the counter, so you'll have to ask for it.

- Want to ride in the nose (front) of the monorail? Simply ask. You may have to wait for one more monorail, but this experience is a thrill for children. The same goes for any ride at WDW. Simply ask to be on the front row, back row, or any row you desire.
- WDW has an entire lingo and philosophy. Everyone that works there (almost 60,000) is considered "part of the show." They are called cast members, and what they wear is called a "costume." When you see them they are "onstage," and when you don't they are "backstage."
- You will find that there are many odd (or so they may seem at first) rules and guidelines at WDW. One example is that you may ask for some scissors so that you can cut a band off your wrist. However, cast members are not allowed to give guests anything sharp or allow anything sharp near them. (Just know that for every rule/policy you come across there is a reason behind it.)
- When traveling to the Fort Wilderness Campground by bus, you have to get off that bus and catch another bus to go into the campground. If you are traveling by car, you will park and catch the bus into the campground. Only registered cars that are paying to stay in the campground are allowed to enter the campground.
- Beignets (been-YAYS), the famous New Orleans pastries, can only be found one place on WDW property, which is at Port Orleans' French Quarter Resort food court. They are the first thing on the left as you walk into the food court.

WDW Calendar of Events

Disney has wonderful special annual events throughout the year. Some require an extra ticket price; however, most don't. It depends on the dates you are traveling. Make sure to check this calendar to see if you will be able to view any of these great events.

CALENDAR OF EVENTS

January		
First week in January at Wide World of Sports	WDW Marathon	The marathon itself takes place all over WDW
Select days at Magic Kingdom	Pirate and Princess Party	Extra ticket charge
February		
Select days at Magic Kingdom	Pirate and Princess Party	Extra ticket charge
The third week at Downtown Disney	Parti Gras	Disney's spin on Mardi Gras
March		
Select days at Magic Kingdom	Pirate and Princess Party	Extra ticket charge
April		
Mid-month at Epcot	Epcot's International Flower and Garden Festival	Celebrity gardeners, Flower Power Concerts from some Oldie-but-Goodie celebrities, and activities for kids like a butterfly house, scavenger hunt, and more
May		
Entire month at Epcot	Epcot's International Flower and Garden Festival	
June		
First week at Epcot	Epcot's International Flower and Garden Festival	
First week all over WDW property	Gay Days	This annual event is not sponsored by WDW
Second weekend at Downtown Disney	VIBE Live!	Celebration of Black Music Month featuring R & B, hip-hop, and soul artists
July		
July 4 at all parks except for Animal Kingdom	Independence Day Celebrations	

September		
First or second week at Magic Kingdom	Night of Joy	Christian music performers
A three-day weekend in midmonth	Walt Disney World Triathlon	
Third weekend at Downtown Disney	Latin Rhythm Nights	
End of month at Magic Kingdom	Mickey's Not-So-Scary Halloween Party	Extra ticket charge
End of month at Epcot	Epcot International Food and Wine Festival	
October		
Entire month at Magic Kingdom	Mickey's Not-So-Scary Halloween Party	Extra ticket charge
Entire month at Epcot	Epcot International Food and Wine Festival	
November		
Through mid-month at Epcot	Epcot International Food and Wine Festival	
Midmonth weekend at Downtown Disney	Jazz Fest	
Midmonth through end of month at Magic Kingdom	Mickey's Very Merry Christmas Party	Extra ticket charge
End of month at Epcot	Holidays Around the World	
December		
Entire month at Magic Kingdom	Mickey's Very Merry Christmas Party	Extra ticket charge
Entire month at Epcot	Holidays Around the World	

≡FAST FACT

BankOne offers an official Disney Visa card. Using this credit card to make your everyday purchases allows you to earn "Disney Dream Reward Dollars" that can be used toward discounts on Disney vacation packages and Disney merchandise. Paying for your Disney vacation (airfares, hotel, rental car, theme park tickets, souvenirs, meals, etc.) with this credit card entitles you to additional discounts. To apply for the card, call ☏(877) 252-6576.

WDW Tours and Special Experiences

Disney offers many fun, interesting, and educating tours of imaginative and the behind-the-scene experiences for guests. Most require entrance into the parks plus the price of the tour. For more information or reservations call (407) WDW-TOUR.

Magic Kingdom Tours

Tours at Magic Kingdom provide guests with a lot of interesting information, history, and fun. Some are suitable to take as a family and others you may want to go solo. Tour sizes are relatively small, so always try to make arrangements to reserve a tour as soon as you can.

Mickey's Magical Milestones

This two-hour tour through Magic Kingdom teaches you tidbits of Magic Kingdom history. It includes a train ride to Mickey's Toontown before it opens to the general public, and you get a surprise visit from Mickey himself, so have your cameras with you. The tour finishes with a backdoor entrance to Magic Kingdom's 3-D movie, *PhilharMagic*. The price is $25 per person and you must be at least ten years old. The tour meets at the garden in front of City Hall on Monday, Wednesday, and Friday at 8:45 A.M. Theme park admission is required.

Family Magic Tour

Take a two-hour interactive imagination tour through Magic Kingdom treasure-hunt-style. Kids love this one! It costs $27 per person and starts at 10:00 A.M. daily. Theme park admission is required.

Keys to the Kingdom

A five-hour tour of Disney history. This is the tour that takes you below Magic Kingdom in the tunnels. The price is $58 per person and includes lunch. The tour starts at City Hall inside Magic Kingdom at 8:30, 9:00, and 9:30 A.M. daily. Theme park admission is required.

The Magic Behind Our Steam Trains

This three-hour tour of WDW trains and history is about Walt Disney's fascination with trains. This tour takes you backstage, and you are given a pin at the end.

The price is $40 per person and you must be at least ten years old. The tour meets at the turnstiles Monday, Tuesday, and Saturday at 7:30 A.M. Theme park admission is required.

Virtual Magic Kingdom Tour

This is a Magic Kingdom tour that you can do at home on the computer. It's free at *www.vmk.com*. Players create their own environments, control characters, and interact with other players from around the globe. When you get to the Magic Kingdom in person, you can log on to a Quest kiosk to win fun stuff.

Animal Kingdom Tours

Tours at Animal Kingdom provide information about certain parts of the park onstage and backstage. They are not meant for smaller children and actually require guests to be at least fourteen to sixteen years old.

Backstage Safari Tour

This is a three-hour backstage tour of Animal Kingdom. It costs $65 per person and you must be at least sixteen years old. No photography is allowed backstage, and theme park admission is required.

Wild by Design

This three-hour walking tour teaches you about the artwork and creative design of Animal Kingdom. Price is $58 per person and you must be at least fourteen years old. It includes a continental breakfast, and theme park admission is required.

Epcot Tours

Epcot offers more tours than any park at WDW. You can swim with dolphins, learn about hydroponics gardening, ride a Segway, visit VIP lounges, and more!

Simply Segway

This is a one-hour class on how to use/drive a Segway Human transporter. Cost is $30 per person and you must be at least sixteen years old and weigh between 100 to 250 lbs. Persons with special needs or expectant mothers are not allowed to participate. Meets at Epcot Guest Relations many times every day except Tuesday. Theme park admission is required.

Behind the Seeds

Take a one-hour walking tour of the Land Pavilion's labs and greenhouses. Video and still cameras are allowed. It costs $12 per adult and $10 per child (ages three to nine). Theme park admission is required.

Epcot Seas Aqua Tour

This is a backstage tour of the Living Seas that lasts for two and a half hours, with thirty minutes in the Living Seas aquarium, so bring a swimsuit. Cost is $100 per person. You must be at least eight years old and ages eight to eighteen must be accompanied by an adult. Scuba certification is not required. Price includes, gear, T-shirt, and a group photo. The tour starts daily at 12:30 P.M. Theme park admission is not required.

Divequest

This program offers certified scuba divers the chance to explore the Living Seas for two and a half hours. You must have proof of current certification. Price is $140 per person. The tour meets daily at 4:30 and 5:40 P.M. and includes refreshments and a T-shirt. A video of your dive is available for $35. Theme park admission is not required.

Dolphins in Depth

This three-hour experience is for guests who want to learn more about the dolphins at the Living Seas. Wetsuits are provided, but you must bring a swimsuit. Showers and amenities are included as well. No cameras or video cameras are allowed, and dolphin interaction is not guaranteed. The price is $150 per person. You must be at least thirteen years old and an adult must accompany children ages thirteen to eighteen. Price includes a photo with a dolphin, refreshments, and a T-shirt. Meets Monday through Friday at 9:45 A.M. at Guest Relations. Theme park admission is not required.

Gardens of the World

Enjoy a three-hour walking horticulture tour of Epcot. The cost is $59 per person and you must be at least sixteen years old. The tour meets at Guest Relations on Tuesdays and Thursdays at 10:00 A.M. During the Flower and Garden Festival it is also offered on Saturdays. Theme park admission is required.

Hidden Treasures

Take a three-hour walking tour of the World Showcase, with lots of peeks behind the scenes. The price is $59 per person. The tour meets at Guest Relations on Tuesdays and Thursdays at 9:00 A.M. Theme park admission is required.

Undiscovered Future World

This walking history tour of Epcot takes four and a half hours and offers lots of backstage peeks and also includes an invitation to sit in the VIP lounge to view IllumiNations later that night. Price is $49 per person and the tour meets at Guest Relations Monday, Wednesday, and Friday at 9:00 A.M. Theme park admission is required.

Combination or Seasonal Tours

Tours that are offered at certain times of the year or include a combination of parks, resorts, and experiences fall under this category.

- **Backstage Magic**

This seven-hour tour visits the backstage areas of Magic Kingdom, Epcot, and Disney-MGM Studios. The price is $199 per person and includes lunch. The tour meets Monday through Friday at 8:45 A.M. at Guest Services at Epcot. Advance reservations for up to two months is recommended. Theme park admission is not required.

- **Disney's Yuletide Fantasy**

This is a three-hour seasonal tour of some parks, resorts, and the holiday warehouse backstage. The price is $69 per person. An adult must accompany guests under the age of sixteen. Theme park admission is not required.

- **Disney's VIP Tour**

A VIP tour can be customized for up to ten guests. The price is $85 to $100 per hour. Call Disney Special Activities at (407) 560-4033.

Other Tours and Adventures

Special adventures and/or tours are offered mostly for the children. Some do not allow adult participation, which allows adults the time to have a massage, relax at the pool, or whatever they desire.

Pirate Adventure

This is a two-hour boat tour and treasure hunt. The price is $28 per child and includes lunch and a goody bag. This tour is for children ages four to ten only. Adults are not allowed. It meets at the Grand Floridian Resort marina at 10:00 A.M. on Monday, Wednesday, and Thursday.

Wonderland Tea Party

This is a delightful tea party with Alice and the Mad Hatter that includes games, refreshments, souvenirs, and a photo. The price is

$28 per child, for ages four to ten only. No adults allowed. It meets daily at 1900 Park Fare at the Grand Floridian Resort from 1:15 to 2:30 P.M.

Grand Adventures in Cooking

A Disney chef helps kids create culinary delights. At the end the kids parade through the lobby and hand out some of their creations to guests. The price is $28 per child, ages three to ten only. No adults allowed. It meets at 1900 Park Fare at the Grand Floridian Resort Tuesday and Friday from 10:00 to 11:45 A.M.

My Disney Girl's Perfectly Princess Tea Party

Sleeping Beauty (Princess Aurora), tells stories, sings songs, and conducts a princess parade. Each girl is given a My Disney Doll, silver bracelet, princess scrapbook page, tiara, and a Best Friend certificate. Gourmet cuisine is available for the princesses and their adult accompaniment.

The price is $200 for one adult and child. The child must be between ages three to eleven. Each additional adult is $65, and $135 for an additional child. It meets in the Garden View Lounge at the Grand Floridian Resort on Monday, Wednesday, Thursday, and Friday from 10:30 A.M. to 12:00 P.M.

Afternoon Tea at the Garden View Lounge

Take tea in the small Garden View Lounge at the Grand Floridian. This is geared for adults or very well-mannered and behaved teenagers. The cost is about $52 for two adults, which does not include the tip. You choose gourmet teas, finger sandwiches, and miniature pastries. Surprisingly, it turns out to be very filling. It is offered daily from 3:00 to 6:00 P.M. and reservations are highly recommended, as there are only twenty small tables.

Bibbidi Bobbidi Boutique

The Bibbidi Bobbidi Boutique located at the Marketplace at Downtown Disney inside the World of Disney store turns little girls ages three and up into a Disney Princess, Pop Princess, or Disney Diva. With the help of a "Fairy Godmother-in-Training," they get a "makeover" that includes hairstyling, makeup, and manicures.

A Coach Package includes hairstyling and shimmering makeup for $35. The Crown Package includes hairstyling, shimmering makeup, and nails for $45. And the Castle Package includes the Crown Package plus a complete costume of your choice with accessories for $175.

They also offer a pirate room with a boys' experience called "Cool Dude," with hairstyling, colored gels/sparkles, build a pirate hat or skull, tattoos, and superhero gear. Call (407) 939-7895 to make a reservation.

WDW Character Meals

You should make reservations for at least one character meal during your WDW visit. Basically, you are paying for you and your children to get up close and personal with many Disney characters. Characters come around to all tables for hugs, autographs, and photos. Prices for character meals range from $18 to $23 per adult and $10 for children three to nine years old.

Magic Kingdom
The Magic Kingdom has three restaurants that offer character meals, for a total of two breakfasts, two lunches, and three dinners.

- **Cinderella's Table** is open for Once Upon a Time Breakfast, Cinderella's Royal Table Lunch, and Dreams Come True Dinner. During breakfast and lunch, several princesses roam the room, while dinner includes a visit from the Fairy Godmother. Reservations are taken three to six months in advance. Tables are not to be pulled together. Only parties of two, three, and four are allowed. If you have a larger party, it's not guaranteed that you will sit near one another.

- **Liberty Tree** is open for Liberate Your Appetite Dinner (4:00 P.M. to park closing). Enjoy a Thanksgiving meal menu with Minnie and friends in Frontierland.
- **Crystal Palace** offers breakfast (8:00 to 10:30 A.M.), lunch (11:30 A.M. to 2:45 P.M.), and a dinner buffet (4:00 P.M. to park closing) with Pooh and friends.

Epcot

There are two restaurants that offer character meals at Epcot. One is buffet-style and the other is service-style. In total, they offer one breakfast, two lunches, and two dinners.

- **Akershus Restaurant** at Norway offers Princess Storybook Dining for breakfast (8:30 A.M. to 11:40 A.M.), lunch (11:40 A.M. to 2:50 P.M.), and dinner (4:20 P.M. to 8:40 P.M.).
- **The Garden Grill** at the Land Pavilion has a circular floor that rotates slowly around. The restaurant is open for lunch (noon to 3:30 P.M.) and dinner (5:00 P.M. to 8:00 P.M.), with Mickey, Minnie, Chip, and Dale.

Disney-MGM Studios

At the moment, Disney's MGM Studios only offers one breakfast and lunch buffet character meal. More are on the way.

- **The Hollywood and Vine** offers a buffet breakfast (8:00 to 11:20 A.M.) and lunch (11:40 to 2:25 P.M.) with Jo Jo and Goliath, and lunch with June and Leo.

Animal Kingdom

Even though Animal Kingdom only has one character meal restaurant, they offer breakfast, lunch, and dinner.

- **Restaurantosaurus** in Dinoland offers Donald's Breakfastosaurus, and lunch and dinner buffets with Donald and friends. The restaurant is open according to Animal Kingdom's opening and closing hours.

WDW Resort Character Meals

Five of Disney's resorts offer character meals, so you wouldn't have to travel very far if you're staying at one of these resorts.

- **Grand Floridian Resort & Spa.** The restaurant 1900 Park Fare offers buffet breakfast with Mary Poppins, the Mad Hatter, Alice, Pinocchio, Tigger, and more from 7:30 A.M. to 11:00 A.M., and Cinderella's Gala Feast Buffet Dinner with Cinderella, Prince Charming, Fairy Godmother, and more from 5:00 P.M. to 9:00 P.M.
- **Polynesian Resort.** Breakfast is available at O'hana's with Mickey and friends, from 7:30 A.M. to 11:00 A.M.
- **Contemporary Resort.** Chef Mickey's offers a buffet breakfast (7:00 A.M. to 11:30 A.M.) and dinner (5:00 P.M. to 9:30 P.M.) with Mickey and friends.
- **Beach Club.** Cape May Café offers a buffet breakfast with Minnie, Goofy, and more.
- **Swan Resort.** Gulliver's Grill offers a prime rib, grilled fish, and lobster dinner buffet with Mickey and friends. Saturday breakfast and lunch are offered at the adjoining (and more casual) Garden Grove Café with Mickey and gang.

WDW Dinner Shows

There are four dinner/meal shows on WDW property. Two of the dinner shows, the Hoop-Dee-Doo Musical Revue and the Spirit of Aloha Dinner Show, have been going strong for over twenty-five years. Starting in 2007 these two shows will have tiered seating and for the first time you'll be able to choose where you want to sit in three categories.

Hoop-Dee-Doo Musical Revue

This rip-roaring fun western-themed dinner show at Pioneer Hall in Fort Wilderness offers down-home country food and unlimited beer, wine, sangria, and soft drinks. This is the best dinner show at Disney, and they take reservations up to two years in advance. The cost is $50 for adults and $25 for ages three to eleven. There are three shows nightly at 5:00 P.M., 7:15 P.M., and 9:30 P.M.

Spirit of Aloha Dinner Show

Enjoy a luau in an open-air covered theater in Luau Cove on the Polynesians beach. It includes Polynesian food and unlimited beer, wine, punch, and soft drinks. The cost is $50 for adults and $25 for ages three to eleven. There are two shows nightly (5:15 and 8:00 P.M.) from Tuesday to Saturday. Shows are canceled if temperatures fall below 50 degrees.

Mickey's Backyard BBQ

This seasonal dinner is at the Settlement (outdoor pavilion) at the Fort Wilderness Campground. It includes a live country band, line dancing with Mickey and friends, down-home barbecue, and unlimited beer, wine, sangria, and soft drinks. The cost is $40 for adults and $25 for ages three to eleven. Weather permitting, it is available on Tuesdays and Thursdays, March through December.

House of Blues Gospel Brunch

This spirited brunch buffet is combined with several onstage gospel performances. The cost is $33.50 for adults and $17.25 for ages three to nine. There are two brunch shows, at 10:30 A.M. and 1:00 P.M.

WDW Cruises

There are several cruises offered at WDW. Groups can divide the cost up evenly to save money. It's an experience you're sure not to forget for a long time.

The *Grand 1*

The *Grand 1*, a 45-foot yacht, can be rented for $350 an hour for up to twelve people. It's docked at the Grand Floridian, but will pick you up if you're staying at the Polynesian, Contemporary, or Wilderness Lodge. It includes a captain and deckhand and is perfect for the nighttime fireworks at Magic Kingdom.

Magic Kingdom Wishes Cruise

A driver takes up to eight guests on a 21-foot Tracker Pontoon for $200. The price includes water, soda, and bagged snacks. Guests may also order private dining to be delivered to the cruise.

Magic Kingdom Wishes Premium Cruise

Rent a 25-foot Tracker Pontoon for $250 for up to ten guests. The price includes water, soda, bagged snacks, and audio feed of Magic Kingdom's fireworks show, Wishes. Guests may also order private dining to be delivered to the cruise.

Magic Kingdom Wishes Celebration Cruise

This cruise is the same as the Magic Kingdom Wishes Cruise plus decorations. The price is $220. To make it the same as the Premium Cruise with decorations add $50.

The Breathless

The Breathless, at the Yacht & Beach Club Resort marina, can be rented for $235 an hour for up to seven people. A driver is included and the best time to book is for Epcot's IlluminNation shows at night.

IllumiNations Basic Cruise

Invite up to ten guests to take a cruise on a pontoon boat for a cost of $250. The price includes a driver, water, soda, and bagged snacks. Guests may also order private dining to be delivered to the cruise.

IllumiNations Celebrations Cruise

This is the same as IllumiNations Basic Cruise plus decorations. The price is $275 and guests may also order private dining to be delivered to the cruise.

WDW Activities

Staying at WDW doesn't have to be all about the parks. There are many activities to keep you busy. If you have bought a package, check to see if these activities are included in your price.

Golf

The WDW Resort offers ninety-nine holes of what Disney calls the world's greatest golf. The resort offers five championship eighteen-hole courses and a nine-hole walking course.

GOLF COURSES ON WALT DISNEY WORLD RESORT			
Course	Par/Yards	Rating	Slope
Eagle Pines	72/6,772	72.3	131
Lake Buena Vista	72/6,820	72.7	128
Magnolia	72/7,190	73.9	133
Oak Trail	36/2,913	N/A	N/A
Osprey Ridge	72/7,101	73.9	135
Palm	72/6,957	73.0	133

In addition to the golf courses, the WDW Resort contains three full-service pro shops, four driving ranges, and four practice putting greens. If you don't feel like packing up your own clubs and bringing them with you to Orlando, all Disney courses rent Callaway golf clubs and FootJoy shoes. Private golf instruction from Disney's PGA professional staff is available by appointment, but you'll want to schedule your lessons as far in advance as possible. Keep in mind, proper golf attire is required on all of Disney's golf courses. Shirts with collars and Bermuda-length shorts are part of the dress code.

WDW Resort guests can reserve tee times up to ninety days in advance, and day guests can reserve up to thirty days in advance by calling (407) WDW-GOLF (939-4653). All reservations must be guaranteed with a major credit card.

For more information about the golfing opportunities available at the WDW Resort and for current rates, call (407) WDW-GOLF, or visit the special Web site at *www.golf.disneyworld.com*. Special golf vacation packages are also offered throughout the year. Call (407) 939-7677 for travel package information. January through April is the busiest golfing season at Disney.

Miniature Golf

If mini-golf is more your thing, there are miniature golf courses on WDW Resort property. For example, there's the family-oriented Fantasia Gardens Miniature Golf and Garden Pavilions, which offers two whimsical eighteen-hole miniature golf courses and a 22,000-square-foot outdoor meeting facility located near Epcot and the Disney-MGM Studios.

FAST FACT

Complimentary taxi vouchers (through Yellow Cab) are provided for Walt Disney World Resort guests who are coming to play golf at one of Disney's golf courses. The valet/concierge desk or Bell Services will summon a cab for you. The Pro Shop at the golf course will assist you in returning to your resort.

Disney's Wide World of Sports Complex

In addition to the ESPN Club and ESPN Store at Disney's Board-Walk, the WDW Resort also offers Disney's Wide World of Sports complex, which hosts all sorts of professional and amateur sporting events throughout the year and is the permanent training location for the Harlem Globetrotters. Tickets to the premium sporting events that take place at this complex can be obtained by calling TicketMaster at (407) 839-3900.

Disney's Wide World of Sports is a 200-acre complex that contains sports fields, baseball diamonds, tracks, tennis courts, basketball courts, and a 7,500-seat stadium, designed to accommodate professional teams and amateurs alike in more than thirty different sports.

A flat one-price daily admission gives guests access to watch as many nonpremium events as they'd like throughout the day and tour the complex. For ticket prices and admission information, see Chapter 3.

To reach Disney's Wide World of Sports, take the WDW bus service, or by car, take I-4 to The Magic Kingdom exit (25), then follow the signs. Parking is free. The D-Sports Shop located in the complex sells a wide range of official NBA, NFL, MLB, and NHL merchandise and clothing. There are also several other sports-oriented shops that sell equipment, apparel, memorabilia, and souvenirs.

⊕ HOT SPOT

The NFL Experience is an exciting attraction for football fans of all ages. This interactive football playground allows fans to kick the ball through uprights, throw footballs at targets, and test their speed in the forty-yard dash.

Drive a Racecar

Champion driver Richard Petty has teamed up with Disney to offer the Richard Petty Driving Experience at the Walt Disney World Speedway. Now you can experience what it's like to drive an actual two-seat stock car around a professional track at speeds of up to 145 miles per hour.

The basic Riding-Along Experience ($89 to $125) allows you to be in the passenger seat of a two-seat stock car as a professional driver takes you for three laps around the track. The Rookie

Experience ($349 to $499) puts you in the driver's seat for eight laps around the one-mile tri-oval track, in a car that can reach 125 miles per hour. The upgraded King's Experience ($749 to $1,199) offers sixteen laps of driving divided into two eight-lap sessions. The Experience of a Lifetime ($1,199 to $1,249) allows you to participate in a thirty-lap program (which is divided into three ten-lap sessions). You'll receive professional instruction designed to teach you the basics of racing.

The Walt Disney World Speedway is open to spectators, who can watch nonprofessional races, free of charge, between 9:00 A.M. and 5:00 P.M. daily (weather permitting). For more information about the Richard Petty Driving Experience, call (800) BE-PETTY or visit the Web site at *www.1800bepetty.com*.

Tennis Anyone?

Disney's Wide World of Sports complex offers several clay courts, plus there are over twenty-five additional courts located at the various WDW Resort hotels. Disney's Racquet Club at the Contemporary Resort offers six courts, plus a pro shop and private instruction. Court time can be reserved between 8:00 A.M. and 8:00 P.M. daily. Some lighted courts are available and are open until 9:00 P.M.

Other court locations include: Disney's Grand Floridian Resort & Spa (two clay courts), Disney's Fort Wilderness Campground (two hard courts), Disney's Yacht Club Resort and Disney's Beach Club Resort (two hard courts), Disney's Old Key West Resort (three hard courts), and Disney's Saratoga Springs Resort & Spa. All are lighted for night play.

For the best court times, you'll have to plan ahead. Reservations are taken up to one year in advance for the courts at Disney's Racquet Club, as well as at many of the other WDW Resort hotel locations. For many of the courts, the rental fee is $15 per hour; however, some of them are free of charge.

For more information about Disney's Racquet Club and where you can play tennis at the WDW Resort, call (407) 824-3578. For information about any of the tennis courts at the WDW Resort, call (407) WDW-PLAY.

≡FAST FACT

Private tennis lessons, with a U.S. Tennis Association–certified instructor, are available at Disney's Racquet Club for $50 per hour. To play against a pro, without receiving instruction, costs $45 per hour. Racquets and ball machines can both be rented for an additional fee.

Row, Row, Row Your Boat

At various locations throughout the WDW Resort, you can rent various types of boats by the half-hour or by the hour. Renting a boat is a wonderful and relatively inexpensive way to spend a morning or afternoon enjoying the outdoors, without dealing with crowds at one of the Disney theme parks.

Boats available for rent include canoes, canopy boats, pedal boats, pontoon boats, sailboats, and speedboats. You can also go parasailing or waterskiing. Many of these boating activities can be done from the various hotels located along the Seven Seas Lagoon, Crescent Lake, or Buena Vista Lagoon. To rent any of the boats at the WDW Resort, you must be a guest at any WDW Resort hotel and have a valid driver's license or passport. No privately owned boats are allowed to be used anywhere on WDW property. Some restrictions apply in regard to minors renting boats. Check with any WDW Resort hotel for details or to reserve a boat.

There's Even Bass Fishing

Back in the mid-1960s, Bay Lake, which is located on Disney property, was stocked with 70,000 bass. Well, those fish have multiplied, making for a wonderful fishing opportunity. If you want to partake in the fishing activities, you must sign up for one of the Fishing Excursions that take place throughout the day. Reservations are required. Call (407) 828-2204 (Downtown Disney Fishing Excursion), (407) 934-5409 (The Fishing Hole), or (407) 824-2621 (WDW Golf and Recreation Reservations).

TRAVEL TIP

Dockside fishing is offered at Fort Wilderness Campground and at Port Orleans Riverside. Cost is nominal and also has a catch-and-release policy.

All fish that are caught must be released. Fishing equipment is provided. The price for a two-hour Fishing Excursion ranges from about $50 to $70 per person. Up to five people can participate in each excursion. The cost of a five-person tour is $160, with a departure in early morning, midmorning, or afternoon.

Spas

If an afternoon of indulging yourself sounds more like your cup of tea, WDW has three spas on property to choose from. You will find them at the Grand Floridian Spa & Health Club, the Spa at Saratoga Springs, and Manadra Spa at the Dolphin. Spa treatments are available at Animal Kingdom Lodge, BoardWalk, Contemporary, Coronado, Wilderness Lodge, and the Yacht Club.

Horse and Carriage Rides

Three WDW resorts offer-horse-and carriage rides: Fort Wilderness Campground, Port Orleans Riverside, and Saratoga Springs. The cost is $35 for thirty minutes. You can only pay cash or use your room card for payment. Any food or beverages you care to bring are allowed. Simply make reservations at any front desk or concierge desk.

Movie Theater

While escaping to the movies is something that you can do at home, you may find yourself with a rainy day here and there while on WDW property and looking for something to do indoors. At Downtown Disney there is an AMC movie theater with twenty-four screens.

The theaters have sport-stadium seating and theaters one and two have balconies.

The Top Free Things at WDW

You don't have to spend a lot of money at WDW to have a good time. Try some of these free activities:

- **Resort hop.** All of the resorts at WDW are wonderfully theme-detailed and each offers a unique experience. As a guest, you are more than welcome to resort hop. The very best time to do this is during the holidays.
- **Pool hop.** Disney doesn't come right out and say that you can pool hop, but you can. Some of the deluxe resorts frown on it, but if you do decide to pool hop, be smart about it and simply blend in. Use the resort towels and only carry one bag with you. You will also be able to use your guest resort ID for food, drinks, and merchandise. Take note that the Yacht & Beach Club will not let you in their pool area unless you show a resort ID from those two resorts.
- **Orchestra at Grand Floridian.** An orchestra plays in the lobby of the Grand Floridian from 5:00 to 8:00 P.M. every day. You can sit in the grand lobby or Mizner's lounge on the second floor.
- **Bob Jackson.** Everyone should see Bob Jackson, the Piano Guy, at least once. He plays at the Port Orleans Riverside in the River Roost Lounge Wednesdays through Saturdays 8:30 P.M. to midnight. He's like a cartoon character come to life, and children as well as adults go crazy over him.
- **Elliot Dyson.** Every Wednesday through Saturday night from 8:00 P.M. to midnight Elliot Dyson plays at the Scat Cat Lounge at Port Orleans French Quarter. This talented musician has about ten instruments onstage and plays them all and sings! He's not to be missed.

🧳 TRAVEL TIP

To catch both family musical acts at the Port Orleans, see Bob Jackson at Riverside for his first set then take a boat ride down to the French Quarter and catch Elliot Dyson. You can walk along the river to the French Quarter as well.

- **Outdoor movie and campfire.** Every night (weather permitting) Fort Wilderness Campground plays an outdoor movie on a big screen. Families gather under the stars and sing campfire songs around a fire. You can bring your own marshmallows and hot dogs or buy them there for a nominal fee. They even sell s'more kits! After sunset the movie starts and families can bring their own snacks or buy them at the concession stand. Oh, and every once in awhile Chip and Dale might make an appearance.
- **Old Faithful.** Every half-hour the Wilderness Lodge's version of the geyser Old Faithful erupts. Afterward you can head into the lobby and sit in rocking chairs in front of the largest fireplace you've ever seen. For the kids you can ask the front desk for an activity goodie bag filled with crayons, coloring book, and a list of places where you can search for Hidden Mickey's while there.
- **Ride in the front of the monorail.** Simply ask to ride in the nose of the monorail and they will let you. Maximum capacity is four. After going around and around the Magic Kingdom and resorts, hop on the Epcot monorail for a longer trip.

WDW Ideas for Special Occasions

If you are visiting WDW during a special occasion such as a birthday, anniversary, etc., you will be happy to know that there are some extra-special things you can do to fit all budgets. Certain ideas will apply to children more than adults and visa versa.

- While at Magic Kingdom, Epcot, or Disney-MGM Studios, stop by guest services and tell them that it's your birthday, and they will give you a birthday button to wear.
- While visiting any restaurant on WDW property, always tell the server about a special occasion and the restaurant will do something special for you. If nothing seems to happen, ask to speak to a manager. If it's a popular restaurant, they will need to know about the special occasion when you make the reservation.
- Winter Summerland Miniature Golf offers two-hour birthday parties for around $20 per person, which includes up to ten guests, cake, pizza, goodie bags, beverages, and golf.
- If you would like to have a full-size specialty cake made, the closest grocery store to WDW is Goodings. Call them at (407) 827-1200. They will deliver your cake to the front desk of your WDW resort.
- Arrange a horse-and-carriage ride and bring a goody basket.
- Take a sunset boat ride on any of the water taxis on WDW property.
- Blizzard Beach Water Park charges $15 per person with a maximum of thirty people for a party that includes pizza, cake, and beverages.
- Choose any of the cruises found in this chapter.
- Take a breathtaking sunrise hot-air balloon ride over WDW. What better way is there to wake up the birthday person and whisk them off to a surprise? Disney does not provide this service, but Orange Blossom Balloons does and has since 1983. Call them at (407) 239-7677 or visit their Web site at *www.orangeblossomballoons.com*. You'll need to make reservations at least two weeks in advance.
- Anyone celebrating a birthday would enjoy dinner at Downtown Disney before or after the Cirque du Soleil show. There's

also a water taxi that very few people know about at Downtown Disney. It sails back and forth from one end of the island to the other (Cirque du Soleil to/from Rainforest Café) until 11:00 P.M. (weather permitting). The searchlights crisscrossing high in the sky is all very exciting.

- If it's Wednesday through Saturday go to the Port Orleans Resort to see free live entertainment at the French Quarter and the Riverside Resort.
- For a price, divers will dive into a tank at the Living Seas, while you are dining at the Coral Reef, and hold up a sign with a message of your choice. Simply prearrange this.
- Dial "0" on any WDW phone and ask for the special "Happy Birthday" message.

For a price, basically anything your imagination can come up with can happen on WDW property. For more ideas, sit at a lounge or bar at WDW, tip the bartender well, and he or she will provide you with an enormous amount of information about celebrations and surprises.

CHAPTER 5

Introduction to the Magic Kingdom

IF THIS ISN'T YOUR FIRST TRIP to the Magic Kingdom, but you haven't been to this park in years (or decades), what awaits you is a combination of nostalgic rides, shows, and attractions, and a whole new set of entertaining experiences. This chapter provides information that will help you get ready to visit the Magic Kingdom.

Getting to and from the Magic Kingdom

Getting to the Magic Kingdom is easy, especially if you're staying at one of the Magic Kingdom Resort hotels. These include, the Contemporary Resort, the Polynesian Resort, and the Grand Floridian Resort. From these three deluxe resorts you can simply ride the monorail or a water taxi to Magic Kingdom. If you are staying at the Wilderness Lodge Resort or Fort Wilderness Campground you can ride a water taxi or bus to Magic Kingdom. For all other WDW resorts simply ride a WDW bus, which lets you off directly in front of Magic Kingdom. If you are driving into the Magic Kingdom you will pay $9 to park, then ride a tram to the Ticket and Transportation Center (TTC). WDW Resort guests do not have to pay for parking. Simply show your resort ID. Once at the TTC you'll have two modes of transportation to choose from to get to the Magic Kingdom. You can either take the monorail or a very large two-level ferryboat. Once the ferryboat launches, it will take four to six minutes to make it across the Seven Seas Lagoon. The monorail departs from the TTC every three minutes or so. However, keep in mind that there are two monorails, so it's important to choose the correct one. One monorail goes to Epcot and the other rides in a circle around the Seven Seas Lagoon to Magic Kingdom and the Magic Kingdom Resorts.

The WDW Transportation bus system takes guests to and from all of the Disney hotels as well as the various other theme parks and attractions located in the entire resort. While the bus system will, in fact, take you anywhere within the resort complex that you need to go, it's not a terribly fast service, so plan on spending at least thirty minutes to one hour traveling each time you need to use this free bus service.

Independent taxi service is available (for a fee, of course). Taking taxis eliminates the wait times involved with taking a WDW Transportation bus, as well as the parking hassles if you drive your own car, but is very expensive compared to other options.

═FAST FACT

No matter where you need to get to within the WDW Resort, the WDW bus system will get you there. This complimentary service features over 230 buses that operate continuously in order to transport guests between theme parks, the Disney hotels/resorts, and around the resort property.

If you're being dropped off by someone (in a car), you'll need to go to the parking lot of the Ticket and Transportation Center and then take the monorail or ferryboat to the Magic Kingdom. The driver will have to pay the daily parking fee; however, this fee will be refunded if the driver stops at the Exxon gas station near the exit of the parking lot and presents the parking receipt to the attendant within one hour.

First Things First

Admission to the Magic Kingdom (or any theme park) requires a ticket. For details about the various ticket and pricing options for visiting the Magic Kingdom and all of the theme parks within the WDW Resort, see Chapter 3.

Whenever you leave the Magic Kingdom, be sure to have your hand stamped as you exit in order to be granted readmission into the park later that day or evening. The hand stamps are designed to be water-resistant, so don't worry if your hand gets wet if you choose to return to your hotel in the middle of the day to go swimming, and then want to return to the Magic Kingdom later that evening. Try to refrain, however, from scrubbing your hands clean with soap until your day's visit to the Magic Kingdom is totally complete. Your ticket stub will also be needed.

What to Bring

Make sure you wear comfortable broken-in shoes! Try to avoid carrying too much stuff with you. You'll enjoy your visit more if your hands are as free as possible. Consolidating everything into one community backpack is a good idea. Depending on the weather, you might want to take along a jacket (you can always store it in a locker or tie it around your waist). It may seem odd to pack a lightweight jacket or long-sleeved shirt especially in the hot summer months, but indoor environments can sometimes be overcooled. Don't forget to bring your camera, along with plenty of film and batteries. Avoid having to purchase high-priced film, batteries, or camera supplies in the park.

In case of rain, plan on getting a bit wet. Wear a raincoat or plan to purchase a bright yellow Mickey Mouse poncho (for about $6). Avoid bringing an umbrella into the park. You'll find it frustrating trying to walk around the crowded park with an open umbrella. During a rainstorm, crowds will be less; however, some outdoor rides and attractions will be closed, and some parades and shows might be canceled. Planning for bad weather is important, but when it's sunny (or even slightly overcast), make sure you protect yourself and those you're traveling with by applying plenty of sunscreen. Also, wear a hat to protect your face from the sun.

TRAVEL TIP

One good rule is to always travel against the crowds. For example, many rides and attractions will have two lines. Statistics show that people automatically head to the right. You'll probably find that the line to the left will be shorter.

Choose a Place to Meet

As soon as you arrive at the Magic Kingdom, choose a place where you'll meet up with the other people in your group if you get separated. Two ideal meeting places are in front of City Hall or at the Hub (in front of the Walt Disney and Mickey Mouse statue). Decide to meet on the half-hour if you become separated. Adults can leave written messages for each other at City Hall. However, most people carry cell phones and simply contact each other this way. Walkie-talkies can be very useful as well.

≡FAST FACT

The very best time to visit the park and not have to deal with huge crowds is on Sunday morning.

If you're traveling with children, upon arriving at the Magic Kingdom, set some ground rules. Instruct the kids to stay close to you (the parent or adult) at all times. Let children know that if they get lost not to panic. All they have to do is find anyone wearing a Disney nametag and tell them that they are lost. The cast member will call the appropriate people and take the child to lost and found.

Kid Switch Policy

Not all of the rides and attractions within the Magic Kingdom are suitable for young children. If two adults are traveling with young kids, but both adults want to experience a ride that's not suitable for the kids, they can take advantage of the Kid Switch policy offered at all of the Disney theme parks.

The Kid Switch policy gives both adults (Mom and Dad, for example) the opportunity to enjoy the various thrill ride attractions that aren't suitable for kids, without the double wait. To take advantage of this policy, one parent waits in line with a small child while the other parent rides the attraction. When the first adult exits the attraction and returns to the loading area, he/she takes custody of the child while the second parent rides—without having to wait in line.

Dining in the Magic Kingdom

If you're looking for a fine-dining experience, you'll find fancy restaurants located in many of the WDW Resort hotels, as well as in Epcot, the Disney-MGM Studios, Downtown Disney, and Disney's BoardWalk Inn. This isn't really the park to visit for a very special meal. However, for a basic, family-oriented dining experience, the Magic Kingdom offers a variety of restaurants and snack shops. Smoking is not permitted in any of the park's eating establishments. Outside you may only smoke in designated smoking areas.

The restaurants in the Magic Kingdom will be the most crowded every day between 11:00 A.M. and 2:00 P.M. (for lunch) and between 5:00 P.M. and 7:00 P.M. (for dinner). If you don't mind having a flexible eating schedule and you want to avoid the crowds, your best bet is to hit the Magic Kingdom's most popular attractions during these times, and eat during the nonbusy periods. It's always a good idea to experience the more turbulent rides (Space Mountain, Big Thunder Mountain Railroad, Splash Mountain, etc.) before eating a big meal.

⊕ HOT SPOT

Kids love meeting the Disney characters and no vacation photo album is complete without a shot of Mickey hugging your child. You're guaranteed to meet Mickey and his friends within Mickey's Toontown Fair (an area of the Magic Kingdom) or at any of the character dining experiences offered at certain restaurants throughout.

For additional information about the dining options available in the Magic Kingdom, call (407) WDW-DINE. At some of these restaurants, special meals can be ordered to accommodate most dietary restrictions. If you need special meals prepared, however, you're better off eating at one of the restaurants located elsewhere in the WDW Resort. Salads as well as low-salt, vegetarian, and low-cholesterol meals are available at many of the following snack shops and full-service restaurants in the Magic Kingdom.

Fast Food/Snack Shops

These eating establishments are considerably cheaper than the full-service restaurants in the Magic Kingdom. With a few exceptions, hamburgers, hot dogs, chicken strips/nuggets, salads, soft drinks, bottled water, and ice cream are the typical menu offerings at the following fast-food snack shops:

- **Aloha Isle (Adventureland)**—Dole pineapple "whips" are the snack food available from this kiosk. Plan on spending under $7 per person for a snack.
- **Auntie Gravity's Galactic Goodies (Tomorrowland)**—If you're looking for frozen yogurt and fruit juices that are out of this world, park your rockets here for a snack. Plan on spending under $7 per person for a snack.

- **Aunt Polly's Dockside Inn (Frontierland)**—This is the only place on Tom Sawyer's Island where you can purchase food, including "picnic lunches" featuring a ham-and-cheese sandwich. Plan on spending under $12 per person for a meal.

- **Casey's Corner (Main Street U.S.A.)**—Hot dogs (with many different toppings), French fries, soft drinks, and a wide range of desserts are available for lunch and dinner. Plan on spending under $12 per person for a meal.

- **Columbia Harbor House (Liberty Square)**—Fried chicken strips and fried fish, clam chowder, sandwiches, and other fast-food items are on the menu. Plan on spending under $12 per person for a meal.

- **Cool Ship (Tomorrowland)**—This is a drink-only kiosk. Coca-Cola and other sodas are served. Plan on spending under $4 per person for a drink. Because this is a kiosk and not a restaurant, only cash is accepted here.

- **Cosmic Ray's Starlight Café (Tomorrowland)**—Traditional burgers, vegetarian burgers, chicken entrées, soups, tossed, chef, and Caesar salads, and sandwiches are available at this cafeteria-style dining location. On the stage in this indoor (air-conditioned) café is an Audio-Animatronic alien (Sonny Eclipse) who performs an ongoing musical act that kids will enjoy watching while they eat. Plan on spending under $12 per person for a meal.

- **Enchanted Grove (Fantasyland)**—Slushes and soft-serve ice cream may be the perfect snack on a hot day. Plan on spending under $7 per person for a snack.

- **Frontierland Fries (Frontierland)**—In addition to a variety of cold drinks, this is one of the few places within the WDW Resort where McDonald's French fries are available. They're a favorite snack among kids. Plan on spending under $7 per person for a snack.

- **Launching Pad at Rockettower Plaza (Tomorrowland)**—Various snack-food items, beverages, and smoked turkey legs are available. Plan on spending under $7 per person for a snack.

- **Main Street Bakery (Main Street U.S.A.)**—Freshly baked goods, including cookies and pastries, various flavored gourmet coffees, and cold beverages are available here. If you choose to order a bagel and cream cheese, you'll be given an extremely small amount of cream cheese. Additional cream cheese costs extra, and you'll quickly discover that while the baked goods are fresh, the bagels aren't made on-site. Plan on spending under $7 per person for a snack.

- **Mrs. Potts' Cupboard (Fantasyland)**—Slushes, soft-serve ice cream, and sundaes are served here. Plan on spending under $7 per person for a snack.

- **Pecos Bill Café (Frontierland)**—Burgers, barbecue chicken, hot dogs, wrap sandwiches, and salads are the main entrées available. Plan on spending under $12 per person for a meal.

- **Pinocchio Village Haus (Fantasyland)**—Hamburgers, cheeseburgers, hot dogs, and salads are among this snack shop's most popular selections. Plan on spending under $12 per person for a meal.

- **El Pirata y El Perico (Adventureland)**—It's not Taco Bell, but if you're in the mood for tacos, nachos, hot dogs, and the like, this is the place to stop for a quick Mexican lunch or dinner. Plan on spending under $12 per person for a meal.

- **Plaza Ice Cream Parlor (Main Street U.S.A.)**—Carnation ice cream is the most popular item here. Plan on spending under $7 per person for a snack.

- **The Plaza Pavilion (Tomorrowland)**—Individual pan pizzas, fried chicken strips, and salads are among the main entrées served at this location. Plan on spending under $12 per person for a meal.

- **Scuttle's Landing (Fantasyland)**—Shaved ice and drinks are sold here. Plan on spending under $5 per person for a snack. This is a favorite snack stop among kids with a sweet tooth looking to cool down on a hot day.

- **Sleepy Hollow (Liberty Square)**—Various types of snacks and beverages can be consumed here if a light, informal snack or meal is what you're looking for. Cappuccino, espresso, and gourmet coffee are served. Plan on spending under $7 per person for a snack.

- **Sunshine Tree Terrace (Frontierland)**—Nonfat frozen yogurt, cappuccino, espresso, and various citrus drinks and snacks are available. Plan on spending under $7 per person for a snack.
- **Toontown Farmer's Market (Toontown)**—Fresh fruit, snacks, and drinks are served. This is one of the few places where truly healthy snacks can be purchased within the Magic Kingdom. Plan on spending under $6 per person for a snack.

Also located throughout the park are wagons and snack kiosks that serve a variety of specialty items, including sodas, bottled water, juices, popcorn, ice cream, turkey legs, eggrolls, pretzels, and fresh fruit. The turkey legs are extremely popular. Genuine McDonald's French fries can also be purchased from a kiosk across from Pecos Bill Café in Frontierland.

Restaurants

If you're looking for a complete meal in a full-service, sit-down restaurant, the following eating establishments are offered within the Magic Kingdom. Plan on spending between $15 and $25 per person when eating at any of these restaurants. To make a same-day lunch or dinner "Preferred Seating" reservation, call (407) WDW-DINE, visit City Hall, or drop by the individual restaurants as early in the day as possible.

- **Cinderella's Royal Table (The Castle)**—This is a character meal restaurant. They have a Once Upon a Time Breakfast, Cinderella's Royal Table Lunch, and Dreams Come True Dinner. During breakfast and lunch several princesses roam the room, and dinner features the Fairy Godmother. Reservations are taken three to six months in advance, so plan accordingly.

Tables are not to be pulled together. Only parties of two, three, and four are allowed. If you have a larger party, it's not guaranteed that you will sit near one another.

- **The Crystal Palace (Main Street U.S.A.)**—This is a character buffet restaurant with Pooh and friends. The menu at this restaurant changes throughout the year; however, American cuisine and seafood are served. Breakfast (8:00 to 10:30 A.M.), lunch (11:30 A.M. to 2:45 P.M.), and dinner buffet (4 P.M. to park closing) Reservations are recommended.

- **Liberty Tree Tavern (Liberty Square)**—This is a full-service character restaurant that offers a large menu of American favorites. Minnie and friends will also walk around to your table. Reservations are suggested. It's open only for dinner.

- **Plaza Restaurant (Main Street U.S.A.)**—An ideal place to stop for lunch, this restaurant offers a large selection of salads, grilled deli-style sandwiches, gourmet burgers, and other light entrées. For dessert, ice cream sundaes, milkshakes, and old-fashioned ice cream sodas are served. A full dinner menu is available. The service is fast, so you can get back into the Magic Kingdom quickly and continue enjoying your day. Reservations are suggested.

- **Tony's Town Square (Main Street U.S.A.)**—Italian lunch and dinner entrées are what you'll find at this "old New York"–style restaurant. Reservations are suggested.

Just outside of the Magic Kingdom, picnic facilities are available (free of charge) if you bring your own food to the park. Guests, however, are not encouraged to bring their own food or drinks into the Magic Kingdom. If you happen to hide a sandwich, piece of fruit, or a candy bar in your jacket pocket or purse, you're not going to be arrested by the Disney Police. If you get caught trying to smuggle a picnic basket of goodies into the park, you'll be asked to store it in a locker or return it to your car.

Chewing gum is not sold anywhere in the Magic Kingdom. If you choose to bring your own chewing gum, please be considerate of other guests and dispose of it in a trash can when you're done chewing it.

Capturing Your Memories on Film

Disposable cameras, Kodak film, a selection of Kodak digital cameras, batteries, and other camera accessories are sold at Exposition Hall within Town Square (along Main Street U.S.A.). Here, two-hour film developing is available, and you can rent video camcorders. If you bring your own camcorder and the battery dies, the Kodak Camera Center will recharge your battery free! Keep in mind, however, that the prices on film and batteries aren't cheap. You can save a lot by buying your film, batteries, and camera accessories outside of WDW.

⊕ HOT SPOT

At every park you will encounter professional photographers wanting to take your photo. This is called the PhotoPass program. You're not obligated to buy, but once people see how great the photos look, most do. Your first photographer will give you a PhotoPass, and whenever you get your photo taken by another photographer, present the pass and she'll scan it. All your photos from that pass are viewable online for one month. The Web information can be found on the PhotoPass.

Calling All Pin Collectors

Throughout the entire WDW Resort, one hobby that an ever-growing number of guests adopt during their visit is pin collecting. Disney continues to issue collectible and commemorative enamel pins relating to special events at WDW, as well as pins for each ride, attraction, show, parade, and Disney character.

There are literally thousands of pins to choose from and collect, ranging in price from $6.50 to $8.50. Serious collectors, however, will sometimes pay hundreds of dollars for limited-edition and extremely rare pins on the secondary collector's market.

You'll find Disney Pin Traders' kiosks in every WDW theme park as well as in the Disney hotels. You can also purchase special lanyards, display cases, hats, frames, and books to showcase your pin collection. Guests are also encouraged to trade pins with Disney cast members and each other.

Visit *www.officialdisneypintrading.com* for a complete overview of Disney Pin trading, including news about pin releases, a calendar of upcoming events, and a guide to pin-trading etiquette. Different pins are offered at each Disney theme park as well as aboard Disney Cruise Lines. To obtain hard-to-find pins for your collection, also check out *www.DisneyAuctions.com*. Pin collecting is a fun, relatively inexpensive, and addicting hobby for people of all ages.

═FAST FACT

The Walt Disney World Resort releases more than 350 new pins per year, including ten to twelve limited-edition pins, ten to twelve core pins, and five to ten special-event pins per month. There are more than eighty locations on WDW property that sell pins, including forty Official Pin Trading Stations.

While visiting WDW, you can participate in organized pin-trading events. For example, Mickey's Pin Trading Nights take place from 7:00 P.M. to 10:00 P.M. on Thursday nights at Disney's All-Star Sports Resort, on Friday nights at Disney's Contemporary Resort, and on Sunday nights at Disney's BoardWalk Inn.

CHAPTER 6

Exploring the Magic Kingdom

THE HEART AND SOUL of the Walt Disney World Resort is the place that probably most resembles Walt Disney's original dream for a theme park—the Magic Kingdom. This chapter will provide you with an attraction-by-attraction tour of the family-oriented rides, shows, and attractions within the Magic Kingdom, plus explain how you can make the most of your time visiting this popular theme park.

Park Overview

This area of the resort is modeled after Disneyland (in Anaheim, California), and while it's only one of several theme parks that now make up the entire WDW Resort, this theme park can easily provide at least one or two full days (and evenings) of fun-filled entertainment, especially if you're traveling with kids. Out of all the theme parks and activities available at the WDW Resort, the Magic Kingdom is most likely what kids will enjoy the most, since most of the rides and attractions, especially in Fantasyland and Mickey's Toontown Fair, are designed with kids in mind.

Like Disneyland, Walt Disney considered the Magic Kingdom to be a giant stage in which guests participate in every aspect of their entertainment. Many of the rides, shows, and attractions in the Magic Kingdom are based on classic Disney stories and movies, and like Disneyland (which was built first), the Magic Kingdom is divided up into distinctly themed lands—Adventureland, Liberty Square, Frontierland, Fantasyland, Mickey's Toontown Fair, Tomorrowland, and Main Street U.S.A. These lands are composed of rides, shows, attractions, restaurants, snack shops, gift shops, outdoor entertainers, and specially designed architecture that make you feel totally immersed in the theme park experience.

≡FAST FACT

As you walk down the center of Main Street look closely at the ground and you'll see a series of "pucks" embedded in the street. These are sensors that are used for the parade floats. They send information back to a centralized computer so that the music stays synchronized with the parade.

Guests enter through the main entrance, pass under the Walt Disney World Railroad, and find themselves on Main Street U.S.A. This street, which is the Magic Kingdom's parade route, is lined with shops, restaurants, and plenty of delightful surprises, like the Main Street vehicles, street performers, and musicians.

As guests wander down Main Street U.S.A., the sight ahead is Cinderella's Castle—the most famous landmark in the WDW Resort and reportedly the most photographed building in the world. This 180-foot-tall castle is the entrance to Fantasyland and is located just past the Hub, where an almost life-size statue of Walt Disney and Mickey Mouse is displayed. This circular park (complete with benches and beautiful landscaping) is known as the Hub because it's located in the center of the Magic Kingdom. From this location, guests can easily locate the entrances to each of the Magic Kingdom's themed lands (with the exception of Mickey's Toontown Fair).

Main Street U.S.A.

Located along Main Street U.S.A. are all sorts of interesting shops that offer a wide selection of souvenirs, gifts, and memorabilia, along with film and various other necessities. These shops are most crowded first thing in the morning and just before the park closes. Don't forget, anything you purchase can be held at a pickup location near the exit of the Magic Kingdom, stored in a locker, or delivered to your WDW Resort hotel. You probably don't want to carry around your purchases throughout the day.

Many of these shops are fully air-conditioned, so if the sun and heat outside become too overwhelming, come inside, browse, and cool off. For your convenience, the shops along Main Street U.S.A. tend to stay open up to one hour later than the rest of the park.

Boulevard Entertainment

Throughout the day, guests are entertained by sidewalk performers, including Dapper Dan's Barbershop Quartet, Rhythm Rascals Band, Casey's Corner Piano, and other talented performers who all add ambiance to Main Street U.S.A. and surrounding areas.

⊕ HOT SPOT

Did you know that you can get a haircut at the Harmony Barber Shop on Main Street in Magic Kingdom? The barber shop is open every day for haircuts and beard and moustache trims. It's for walk-in service only. Look for the red and white pole near the Car Barn. Babies that get their first haircut receive a complimentary Mickey Ear cap.

Wishes Fireworks Show

Ages 2–4:	★★
Ages 5–10:	★★★
Ages 11–15:	★★★
Ages 16–Adult:	★★★

For a reminder of the rating system, see page xiv)

For as long as the Magic Kingdom has been open, a nightly fireworks show has been offered. The Wishes show (which debuted in late 2003), however, is the best fireworks display ever offered in the park. It takes place almost every night high above Cinderella's Castle. The fireworks are choreographed and synchronized to popular Disney tunes, particularly the song "When You Wish upon a Star." With its unique star-shaped fireworks, Wishes is truly breathtaking, so don't miss it! The best viewing locations can be found along Main Street U.S.A., toward (and around) the Hub. Basically, if you have a good view of the top of the castle, you'll see the entire fireworks show clearly. If you're traveling with kids, the fireworks will be less noisy if you watch the show from along Main Street U.S.A., but stand closer to the train station near the park's entrance (as opposed to near the castle). This is a twelve-minute show featuring more than 655 pyrotechnics.

✔ This is a must-see attraction.

TRAVEL TIP

If you are a guest at the Contemporary, Polynesian, or Grand Floridian, you will be able to see Wishes from your resort or onboard a boat if you desire.

Main Street Cinema

Ages 2–4:	★
Ages 5–10:	★
Ages 11–15:	★★
Ages 16–Adult:	★★

If you're in the mood to catch Mickey Mouse in his very first animated features, drop in to this old-fashioned cinema located along Main Street U.S.A. Mickey's movies are shown continuously, so you're free to come and go as you please.

There's seldom a crowd at this attraction, and since the theater is air-conditioned, dropping in for a few minutes is a great way to cool off and experience some of Walt Disney's classic animation. There are no seats in this small theater, but there is an area where kids can sit on the floor.

Main Street Railroad Depot

Ages 2–4:	★★
Ages 5–10:	★★
Ages 11–15:	★★
Ages 16–Adult:	★★

This is the main station for the Walt Disney World Railroad, which follows a circular track around the perimeter of the Magic Kingdom. Here's your chance to ride in an authentic 1920s steam train and get a tour of the Magic Kingdom at the same time. You can get on and off at any of the train stations, or take a ride completely around the park. (It takes about twenty minutes to complete the 1.5-mile journey.)

⊕ HOT SPOT

While you are walking around Magic Kingdom there is a world underneath you. These are the tunnels you hear so much about. The tunnels themselves are nothing spectacular, just good planning. The tunnels are just like a basement in a house and contain everything needed to support the workers in the park: cast member entrances, lockers, dining, restrooms, showers, etc. Cast members simply pop up into the land that their costume matches.

SpectroMagic Parade

Ages 2–4:	★★★
Ages 5–10:	★★★
Ages 11–15:	★★★
Ages 16–Adult:	★★★

In 1991, the Main Street Electrical Parade was replaced by the Spectro-Magic Parade. Floats and popular Disney characters are covered with thousands of fiber-optic lights that flash in a rainbow of colors as this parade travels down Main Street U.S.A. accompanied by popular Disney music.

This is a family-oriented parade that's presented in the evenings and shouldn't be missed. One good viewing location is from the porch of the Visitor's Center, located near the train station, opposite City Hall. Otherwise, you can catch this parade from anywhere along Main Street U.S.A. Be sure to arrive early to stake out your viewing location, especially if the park is crowded. If two shows are presented the evening of your visit, the crowd for the second performance will be much smaller.

✔ This is a must-see attraction.

Share a Dream Come True Parade

Ages 2–4:	★★
Ages 5–10:	★★★
Ages 11–15:	★★★
Ages 16–Adult:	★★

The Share a Dream Come True Parade features favorite Disney characters riding inside giant snow globes. This parade is more kid-oriented, although it'll appeal to people of all ages and help get you into the Disney spirit as you spend your day in the Magic Kingdom.

Performed daily, typically at 3:00 P.M., this parade lasts about fifteen minutes and features more than 110 cast members, including many of your favorite Disney characters.

═FAST FACT

Hard to believe, but the snow globes in the Share a Dream Parade are not air-conditioned! They can't be cooled inside for fear of condensation.

Town Square Exposition Hall

Located on the right side of Main Street U.S.A., just after you pass under the train tracks, you'll find the Town Square Exposition Hall.

What's offered within this attraction changes periodically. The movie theater inside (which typically offers a behind-the-scenes look at Walt Disney and/or Disney animation) is fully air-conditioned and comfortable seating is provided. There's also the AAA Travel Center/Information Desk inside this building along with a camera shop. It's here you can purchase the photos taken of you and your family by Disney cast members when you enter the park.

Adventureland

As you already know, the Magic Kingdom is divided into various themed areas. Starting with Adventureland, here's a rundown of the rides, shows, and attractions you'll find in this area of the theme park. Anything that's specifically targeted to young kids (and not necessarily teens or adults), however, is described in the next chapter.

The Jungle Cruise

Ages 2–4:	★
Ages 5–10:	★★★
Ages 11–15:	★★★
Ages 16–Adult:	★★

This is one of the Magic Kingdom's original rides that opened in 1971. Safari boats modeled after the movie *The African Queen* starring Humphrey Bogart and Katherine Hepburn carry guests down a man-made river. You'll see life-size Animatronic animals as you embark on a ten-minute journey. You should definitely experience the Jungle Cruise during daylight hours. Be prepared to hear corny jokes from your tour guide.

≡FAST FACT

The river water in the Jungle Cruise is dyed brown to give it an authentic African river look. Without the dye the depth would seem very shallow, ruining the illusion that you are in deep African river water.

Pirates of the Caribbean

Ages 2–4:	★
Ages 5–10:	★★★
Ages 11–15:	★★★
Ages 16–Adult:	★★★

Since 1973, this boat ride has taken guests on a magical journey to a port on the Spanish Main. You'll be singing "Yo ho, yo ho; a pirate's life for me" along with the life-size Audio-Animatronic pirates as you experience this enjoyable ten-minute cruise. While it's no longer state-of-the-art and isn't a thrill ride, Pirates of the Caribbean is one of the Magic Kingdom's most popular rides. Also, Captain Jack Sparrow has been added to the attraction.

✔ This is a must-see attraction.

⊕ HOT SPOT

When this ride first opened, it featured pirates chasing the women of the town. Women activist groups complained about this so much that Disney changed it around so that the women now chase the pirates.

Ages 2–4:	N.S.
Ages 5–10:	★★★
Ages 11–15:	★★★
Ages 16–Adult:	★★★

Swiss Family Treehouse

Inspired by the 1960 Disney film *Swiss Family Robinson*, this is a giant tree house that guests of all ages are welcome to climb and explore. This tree contains over 300,000 lifelike polyethylene leaves that appear to grow on 1,400 man-made branches. Children in particular will enjoy exploring the hidden areas located in this tree house. This is a climbing activity, so guests with health concerns or physical limitations should be cautious.

The Enchanted Tiki Room—Under New Management

Ages 2–4:	★
Ages 5–10:	★★★
Ages 11–15:	★★★
Ages 16–Adult:	★★★

Originally, this was one of the first Disney attractions ever to utilize Audio-Animatronics (robotic characters that seem lifelike). A version of this show was first introduced at Disneyland back in 1963. It featured 225 Audio-Animatronic birds that sang and entertained guests during a seventeen-minute performance that was extremely cute.

Back in 1998, this attraction was reworked. While the concept is pretty much the same, this attraction is now "hosted" by Audio-Animatronic adaptations of Iago (from Disney's *Aladdin*) and Zazu (from *The Lion King*). So, if you haven't visited the Magic Kingdom in the past few years, seeing this new show will provide a new entertainment experience, yet rekindle a touch of Disney nostalgia.

The Magic Carpets of Aladdin

Ages 2–4:	★★
Ages 5–10:	★★★
Ages 11–15:	★★
Ages 16–Adult:	★

Here's your chance to hop aboard a magic carpet and see Agrabah in style. Based on Disney's Aladdin, guests climb aboard moving vehicles (four people per carpet), which they then control. Carpets can move up and down, plus pitch forward and backward. During the ride, water gets shot at guests by spitting camels. (Don't worry, you'll hardly get wet.) This ride is very similar to Dumbo the Flying Elephant, but has a different theme.

⊕ HOT SPOT

Throughout the day, at specific times that are listed within the Magic Kingdom Guide Map, Disney characters will make appearances throughout the park. Look for the white-gloved Mickey Mouse hand icons on the map.

Frontierland

Here's a rundown of what you'll experience in this area of the Magic Kingdom, which was inspired by America's early days of exploration and expansion.

Big Thunder Mountain Railroad

Ages 2–4:	N.S.
Ages 5–10:	★★
Ages 11–15:	★★★
Ages 16–Adult:	★★★

Don't confuse this fast and furious runaway train ride with the Walt Disney Railroad. This is a four-minute, high-speed, fast-turning thrill ride up, down, and around a man-made mountain. Along this ride's 2,780 feet of roller coaster track, over twenty Audio-Animatronic characters and over $300,000 worth of genuine mining antiques help to add a sense of authenticity. To truly experience this ride, check it out after dark. Guests must be at least 40 inches tall to experience Big Thunder Mountain Railroad, and anyone who suffers from heart or back problems or is pregnant should skip it. This is one of the attractions in the Magic Kingdom that teens and adults won't want to miss.

✔ This is a must-see attraction.

⊕ HOT SPOT

When most people are watching the fireworks at night the lines are short for Big Thunder Mountain Railroad. So if you time it right, you can get fantastic view of the show from the top of the 197-foot mountain right before you plummet down.

Frontierland Shootin' Arcade

Ages 2–4:	N.S.
Ages 5–10:	★
Ages 11–15:	★
Ages 16–Adult:	★

Replica rifles that use infrared bullets are used in this old-west-style shooting gallery. Get ready for the unexpected if you hit your targets. (If you want to test your aim, it'll cost you fifty cents. Like all of the arcades, shooting costs aren't included in the price of your admission to the Magic Kingdom.)

Country Bear Jamboree

Ages 2–4:	★★
Ages 5–10:	★★★
Ages 11–15:	★★★
Ages 16–Adult:	★

Country music is performed by a group of about twenty life-size Audio-Animatronic bears and creatures. Young kids and adults will find this show charming, while the teen set will probably find it a bit hokey. This seventeen-minute show will have you singing and clapping along. Shows are continuous, and there's excellent visibility from all seats in the theater, so don't worry about trying to get preferred seating in the front or center of the auditorium.

Splash Mountain

Ages 2–4:	N.S.
Ages 5–10:	★
Ages 11–15:	★★★
Ages 16–Adult:	★★★

This light-hearted flumelike boat ride starts out totally calm and mellow, as guests are entertained by dozens of singing Audio-Animatronic characters from Disney's animated classic *Song of the South*. "Zip-a-Dee-Doo-Dah" is the theme song of this ride, which tells the story of Brer Rabbit as he tries to locate his "laughing place."

Brer Rabbit gets the last laugh, however. At the end of this ride, you'll be sent cruising down a 52-foot drop at a 45-degree angle, traveling in excess of 40 miles per hour. In all, this is a rather calm eleven-minute boat ride. It's only the very last few seconds that constitute the thrill-ride element. Splash Mountain is definitely one of the Magic Kingdom's very best attractions, from both an entertainment and a thrill-providing standpoint. It's not suitable for young children (under 44 inches tall), nor should it be experienced by anyone with back or heart problems or who can't endure the final drop at the end of the ride.

✔ This is a must-see attraction.

≡FAST FACT

Chances are, you will get a bit wet at the end of this ride, so be sure that you cover up your camera equipment and snugly stow your belongings. As you're taking the final plummet, be sure to smile! Color 8" × 10" photos of your plunge are available as you exit this ride, for an additional fee.

Tom Sawyer Island

Ages 2–4:	★
Ages 5–10:	★★
Ages 11–15:	★★★
Ages 16–Adult:	★★

This man-made island is located in the center of the Rivers of America. To reach this island, you'll need to hop aboard one of the Tom Sawyer log rafts, which depart regularly. The island is open during daylight hours only. Kids especially will love exploring Injun Joe's Cave, Harper's Mill, and Fort Sam Clemens. The island is filled with dirt paths to follow, bridges to cross, and lots of places to explore. Kids who know the story of Tom Sawyer and Huck Finn will enjoy this attraction the most.

Liberty Square

Give me liberty or give me Mickey! Patriotic tourists, thrill seekers, and fun-loving vacationers alike will find a lot to experience in this area of the Magic Kingdom.

Goofy's Country Dancin' Jamboree

Ages 2–4:	★★
Ages 5–10:	★★★
Ages 11–15:	★★★
Ages 16–Adult:	★★

Goofy and his pals host a fun and upbeat musical show for young guests several times a day in the world-famous Diamond Horseshoe Saloon. Check the Guide Map: Magic Kingdom for showtimes.

Davy Crockett Keel Boats

Ages 2–4:	N.S.
Ages 5–10:	★
Ages 11–15:	★★
Ages 16–Adult:	★★

Head for the dock near the Haunted Mansion and climb aboard one of these keel boats for a ride around Tom Sawyer's Island (along the Rivers of America).

Liberty Square Riverboat

Ages 2–4:	★★
Ages 5–10:	★★
Ages 11–15:	★★
Ages 16–Adult:	★★

The *Richard F. Irvine* is a real stern-wheeler steamboat that was built at Disney World and named after one of its designers. This boat picks up passengers and takes them for a fifteen-minute ride around the Rivers of America (a half-mile-long cruise), giving a great view of Tom Sawyer's Island and many other sites in the Magic Kingdom.

For the best view of the park, climb to the upper deck during the cruise. This is a great way to get off your feet for a while, and at the same time, experience the ambiance of the Magic Kingdom.

The Hall of Presidents

Ages 2–4:	N.S.
Ages 5–10:	★
Ages 11–15:	★★
Ages 16–Adult:	★★★

This attraction is sort of like visiting a high-tech museum in which Audio-Animatronic re-creations of America's presidents actually teach guests history. Kids will most likely get bored by this twenty-minute presentation; however, adults will find it both highly patriotic and extremely interesting. Advanced Audio-Animatronic technology is used to make several of the presidents, including George W. Bush (the newest addition to this attraction), come to life on the stage. President George W. Bush makes an inspirational ninety-second speech (which he actually recorded for this attraction) about freedom to create, to prosper, and to dream.

This presentation is shown in an air-conditioned theater. In fact, even the waiting room is air-conditioned. As you're spending time in the waiting room, browse around and check out the historical paintings on the walls. Take a look back at American history in this educational and inspirational attraction.

The Haunted Mansion

Ages 2–4:	N.S.
Ages 5–10:	★★
Ages 11–15:	★★★
Ages 16–Adult:	★★★

Yes, this is a haunted house that's jam-packed with all sorts of awesome special effects, but this ride is designed to provide family-oriented entertainment, so don't expect anything too scary. During much of your eight-minute tour of this mansion, you'll be riding in a moving love seat. This is definitely one of the Magic Kingdom's most technologically advanced rides in terms of the special effects. As you enter the house, be sure to read the rather bizarre inscriptions on the tombstones.

As you wait outside of the mansion for your tour, you'll be covered by an awning, so you won't be exposed to direct sun or rain. Be sure to notice the somber costumes worn by Disney cast members working at this attraction. When you're escorted into a small room that appears to stretch, be sure to look upward, especially just after the lights go out. The ride portion of this attraction begins as you exit the small room (which is really an elevator). You'll be loaded into two-person vehicles that look like love seats.

When your tour begins, check out the "animated" statues in the library. Other awesome effects to be on the lookout for are the woman's head in a crystal ball and the ghosts in the ballroom (be sure to look all around this room, including near the floor and ceiling). Near the very end of your tour, look into the mirror to see who (or what) is sitting between you and the living person you're sitting next to in this final haunting special effect.

✔ This is a must-see attraction.

Tomorrowland

When the Magic Kingdom first opened in 1971, this land was designed to offer guests a peek into the future. This area of the park changes more than any other area because existing rides are always replaced by newer, more state-of-the-art rides and attractions that continue to offer a futuristic theme.

Stitch's Great Escape

Ages 2–4:	★
Ages 5–10:	★
Ages 11–15:	★
Ages 16–Adult:	★

Stitch's Great Escape replaced the ExtraTERRORestrial Alien Encounter attraction in 2003 because it was considered too frightening. This all-new attraction is loosely based on the animated film *Lilo & Stitch* but is not very good. First you are held firmly in place by a special seat, then Stitch breaths on your neck and some slime (water) hits your face. Spend your time at Buzz Lightyear's Space Ranger Spin across the way instead.

TRAVEL TIP

Guide Map: Magic Kingdom is a full-color map and brochure provided free of charge when you enter that park. It lists all of the rides, shows, attractions, times of parades, and other information about the park. The red dotted line on the map indicates the parade route. You can pick up a free Guide Map for each of the Disney theme parks.

Space Mountain

Ages 2–4:	N.S.
Ages 5–10:	★★
Ages 11–15:	★★★
Ages 16–Adult:	★★★

Since 1975, this has been one of the most popular rides in all of WDW, and with good reason. Space Mountain is a high-speed indoor roller coaster that uses some special effects to make you feel like you're seated in a rocket that's racing through space. In reality, you'll be traveling about 28 miles per hour.

This entire ride is experienced in almost total darkness, so you won't see what's coming. This is an awesome thrill ride. For those who don't normally enjoy roller coasters, this one offers a lot of high-speed sharp turns, but very few drops, making it exciting, but a bit tamer than a typical roller coaster. The ride itself lasts under three minutes, but the wait is usually about one hour (or more). Space Mountain is one of those rides you don't want to miss, so plan your time in the Magic Kingdom accordingly.

The best times to experience this ride are during one of the parades, or during peak lunch or dinner hours. Space Mountain is not suitable for very young children (there is a height restriction of 44 inches and children under the age of seven need an adult to ride with them) or anyone with heart, back, or other medical problems. Pregnant women should also sit this one out. As soon as the park opens, race to this ride for the shortest wait.

✔ This is a must-see attraction.

═FAST FACT

Space Mountain wins for the most guest lost items that drop to the floor during the ride. Please make sure keys, bags, tickets, wallets, etc., are firmly secured because they will not be able to shut down the ride to look for your stuff.

Astro Orbiter

Ages 2–4:	N.S.
Ages 5–10:	★★
Ages 11–15:	★★
Ages 16–Adult:	★

Here's one way to get a great view of Tomorrowland and at the same time enjoy a mild thrill ride. Guests sit in rocket-shaped cars that go up and down as they travel around in circles high above ground level. The line for this ride moves very slowly. If there's a long wait, either return later in the day or skip this ride.

The Laugh Floor Comedy Club

Ages 2–4:	★★
Ages 5–10:	★★★
Ages 11–15:	★★★
Ages 16–Adult:	★★

This show replaced the long-running Timekeeper show. Inspired by Disney-Pixar's *Monsters, Inc.*, guests match wits with the one-eyed hero, Mike Wazowski, and his friends. The indoor theater holds 400 people. A must see for *Monsters Inc.* fans.

Walt Disney's Carousel of Progress

Ages 2–4:	★
Ages 5–10:	★★
Ages 11–15:	★★★
Ages 16–Adult:	★★★

This classic WDW attraction was revamped in 1996 but is still as charming as when it first began entertaining guests in 1975. Guests are seated in a theater-like room that actually rotates around a 360-degree stage. Each time the theater moves, a new scene featuring an Audio-Animatronic American family is seen. Guests follow this family through the twentieth century and explore some of the major technological advances that have occurred in the home during the early 1900s, 1920s, 1940s, and present day. The final scene depicts technology that we might be seeing in the not-too-distant future. "A whole new century is waiting for us" and "Tomorrow is just a dream away" are two of the themes of this attraction.

≡FAST FACT

Walt Disney himself created the Carousel of Progress, which has been seen by more people than any other show in U.S. history. Walt requested that this exhibit never be removed from Tomorrowland, so it will always be there.

Tomorrowland Transit Authority

Ages 2–4:	★
Ages 5–10:	★
Ages 11–15:	★★
Ages 16–Adult:	★★

For a ten-minute, rather relaxing tour of Tomorrowland, climb aboard Tomorrowland's energy-efficient, pollution-free mass-transit system that travels about 10 miles per hour and follows a mile-long track. You'll get a sneak peek inside Space Mountain and pass by just about all of Tomorrowland's other rides and attractions.

Tomorrowland Indy Speedway

Ages 2–4:	★
Ages 5–10:	★★★
Ages 11–15:	★★★
Ages 16–Adult:	★

People of all ages (who meet the 52-inch height restriction) can drive these sports cars along a 2,000-foot-long track— whether or not they have a real-life driver's license. These gasoline-powered cars have rack-and-pinion steering and disk brakes, but they're confined to a track that keeps the driver totally safe. Drivers can reach cruising speeds of about 7 miles per hour as they take a single lap around the track.

The ride lasts about five minutes and gives young people a true feeling of being in the driver's seat of a car. Drivers beware: Even in these cars, minor fender benders are common, especially if you get stuck behind a slow driver.

Buzz Lightyear's Space Ranger Spin

Ages 2–4:	★
Ages 5–10:	★★★
Ages 11–15:	★★★
Ages 16–Adult:	★★★

Designed with kids in mind, this attraction lets young guests take on the role of Space Rangers as they join their hero, Buzz Lightyear, on an adventure to save the universe's crystollic fusion cell supply (i.e., batteries). Riders climb aboard a ZP-27 space cruiser and take a lighthearted voyage through ten interactive scenes. While the vehicles move forward by themselves as the adventure unfolds, riders can make their vehicles spin, since there are things to see all around. Using a light gun (attached to the vehicle), riders can shoot at targets in order to obtain the highest possible score.

 TRAVEL TIP

The most points you can score is 999,999. If you want to get a secret head start on points, as soon as you enter the first room look to your left and you will see a big orange robot. Spin around and shoot the target on his left arm to get 100,000 points. As you are leaving the room, look up because there's a "Z" target on the ceiling worth 100,000 points as well.

The Galaxy Palace Theater

Ages 2–4:	★★
Ages 5–10:	★★★
Ages 11–15:	★★★
Ages 16–Adult:	★

Mickey Mouse and his Disney pals entertain guests with plenty of colorful costumes, singing, and dancing. Performances are held throughout the day, but showtimes vary based on the time of year and on weather conditions. On sunny days, make sure you apply plenty of sunblock (and wear a hat). This is an outdoor amphitheater, so you'll be exposed to the sun. Be sure to arrive about twenty minutes early to ensure that you get a good seat. The show offered here changes periodically.

Shop 'til You Drop

Located throughout the Magic Kingdom are dozens of shopping opportunities, including specialty shops, general gift shops, and plenty of souvenirs to choose from. All of the shops in the Magic Kingdom offer complimentary package delivery to your WDW Resort hotel. For an additional fee, your purchases can be shipped (via FedEx) to any location worldwide. Keep in mind that even though FedEx is being used for shipping, it could take up to two weeks for your items to arrive at their destination, due to order processing delays at Disney World. Before shipping your items, ask how long it'll take for the order to be processed.

⊕ HOT SPOT

While you can buy Disney-themed hats at virtually any shop within WDW, the only place to pick up monogrammed Mickey ears (like the ones worn by the original Mouseketeers on *The Mickey Mouse Club*) is at the Chapeau, at the end of Main Street U.S.A. The hats can be monogrammed while you wait, and they remain one of the best bargains at the park in terms of a memorable and personalized souvenir.

If you find something you really like but can't afford at the moment, or you don't want to lug it home, you can order any item available from any WDW shop by calling (407) 363-6200 during business hours. Many of the items available at Walt Disney World are not sold at any of the Disney Stores and are not available from the Disney Catalog.

CHAPTER 7

Kid-Oriented Areas of the Magic Kingdom

WHILE THE ENTIRE WDW RESORT was created to entertain and inspire people of all ages, there are certain lands within the Magic Kingdom specifically designed for young children under the age of twelve (along with their parents). Thus, if you're traveling with young people, plan on spending extra time within these areas.

Fantasyland

This area of the Magic Kingdom offers many attractions specifically for young kids, featuring some of Disney's classic characters from movies like *Snow White and the Seven Dwarfs, Cinderella, Peter Pan, Alice in Wonderland*, and *The Little Mermaid*. Anyone traveling with young kids should plan on spending at least one full day experiencing everything that Fantasyland has to offer.

 TRAVEL TIP

During peak travel times (especially holidays), plan on allocating an average of forty-five minutes per ride or attraction. This includes wait times.

Cinderella's Castle

Ages 2–4:	★★★
Ages 5–10:	★★★
Ages 11–15:	★★★
Ages 16–Adult:	★★★

For a reminder of the rating system, see page xiv.

This is the best-known landmark in all of the WDW Resort and many say the most photographed building on earth. Inside the castle is a glass tile mosaic mural that tells the story of Cinderella. This castle is 180 feet tall and is twice the height of Sleeping Beauty's Castle located at Disneyland.

Kids especially will enjoy eating breakfast, lunch, or dinner with Cinderella in the castle at Cinderella's Royal Table. Make your reservations at least three to six months in advance.

✔ This is a must-see attraction.

Cinderella's Surprise Celebration

Ages 2–4:	★★★
Ages 5–10:	★★★
Ages 11–15:	★★
Ages 16–Adult:	★

Several times throughout the day (see the Guide Map: Magic Kingdom brochure for details), Cinderella's Surprise Celebration takes place on the castle's front stage. This is a musical show that stars Cinderella and other classic Disney characters. After the show, there's a meet-and-greet opportunity that provides an awesome chance for parents to photograph their kids in front of the castle with the various characters, or for kids to collect their autographs.

TRAVEL TIP

Young kids in particular (ages four to ten) love meeting the Disney characters and getting their autographs. For about $6, you can purchase an official Disney Autograph Album (from any Disney gift shop) that your child can transform into a personalized souvenir by collecting the autographs of the characters they meet within the parks and Disney hotels.

Cinderella's Golden Carrousel

Ages 2–4:	★★
Ages 5–10:	★★★
Ages 11–15:	★★
Ages 16–Adult:	★

This is one of the world's largest carrousels, and one of the Magic Kingdom's original attractions. Cinderella's Golden Carrousel holds seventy-two hand-carved horses that are truly works of art that guests of all ages can ride. Along with the exquisitely decorated horses, the entire carrousel features medieval décor. This ride was built in 1917 and was acquired from an amusement park in New Jersey that's no longer in existence. It has since been totally refurbished and modernized, but it still has its original beauty and charm. The ride itself lasts about two minutes.

⊕ HOT SPOT

Behind the castle is a sword stuck in a stone. A Stone Ceremony takes place several times daily in this area by Merlin the Magician. Merlin chooses a child from the audience to pull the magical sword, Excalibur, from the stone. He or she is then appointed "temporary ruler of the realm."

Dumbo the Flying Elephant

Ages 2–4:	★
Ages 5–10:	★★★
Ages 11–15:	★★
Ages 16–Adult:	★

The Magic Kingdom's younger guests can fly high above Fantasyland in cars shaped like Dumbo (the elephant), who uses his oversized ears to fly. Inspired by Disney's animated movie *Dumbo*, this two-minute ride is for kids only.

"it's a small world"

Ages 2–4:	★★★
Ages 5–10:	★★★
Ages 11–15:	★★★
Ages 16–Adult:	★★★

Whether you're spending one hour or several days exploring the Magic Kingdom, this is one attraction that nobody should miss. It's been called the "happiest cruise that's ever sailed," and you'll quickly discover that this description is totally accurate.

This is a colorful, ten-minute boat ride that takes guests through several large indoor areas filled with Audio-Animatronic children from around the world, all singing "it's a small world" in different languages. "it's a small world" is absolutely delightful and is well worth waiting in line to experience. (There's almost always a shorter wait if you get into the left line queue.) During the ride, be sure to look upward as well as to the sides, because there are exciting and adorable things happening all around you. Kids love the laughing hyenas, about five minutes into the ride, while adults will find the final scene on the ride extremely heartwarming.

As they leave, many people feel inclined to toss a coin into the water and make a wish. If you're traveling with someone in a wheelchair, special boats are available (upon request) to accommodate wheelchairs.

✔ This is a must-see attraction.

≡FAST FACT

"it's a small world" was created by Walt Disney and his team of Imagineers for the 1964–1965 New York World's Fair, and was later added to Disneyland, and then to the Magic Kingdom at WDW, where it continues to entertain guests.

Mad Tea Party (a.k.a. "The Teacups")

Ages 2–4:	N.S.
Ages 5–10:	★★★
Ages 11–15:	★★★
Ages 16–Adult:	★★

Inspired by Disney's *Alice in Wonderland*, this ride is virtually guaranteed to make you totally dizzy. It's the type of ride that most kids love, but that's suitable for anyone who has the stomach for it. Guests sit in oversized teacups that spin around each other. At the same time, individual guests can make their own teacup spin around its own axis. The ride lasts about two minutes and is best experienced on an empty stomach.

Peter Pan's Flight

Ages 2–4:	N.S.
Ages 5–10:	★★★
Ages 11–15:	★★★
Ages 16–Adult:	★★★

Guests ride in pirate galleons over London on a nonstop, three-minute journey to Never Never Land, where Captain Hook and the Lost Boys will be waiting. Think of this ride as an animated, three-dimensional storybook that tells a condensed version of the Peter Pan story. This ride is definitely kid-oriented and will be of little interest to adults traveling without young kids. Don't be surprised if this ride has one of the longest lines in Fantasyland. This attraction may be too scary for very young children.

Snow White's Scary Adventures

Ages 2–4:	N.S.
Ages 5–10:	★★★
Ages 11–15:	★★★
Ages 16–Adult:	★

Young guests in particular will enjoy this three-minute ride, which depicts several popular scenes from Disney's *Snow White and the Seven Dwarfs* animated classic. The Audio-Animatronic dwarfs are really cute, but kids might get a bit scared by the wicked witch's multiple appearances, so it's a good idea to prepare children by telling them what to expect. Once again, this ride should be experienced by people traveling with kids; otherwise it could be skipped. This attraction may be too scary for very young children.

The Many Adventures of Winnie the Pooh

Ages 2–4:	★★★
Ages 5–10:	★★★
Ages 11–15:	★★
Ages 16–Adult:	★

This colorful ride takes guests on a whirlwind visit with the classic Winnie the Pooh characters from the Hundred Acre Wood. As guests ride in honey pot–shaped vehicles, they bounce along with Tigger, float through a floody place with Piglet, and then enter the mysterious world of Heffalumps and Woozles. Colorful Animatronic figures and three-dimensional sets are used to convey the story line of this adventure.

Mickey's PhilharMagic

Ages 2–4:	★★
Ages 5–10:	★★★
Ages 11–15:	★★★
Ages 16–Adult:	★★★

This 3-D movie takes place in a large, custom-designed theater that actually interacts with visitors. For example, when water shoots on screen, guests will feel droplets of water shot at them. (Don't worry, it's only a few drops. You won't get drenched.)

This movie features state-of-the-art computer animation, tons of special effects, and stars some of Disney's most beloved characters, including Donald Duck. Mickey's PhilharMagic is presented on a 150-foot by 28-foot movie screen. Special 3-D glasses are provided when you enter the air-conditioned theater. The show is presented continuously throughout the day and should not be missed!

✔ This is a must-see attraction.

Mickey's Toontown Fair

People traveling with young children (ages three to twelve) will definitely want to check out the Magic Kingdom's newest land, which was designed specifically for kids. This area features many of Disney's classic characters, including Mickey Mouse, Minnie Mouse, Donald Duck, and Goofy. Mickey's Toontown Fair is a colorful, cartoonlike town that's a blast for kids, but it offers little of interest to adults. Near the entrance of this area, you'll find Pete's Garage. Here you'll find restrooms and public phones. If you want to meet Mickey Mouse and Minnie, Donald, and Goofy, the best place to do this is within Mickey's Toontown Fair.

⊕ HOT SPOT

Throughout Mickey's Toontown Fair there are a lot of photo opportunities around every corner, so make sure you have enough film and batteries in case you run out.

Donald's Boat

Ages 2–4:	★★★
Ages 5–10:	★★★
Ages 11–15:	★
Ages 16–Adult:	N.S.

Kids get to explore this boat-shaped playground with a nautical theme. This boat is hardly seaworthy, however. In fact, it has so many leaks, kids who explore it are virtually guaranteed to get a bit wet. The shooting fountains offer an excellent way for kids to cool off on a hot day. On cooler days, you might want to instruct your kids to stay dry by avoiding the shooting water. (A cold and wet kid is an unhappy kid.) Otherwise, have a dry change of clothes on hand.

Mickey's Country House and Judge's Tent

Ages 2–4:	★★★
Ages 5–10:	★★★
Ages 11–15:	★★★
Ages 16–Adult:	N.S.

After exploring Mickey's yellow, green, and red country home and yard, visitors get to meet Mickey in person. This is an excellent photo opportunity and a chance for your children to meet the Mouse one-on-one. While Disney characters make appearances every day throughout Walt Disney World, if you want to be guaranteed that your child will meet Mickey (and shake hands, etc.), this is the place to go. The wait, however, could be up to one hour.

Minnie's Country House

Ages 2–4:	★★★
Ages 5–10:	★★★
Ages 11–15:	★★★
Ages 16–Adult:	N.S.

Young guests get to explore Minnie's pink-and-purple country home and then explore the backyard, where Minnie herself will be waiting to greet guests in her gazebo. This is another excellent photo opportunity and a chance to interact with one of Disney's most popular characters. Be prepared to experience a wait to meet Minnie in person.

═FAST FACT

Mickey's Toontown typically opens a little later than the rest of the park and sometimes closes earlier. Be sure to check your Guide Map: The Magic Kingdom brochure or the Information Board (at the end of Main Street U.S.A.) for details and plan accordingly.

The Barnstormer at Goofy's Wiseacre Farm

Ages 2–4:	N.S.
Ages 5–10:	★★★
Ages 11–15:	★★★
Ages 16–Adult:	N.S.

Young people will love Toontown's only thrill ride—a roller coaster with a "cartoon" twist that's fast enough to give young people a bit of excitement, without being too scary. Near the exit of the Barnstormer is a fun snack shop where guests can make their own strawberry shortcake. Kids must be at least 35 inches tall to experience this mild thrill ride.

Toon Park

This playground looks like a 3-D cartoon, and virtually everything within it is made out of foam, including the grass and animal statues. Toon Park is a fun and safe place for your kids to have fun while the adults sit on the sidelines.

Toontown Fair Hall of Fame

Ages 2–4:	N.S.
Ages 5–10:	★★★
Ages 11–15:	★★
Ages 16–Adult:	N.S.

This gallery features many of Disney's most popular characters from animated movies. Guests can also meet and greet multiple Disney characters who appear throughout the day.

Toontown Fair Railroad Station

Ages 2–4:	N.S.
Ages 5–10:	★★★
Ages 11–15:	★★
Ages 16–Adult:	N.S.

Climb aboard the WDW Railroad, which makes stops at Main Street U.S.A. and Frontierland.

⊕ HOT SPOT

Within Mickey's Toontown Fair, the main shopping opportunity is County Bounty, a gift shop that sells Disney-themed merchandise.

Meet the Characters

Ages 2–4:	★★
Ages 5–10:	★★
Ages 11–15:	★★
Ages 16–Adult:	★★

Located between Fantasyland and Tomorrowland, Ariel's Grotto is where you'll usually find Ariel and possibly other characters from Disney's *The Little Mermaid*, who meet guests, take pictures, and sign autographs in an area that looks like Ariel's undersea home. If you're traveling with kids, this area provides excellent photograph and autograph opportunities, and the line typically isn't too long.

The Fantasyland Character Festival is where you'll find a handful of Disney characters who meet and greet guests, sign autographs, and take pictures. While you typically won't find Mickey or Minnie here, at least a few other classic characters show up here throughout the day.

Within the Fairytale Garden in Fantasyland, at several times throughout the day, young guests can hang out with Belle (from *Beauty and the Beast*) as she tells a story about her adventures in a small and intimate setting. Showtimes are listed in the Guide Map: Magic Kingdom brochure. Be sure to arrive early, since space is limited.

Other Kid-Oriented Attractions

The other lands within the Magic Kingdom also offer kid-oriented attractions. In addition, all the parades and shows will appeal to the younger crowd. If you're traveling with kids, the following rides, shows, and attractions should not be missed:

- Astro Orbiter (Tomorrowland)
- Buzz Lightyear's Space Ranger Spin (Tomorrowland)
- Country Bear Jamboree (Frontierland)
- The Magic Carpets of Aladdin (Adventureland)
- Swiss Family Treehouse (Adventureland)
- Tomorrowland Indy Speedway (Tomorrowland)
- Tom Sawyer Island (Frontierland)

Rides Not Suitable for Young Children

Due to the turbulent, thrill-ride nature or themes presented within some of the rides and attractions within the Magic Kingdom, some simply aren't suitable for young kids (under age six). Some of these rides and attractions include Splash Mountain, Big Thunder Mountain Railroad, the Haunted Mansion, Peter Pan's Flight, Snow White's Scary Adventures, Space Mountain, and the Mad Tea Party.

As a parent, you'll need to make a judgment call based on the information provided within this book and after seeing the ride, show, or attraction for yourself once you get to the theme park.

CHAPTER 8

Epcot Offers a Peek at Tomorrow

OUT OF ALL OF the theme parks and things to do and see at the WDW Resort, Epcot is probably the most un-Disney. In other words, you won't be seeing flashy parades and Disney animated characters. What you will find, however, is that Epcot is a theme park designed primarily for teens and adults, offering attractions to entertain, thrill, and educate.

Park Overview

Epcot is really two totally different theme parks in one. There's Future World, which offers rides and attractions, each showcasing or demonstrating human progress in science and technology. And then there's the World Showcase, which is designed to examine the cultural achievements, food, artistic products, and classic architecture of eleven countries from around the world.

Guests of all ages, especially adults, will find Epcot to be educational and thought provoking. This theme park takes an extremely innovative and entertaining approach to teaching people about the world in which we live. Make sure that you wear comfortable shoes when you visit Epcot, because a considerable amount of walking is required.

There's an awful lot to see and do at Epcot. In order to see everything, plan on spending a minimum of two days visiting this park. Ideally, you'll want to spend one full day exploring Future World, and one day visiting the World Showcase pavilions. If you can't allocate this much time to visiting this park, choose a handful of attractions that are of interest to you from each area.

Looking at a map of Epcot, you'll discover that the park is laid out in the shape of an eight. The bottom loop comprises the attractions, shops, restaurants, and rides in Future World. The top loop comprises the World Showcase pavilions, which circle around the World Showcase Lagoon. For parents and educators, Epcot features two Discover Centers in Future World that offer educational resources and products.

≡ FAST FACT

Did you know that EPCOT was an acronym for, *Experimental Prototype Community of Tomorrow*? Walt actually wanted to make it a community of people living with the highest technology, where guests would watch them fishbowl-style. As of January 1, 2006, it was deemed no longer an acronym.

Getting to Epcot

Just like The Magic Kingdom, Epcot is connected to the WDW monorail system, so you can reach this park via monorail by departing from the Ticket and Transportation Center or magic Kingdom. If you're staying at the Grand Floridian, the Contemporary, or the Polynesian, take the monorail from the hotel to the Ticket and Transportation Center, then switch monorails and take the one that goes directly to Epcot's main entrance.

To reach Epcot's World Showcase entrance (a.k.a., "The International Gateway" entrance by France), take a short walk along a paved pathway from the Disney Yacht and Beach Club, Swan, Dolphin, and BoardWalk hotels, or take a water taxi.

🧳 TRAVEL TIP

The World Showcase generally doesn't open until 11:00 A.M., so there's no sense in rushing to the back of the park unless you have made reservations for Norway's Princess character breakfast or an Epcot tour.

From all other WDW Resort hotels, you can take a WDW bus to Epcot's main entrance. If you're arriving at Epcot by car, you'll have to pay $9 per day to park, and then ride a tram to the entrance. Keep your parking ticket so that you can leave and re-enter the parking lot during a single day. Guests who are staying at any WDW Resort hotel and are already paying for parking at their hotel will receive free parking at any of Epcot's parking lots.

Admission to Epcot

Admission to Epcot requires a ticket. For details about the various ticket and pricing options for visiting Epcot and all of the theme parks within the WDW Resort, see Chapter 3.

Same-Day Re-entry

As you leave Epcot, be sure to have your hand stamped as you exit in order to be granted readmission into the park later that day or evening. In addition to the hand stamp, be sure to retain your ticket stub. The hand stamps are designed to be water-resistant, so don't worry if your hand gets wet if you choose to return to your hotel in the middle of the day to go swimming and then want to return to Epcot later that evening. Try to refrain, however, from scrubbing your hands clean with soap until your day's visit to the park is complete.

Hours of Operation

The hours Epcot is open vary throughout the year; however, during much of the year, the park is open from 9:00 A.M. to 9:00 P.M., although there are exceptions. Future World is typically open from

9:00 A.M. to 7:00 P.M., though the popular Spaceship Earth and Innoventions attractions remain open until 9:00 P.M. The World Showcase, on the other hand, typically opens daily at 11:00 A.M. and remains open until 9:00 P.M. During the summer or during a peak holiday period, Epcot's hours are extended. To obtain the exact park operating hours for the dates of your visit, call (407) 824-4321.

What to Bring

Make sure you wear comfortable shoes! Depending on the weather, you might want to take along a jacket (you can always store it in a locker). Try to avoid carrying too much stuff with you. You'll enjoy your visit more if your hands are as free as possible.

Don't forget to bring your camera, along with plenty of film and batteries. Avoid having to purchase high-priced film, batteries, or camera supplies in the park.

≡FAST FACT

Most of the things to see and do within Epcot are located inside. In fact, many of the attractions even allow you to wait in line indoors. You will, however, have to walk outside to go from attraction to attraction in Future World and from pavilion to pavilion in the World Showcase.

In case of rain, plan on getting a bit wet. Wear a raincoat or plan on purchasing an inexpensive Mickey Mouse poncho. Avoid bringing an umbrella into the park. You'll find it frustrating trying to walk around the crowded park with an open umbrella. For an up-to-the-minute weather report for the Orlando area, call (407) 824-4104.

Choose a Place to Meet

As soon as you arrive at either Future World or the World Showcase at Epcot, choose a place where you'll meet up with the other people in your group if you happen to get separated. Choose to meet on the half-hour or on the hour after being separated.

If you're traveling with children, upon arriving at Epcot, set some ground rules. Instruct your kids to stay close to you at all times. They should know that if they get lost, they should immediately contact any Disney cast member.

≡FAST FACT

Over the years guests have come up with their own humorous acronyms for Epcot; Every Person Comes Out Tired, Every Parent Carries Out a Toddler, and Every Pocketbook Comes Out Trashed. Cast members have their own as well; Experimental Polyester Costumes of Torture and Every Paycheck Comes Out Tiny.

There are several good meeting locations in Future World, such as in front of Spaceship Earth or in front of the fountain near Epcot's main entrance. While visiting the World Showcase, you can choose a meeting location in front of a particular pavilion, such as the American Adventure, which is located exactly halfway around World Showcase Lagoon (opposite Future World). Cell phones and walkie-talkie radios are goods sources of communication s well.

Guest Relations

Located near Spaceship Earth is the Epcot Guest Relations building. The Disney cast members here are exceptionally helpful and will answer any and all of your questions regarding what to see and do at Epcot or anywhere at the WDW Resort. You can also make dining reservations here, or borrow a special wireless translator device that will translate the audio portion of many attractions within Epcot into Spanish, Japanese, Portuguese, German, or French.

Future World

Epcot's Future World comprises multiple large buildings that house the various shows, rides, and attractions. This section provides information about everything there is to see and do in this portion of Epcot. Plan on spending between forty-five minutes and three hours at each of these attractions. As you'll see, some of the attractions contain multiple rides, shows, or things to experience. (If the park is extremely crowded, more time may be required.)

Spaceship Earth

Ages 2–4:	N.S.
Ages 5–10:	★★★
Ages 11–15:	★★★
Ages 16–Adult:	★★★

For a reminder of the rating system, see page xiv.

Whether you approach Epcot via car, bus, or monorail, you can't miss seeing this 16-million-pound, 180-foot-tall, silver landmark as you approach the park. Inside this oversize golf ball–like object is an entertaining and informative attraction that explores the history of communication.

Spaceship Earth is the first major attraction you reach once you enter into Epcot's Future World from the main entrance. As a result, the line to experience Spaceship Earth's fourteen-minute-long ride is usually long. Once guests board the Omni-Mover transport inside the geosphere, they're seemingly transported back in time to discover how humans first learned to communicate. Throughout the attraction, Audio-Animatronics, lasers, and all sorts of other special effects are used to showcase communication and communication technology past, present, and future.

As the ride comes to an end, guests disembark from the Omni-Mover and find themselves in the AT&T Global Neighborhood. Guests can also enter this area through a separate entrance. This is a hands-on exhibit that showcases up-and-coming communication technology and offers a firsthand look at equipment like video telephones, and state-of-the-art ways of surfing the Internet.

The best time to experience Spaceship Earth is late afternoon or during the last ninety minutes before Epcot's Future World closes for the day.

Innoventions

Ages 2–4:	N.S.
Ages 5–10:	★★
Ages 11–15:	★★★
Ages 16–Adult:	★★★

The purpose of Innoventions is to showcase technologically advanced products and services from many of the world's technology leaders. Innoventions is a large, hands-on, and visually exciting exhibit that's constantly changing. Its goal is to offer guests a preview of consumer electronics and computer technology that's new, but not necessarily currently available in American homes. What sets Innoventions apart from other attractions at Epcot is that almost everything that's on display is interactive, so you actually get to try things out, not just look at products or see someone else demonstrate them.

Whether you're a computer guru or totally computer illiterate, Innoventions gives people of all ages a chance to learn about current and future technology in a fun, but casual, setting. You're free to visit and walk through only the areas of Innoventions that are of interest to you, and spend as much or as little time as you want in each area. If you happen to see a product you're interested in, helpful people are available at each area of the pavilion to answer your questions or supply you with free informational brochures.

The Land

The overall theme of the Land is an exploration of our planet and how it produces food to support humanity and all of the other creatures living on Earth. The Land is divided up into four separate attractions: Living with the Land, Circle of Life, Food Rocks, and a Greenhouse Tour. Once you enter into this six-acre complex, plan on spending a minimum of one to three hours here.

Living with the Land

Ages 2–4:	N.S.
Ages 5–10:	★★
Ages 11–15:	★★
Ages 16–Adult:	★★★

Living with the Land is a fourteen-minute boat ride that takes guests through a man-made rain forest as well as the Land's massive greenhouses, where plant research is being conducted. All of the plants you see in the greenhouses are alive and real. Along the boat ride, however, to create some of the scenes you'll be seeing, artificial plants and special effects are used. This ride appeals to people of all ages and is meant to be highly educational as well as entertaining.

The Circle of Life

Ages 2–4:	★★★
Ages 5–10:	★★★
Ages 11–15:	★★
Ages 16–Adult:	★★

The Circle of Life attraction located in the Land pavilion is a twenty-minute movie shown on a massive screen (23-inch by 60-inch) that combines live action with animation. This movie stars characters from *The Lion King*. Designed to appeal to younger guests, the attraction focuses on the many dangers that face our environment. Environmental responsibility, demonstrated in ways that kids and adults alike will understand, is a central theme of this movie.

Food Rocks

Ages 2–4:	★★★
Ages 5–10:	★★★
Ages 11–15:	★★
Ages 16–Adult:	★★

Food Rocks is another kid-oriented attraction within the Land pavilion, offering a fifteen-minute concert featuring upbeat music. The setting is a kitchen, and the performers include vegetables, a milk carton, and silverware. While guests will recognize many of the songs that are performed, all of the lyrics have been changed, giving each song a food theme. We're all taught never to play with food, but until you experience this show, you probably haven't thought too much about how entertaining food can be.

Greenhouse Tour

Ages 2–4:	N.S.
Ages 5–10:	N.S.
Ages 11–15:	★★
Ages 16–Adult:	★★★

If you have a green thumb, enjoy gardening as a hobby, or just want to get a close-up look at the exotic plants growing within the Land's greenhouses and see how they're maintained, one-hour guided tours are offered throughout the day.

Reservations for this tour can be made only on the day of your visit, and must be made in person by visiting the tour desk located at the Green Thumb Emporium (found inside the Land pavilion). There's a small fee (under $10 per person) to participate. The tour, however, will appeal mainly to adults interested in gardening and agriculture.

⊕ HOT SPOT

Space for these walking tours is extremely limited, but guests have the unique opportunity to see firsthand how plants are being grown without soil, and learn how NASA and the U.S. Department of Agriculture are working together on research being conducted at Epcot.

Soarin'

Ages 2–4:	N.S.
Ages 5–10:	★★★
Ages 11–15:	★★★
Ages 16–Adult:	★★★

Thanks to a combination of motion simulators and Omnimax movie technology, you'll feel as if you're soaring over California as you're given a beautiful airborne tour of historic landmarks and national parks. You'll see the Golden Gate Bridge, redwood forests, Napa Valley, Yosemite, and other landmarks in a way you've never seen them before. As you experience this realistic movie on the giant screen in front of you, you'll be suspended 45 feet in the air in what's designed to feel like a hang glider. Your movements are perfectly synchronized with the movie.

While there is a mild thrill element to this attraction, it's relatively calm and visually stunning. It's well worth experiencing this four -minute "flight" across California, which allows you to see 180 degrees around you. Unless you're prone to motion sickness, this ride/attraction is suitable for everyone (except very young kids). You should get a FASTPASS for this popular ride as soon as you walk into the park. During peak times, all available FASTPASS tickets for Soarin' will be gone by noon and the only way to see this attraction is standing in a two-hour line.

✔ This is a must-see attraction.

⊕ HOT SPOT

Once you make it to the preloading line of Soarin', ask a cast member if you can please wait for "row number one." Don't ask for the first row or front row because the mechanism picks all rows up, making all rows first rows and front rows. Say row number one, because rows two, three, and four will have silhouetted legs of riders above them dangling above the screen.

The Living Seas

Ages 2–4:	★★★
Ages 5–10:	★★★
Ages 11–15:	★★★
Ages 16–Adult:	★★★

Unless you've had the opportunity to ride in a real-life submarine or go scuba diving in the Caribbean, you haven't seen what life is truly like in the ocean. The Living Seas is much more than just the world's largest fish tank. Some of the world's most renowned oceanographers, researchers, and scientists, along with Disney's Imagineers, have created an attraction that allows guests to get a close-up view of life under the sea without ever having to get wet. What you'll see when you enter this pavilion is nothing short of spectacular.

The attraction begins with a walking tour through a gallery that chronicles man's journey into the oceans, using submarines and deep-sea diving equipment. Next, you'll see a short, two-and-a-half-minute movie that shows some of the deep-sea diving and ocean exploration equipment that's currently being used for research.

Your next stop is Sea Base Alpha, the world's largest aquarium. The reef you'll be seeing is man-made, but the fish and exotic marine life are all real. Sea Base Alpha also offers hands-on activities and interactive video screens that help to explain various oceanographic topics. Once you enter into the Living Seas, plan on spending at least thirty to sixty minutes here. There are many other attractions inside the Living Seas to see as well. Turtle Talk with Crush is an interactive real-time talk with Crush and the audience. Also check out The Seas with Nemo & Friends where you can greet all the *Finding Nemo* friends as they swim amid the marine life in a huge aquarium.

On some evenings around 7:00 P.M., if you're lucky, you'll get to see Mickey Mouse in scuba gear diving into the tank and swimming with the sea life.

Special tours include Epcot Seas Aqua Tour, Divequest, and Dolphins in Depth.

✔ This is a must-see attraction.

Universe of Energy

Ages 2–4:	★
Ages 5–10:	★★
Ages 11–15:	★★
Ages 16–Adult:	★★

The Universe of Energy was one of the original pavilions in Epcot's Future World. In 1996, however, it was totally revamped to provide guests with an entirely new and far more entertaining experience. The forty-five-minute presentation, called Ellen's Energy Adventure, features actress/comedian Ellen DeGeneres and scientist Bill Nye ("The Science Guy"). It's shown every seventeen minutes throughout the day.

As you might have gathered from the name, this attraction explores how energy is created and used around the world. Not only does this attraction explain all of the different options available for creating energy now and in the future, but it does so in a way that's entertaining and not preachy.

Imagination!

Ages 2–4:	★
Ages 5–10:	★★★
Ages 11–15:	★★★
Ages 16–Adult:	★★

The Epcot ride/attraction Journey into Your Imagination, which opened in conjunction with this theme park, has been totally revamped yet again, creating a totally different attraction. The latest ride, Journey into Imagination with Figment, stars the adorable purple dragon, Figment (as in figment of your imagination), and explores the human imagination and our five senses in a fun, whimsical, and musical way. After experiencing the six-minute ride, guests wind up within ImageWorks and Kodak's "What If" Labs. This is a totally interactive, walk-through area that features technological exhibits and activities for people of all ages. The entire attraction, including the wait queue, is located within an air-conditioned building.

Honey I Shrunk the Audience 3-D Movie

Ages 2–4:	★★
Ages 5–10:	★★★
Ages 11–15:	★★★
Ages 16–Adult:	★★★

Also located in the Journey into Imagination pavilion is the Honey, I Shrunk the Audience show, which is loosely based on Disney's *Honey, I Shrunk the Kids* movie. Rick Moranis and Marcia Strassman, along with the kids from this movie series, reprise their roles for this comical fourteen-minute 3-D movie. Ultimately, after the theater is invaded by 3-D movie mice, and you see the onscreen characters miniaturized, the audience itself becomes the unwilling victim of Professor Wayne Szalinski's shrinking machine. This movie is exciting, extremely entertaining, and offers lots of surprises. While you'll be handed special 3-D glasses as you enter into the theater, do not place them over your eyes until you're seated and instructed to do so. The 3-D glasses can be placed directly over prescription eyeglasses.

✔ This is a must-see attraction.

⊕ HOT SPOT

Look for the marker in Epcot showing the exact center of the park. It is located just to the west of Innoventions West on the path that leads straight to the Land Pavilion.

Test Track

Ages 2–4:	N.S.
Ages 5–10:	★
Ages 11–15:	★★★
Ages 16–Adult:	★★★

When you experience this attraction, you take on the role of a test driver for General Motors. Your responsibilities include testing new models of automobiles while they're still in the concept phase. This is a challenging job that takes skill, guts, and a love for speed. That's the premise behind Epcot's thrill ride Test Track.

The preshow/line queue takes place within an industrial-looking test laboratory filled with equipment and vehicle components. There are simulated brake, wheel, suspension, airbag, seat belt, and windshield tests.

As the ride begins, get ready to buckle up and travel along bumpy terrain, through hairpin turns, into freezing cold chambers, and along 50-degree banked curves at speeds up to 65 miles per hour. Guests experience this ride in specially designed six-passenger vehicles that travel along the mile-long track.

✔ This is a must-see attraction.

≡FAST FACT

The four wheels on the test cars in Test Track are an illusion. There are really a total of twenty-two wheels per vehicle. The other eighteen are hidden by the four visible tires and are used at different times throughout the ride. Especially the brake wheels!

Innoventions Fountain

Ages 2–4:	★★
Ages 5–10:	★★
Ages 11–15:	★★
Ages 16–Adult:	★★

Every fifteen minutes, a computer-controlled, fully choreographed shooting water performance is presented at this fountain, located outside in Innoventions Plaza. This short show is nothing compared to IllumiNations: Reflections of Earth (presented nightly), but it offers a nice diversion as you're walking by.

Mission: SPACE

Ages 2–4:	N.S.
Ages 5–10:	N.S.
Ages 11–15:	★★★
Ages 16–Adult:	★★★

Imagine what it would be like if you were an astronaut taking off and then traveling deep into space. Well, the closest thing you'll probably ever get is this high-tech ride/attraction that was created in conjunction with NASA and Hewlett-Packard. Mission: SPACE has replaced the old Horizons pavilion at Epcot and was in development for more than five years. The actual ride lasts about four minutes and uses state-of-the-art centrifuge technology, sophisticated visual imaging, and incredible audio effects to create a very realistic space-flight simulation experience. Basically, you are spinning at around 35 mph; however, while inside the cabin, you never know this. You only feel the effects, which is the skin on your face pulling back and a slight tightening of the chest against your chair. To experience Mission: SPACE, you must be at least 44 inches tall. It's not recommended for anyone who easily gets motion sickness or has known heart issues. You'll definitely want to utilize FASTPASS and not eat beforehand.

✔ This is a must-see attraction.

≡FAST FACT

As of 2006, two people have died after the Mission: SPACE experience. However, both families admitted that there were known heart conditions. Since these incidents the ride now has two versions you can choose. One version has movement and the other does not.

Dining in Future World

The restaurants and snack shops located in Epcot's Future World are open during park hours (but most close at 7:00 P.M.). For exact hours or to make a reservation at any of the full-service establishments, call (407) WDW-DINE. The following are dining options available at Epcot's Future World:

 TRAVEL TIP

In 1997 Disney restaurants stopped taking reservations and started a policy of priority seating. You will call the restaurant or guest services and tell the representative the date and time you would like to dine. You are then given a seating time, and when you arrive at the restaurant you will be given the next available table for your party's size.

- **Coral Reef**—This is a full-service restaurant located in The Living Seas pavilion. The backdrop for this dining room is the attraction's 6-million-gallon aquarium. The majority of the menu items served at this restaurant are seafood dishes. Priority Seating reservations are definitely recommended. Lunch and dinner are served daily.
- **Garden Grill**—This full-service restaurant serves breakfast, lunch, and dinner, hosted by Disney characters, including

Mickey Mouse and Minnie Mouse. Lunch and dinner entrées include chicken, fish, and steak dishes.

- **Electric Umbrella**—Located near Innoventions, this is Future World's largest fast-food dining establishment. Entrées include hamburgers, cheeseburgers, hot dogs, sandwiches, salads, and a variety of snack items and beverages.
- **Fountain View Espresso and Bakery**—Freshly baked items such as croissants and a wide range of extremely tasty desserts are offered at this dining spot located near Innoventions. Espresso, cappuccino, coffee, wine, beer, and other beverages are available.
- **Pure and Simple**—This snack shop, located within the Wonders of Life pavilion, offers a selection of healthy snack foods, like fresh fruit, salads, frozen yogurt, muffins, juices, and oat bran waffles with fruit toppings. Breakfast, lunch, and dinner are served, and counter service is available.
- **Sunshine Season Food Fair**—Located on the lower level of the Land pavilion in Future World, this food court offers soups and salads, as well as baked goods, bagels, fresh fruit, cinnamon rolls, Danish, and other breakfast treats. There's also a barbecue stand, Chinese food stand, a sandwich shop, and the Potato Store. The Beverage House offers a large list of tropical (alcoholic and nonalcoholic) frozen drinks, plus beer, wine, bottled water, and soda.

⸺FAST FACT

Throughout Epcot, you'll find snack carts that sell ice cream, snack foods, and beverages. In the dead of the summer they will keep the ice cream frozen very hard to keep it from melting so fast in the summer sun.

Shopping in Future World

As you probably expect, gift shops and souvenir stands are located throughout Epcot's Future World. Gateway Gifts and the Camera Center are located near the park's main entrance. Here you can pick up souvenirs or film for your camera. You can rent video cameras at the Camera Center, and same-day film processing is available. You will, however, pay a premium if you purchase film or batteries anywhere at WDW or have your film developed at the park.

The Centorium is located in the midst of Innoventions and offers a large selection of Disney character merchandise, gifts, and souvenirs with the Epcot logo. This is the largest gift shop in Epcot.

≡FAST FACT

An animated movie is essentially a collection of painted animation or cartoon cells. A cell is a clear sheet of acetate or nitrate paper. The desired characters are painted onto this paper and then layered on top of a background to create a scene. Then a picture is taken of the cell and the background. It takes thousands of cells to make up a half-hour cartoon.

For Disney fans and collectors, the Art of Disney Epcot Gallery is one of the most exciting shops at Epcot, because Disney animation artwork is on display (and available for purchase), including actual production animation cells and limited edition animation cells. Other Disney collectibles are also displayed in a museum gallery–like setting. Whether you're looking to add to your Disney art collection, you're hoping to start a collection, or you just want to see some of the stunning artwork that's on display, be sure to stop by this gallery for a visit. It'll appeal mainly to adults.

The World Showcase

Each of the pavilions in the World Showcase represents a country and showcases its culture, architecture, food, art, music, and history. These pavilions are staffed by natives of the featured country and offer an authentic look at what each country has to offer. To make your trip around the world more exciting, many of the pavilions offer live shows, musical performances, and some type of ride or movie attraction. Specialty shops are also featured within the pavilions, so you can pick up unique souvenirs that were handcrafted or manufactured in the featured country.

⊕ HOT SPOT

The full-service, fine-dining restaurants within these pavilions are authentic and offer some of the best food available anywhere in WDW. Reservations for these relatively high-priced restaurants are strongly recommended. Call ☎(407) WDW-DINE as far in advance as possible. Same-day reservations are also available, but if you don't mind waiting, you can simply show up for a meal at one of the full-service restaurants.

The World Showcase as a whole is designed more for adults than children, although there's always so much to see and do in this area of Epcot, people of all ages will enjoy the experience of traveling to exotic countries without ever stepping foot on an airplane. These pavilions are described in the order that you'll encounter them if you begin at the main entrance of the World Showcase (approached by coming through Future World) and proceed in a clockwise direction (traveling to the left).

Mexico

A large pyramid-like structure is the home of the Mexico pavilion, where you can experience El Rio del Tiempo: The River of Time. This is a six-minute boat ride that takes a look at life in Mexico past and present. Movies, animated sets, and Audio-Animatronics are used to provide the visuals along the boat trip. The lines for this attraction will probably be long in the morning, so if you wait until late in the day or evening, your wait will be less. Live entertainment is provided both inside and outside of the pavilion throughout the day.

At the Plaza de Los Amigos marketplace area, you can shop for piñatas, sombreros, pottery, colorful paper flowers, and other genuine Mexican souvenirs. For a higher-priced selection of merchandise, visit Artesanias Mexicanas. Products from northern Mexico are showcased at El Ranchito del Norte, while La Familia Fashions offers clothing and accessories for women and children, along with jewelry.

As for the Mexican dining experience offered at this pavilion, San Angel Inn is a second location for a famous restaurant located in Mexico City. Here you'll be able to choose from an assortment of delicious Mexican entrées, including tacos as well as fish, meat, and chicken dishes. This is a full-service restaurant and reservations are strongly recommended. Lunch and dinner are served daily.

A less expensive dining option at the Mexico pavilion is offered at Cantina de San Angel. Here you can snack on various types of filled soft tortillas and other fast-food items. Lunch, dinner, and snacks are served, and counter service is offered. Nearby outdoor tables are provided, or you can enjoy your food as you walk around the World Showcase Promenade.

≡FAST FACT

All cast members that work at World Showcase pavilions are actually from those countries. They sign a contract with WDW for one year to come work in the pavilion of their heritage. They all must know a little of the English language to qualify.

Norway

This pavilion offers you the opportunity to learn about some of the history, culture, and folklore of Norway. The architecture of this pavilion depicts several different styles from around the country, plus from the country's past. For example, one of the main structures is a Norwegian castle that is modeled after a fourteenth-century fortress that can still be seen in Oslo's harbor.

The main attraction of the Norway pavilion is the Maelstrom, a ten-minute ride that uses boats modeled after those used by Vikings over 1,000 years ago. Your journey begins with a look at the country's past and at its ancient folklore. After the boat ride, your look at Norway continues in a theater, where a movie depicting life in modern Norway is presented. This is a popular attraction that's often less crowded in the evenings.

One of the buildings that make up this pavilion is a re-creation of a wooden stave church. Inside you'll discover a gallery that offers scenes and objects designed to help guests better understand this country's culture, including the following:

- **The Puffin's Roost** is a shop that displays an assortment of Norwegian gifts, handmade items, clothing, jewelry, toys, and other souvenirs.
- **Princess Storybook Character Dining** can be found at Akershus Restaurant at Norway for breakfast, lunch, and dinner. Reservations are needed.
- **Kringla Bakeri og Kafe** offers less expensive snacks and candies as well as open-faced smoked salmon, roast beef, and turkey sandwiches. One treat that's sold here is kringles, which are candied pretzels that Norwegians eat on special occasions. Beers from Norway are served. Counter service is available, and nearby outdoor seating is provided.

⊕ HOT SPOT

Greta Waitz, the Norweigen nine-time New York City Marathon winner is immortalized in a statue located on the grounds of the Norway pavilion. The Greta Waitz Lopet race (the largest run for women in the world) is an annual event in Norway.

China

As you approach the China pavilion, you'll quickly notice the authentic architecture and hear the Chinese music that's played constantly near the pavilion so passersby can get a taste of China, even without dropping into the pavilion. Inside the pavilion's Temple of Heaven, live music is performed almost continuously, while in the nearby courtyard, you can catch a performance by a team of highly talented acrobats. This courtyard features landscaping made up of plants that are native to China.

In addition to the live performances, the China pavilion features a Circle-Vision 360 movie, *Reflections of China*, which was updated in late 2003. This presentation shows locations in China that foreigners had never seen prior to this movie's premiere at Epcot. You'll see stunning footage of Beijing's Forbidden City, the Great Wall of China, and many other beautiful locations.

As you leave the movie theater, you'll have a chance to walk through an exhibit of Chinese art. The gallery exhibit changes every six months but always includes pieces from well-known artists that are on loan from private collectors and world-renowned museums.

Your visit to the China pavilion can also include a shopping excursion to the Yonh Feng Shangdain Shopping Gallery, located on the Street of Good Fortune. Here you can purchase authentic Chinese merchandise like silk robes, paper fans, and umbrellas, as well as antiques and other souvenirs.

If you're in the mood for a tasty Chinese lunch or dinner, the Nine Dragons restaurant offers a wonderful full-service dining experience.

The food is prepared in a variety of different cooking styles, including Mandarin, Hunan, Cantonese, and Szechuan. On the menu, you'll find a wide range of entrées listed, along with Chinese teas, beers, and wines. Reservations are strongly recommended.

⊕ HOT SPOT

As you enter the main building in the Chinese pavilion, look down and you'll see nine stones embedded into the floor. The Chinese consider nine to be a lucky number.

For lunch or dinner, the Lotus Blossom Café is Epcot's answer to Chinese fast food. Nearby outdoor seating is provided. The food served here is considerably less expensive than the full-service Nine Dragons restaurant, and you'll finish eating much faster, allowing you to continue exploring the World Showcase.

Germany

The Germany pavilion is a re-creation of a small German village, although the architecture of the various buildings and structures was borrowed from many different areas of the country. On the hour, a glockenspiel located within the pavilion can be heard playing an original tune, and throughout the day, live musical entertainment is often featured.

By exploring the pavilion, you'll encounter several small shops, each featuring unique German items. At Der Bucherwurm, you'll find books about Germany, artwork, and souvenir items. Volkskunst is a small shop that sells clocks and watches, as well as other handcrafted items. If you're looking for a special gift for a child (or a collectible doll for yourself), check out what's offered at Der Teddybar, a lovely toy shop.

No matter what time of year you're visiting Epcot, it's always the Christmas holiday season at Die Weihnachts Ecke, a German Christmas shop that sells ornaments, holiday decorations, and holiday-oriented gift items. Those who collect tree ornaments will be able to purchase some wonderful and unique additions for their collection here.

Participate in a daily wine tasting or take home a bottle of German wine by visiting Weinkeller, a wine shop that offers more than 250 varieties of German wine that were produced and bottled by H. Schmitt Sohne. Crystal jewelry and glass items are offered at Kunstarbeit In Kristal. You'll be able to satisfy your sweet tooth at Sussigkeiten, a confectionery shop that offers many German sweets.

At Glas und Porzellan, you'll find glass and porcelain items made by Goebel. Collectors of Hummel figurines will find a huge assortment of these collectibles on display, plus there's often a Goebel artist on hand answering questions and demonstrating how these pieces are hand-painted. This is a wonderful shop for adults to browse through, even if you have no intention of making a purchase.

Lunch and dinner are served daily at the Germany pavilion's fine-dining restaurant, called Biergarten. Guests sit at large tables (often with total strangers) and can enjoy a selection of authentic German cuisine and drink German beer. Live entertainment is offered every half-hour. At Sommerfest, bratwurst sandwiches are the specialty, but you'll also find treats like soft pretzels, apple strudel, and other German snacks. Counter service is provided and nearby outdoor seating is available. Located in between the Germany and China pavilions is a snack shop that offers soda, bottled water, frozen yogurt, and ice cream.

⊕ HOT SPOT

Every half-hour there is live German entertainment on the dining-room stage inside. If you don't care to eat, grab a refreshing beverage outside of the pavilion and carry it inside to watch the show. Simply walk in and turn to the left past the hostess stand. These tables are meant for guests just passing through.

Italy

In addition to fine Italian food, guests get a true taste of Italy when they visit this pavilion. In the courtyard of this pavilion, not only will you see and hear live music performed, but you'll also get a chance to see the Living Statues. Performers stand motionless and periodically change positions. Despite the best efforts of guests to distract these performers, they remain expressionless and motionless except to change positions.

Delizie Italiane is a marketplace area that sells chocolates and other sweets, while La Cucina Italiana is a gourmet shop that offers Italian pastries and dessert items. Take-home gourmet food items and accessories are also sold here. For more expensive gifts, such as glassware or porcelain figurines, be sure to visit La Bel Cristallo ("The Beautiful Crystal"). Jewelry made from silver and gold, along with other items, is sold at La Gemma Elegante.

An authentic and delicious Italian dining experience is offered during lunch and dinner hours at L'Originale Alfredo di Roma Ristorante. The specialty of the house is fettuccine, although you'll find a range of Italian entrées available. The kitchen of this restaurant is located behind a large glass window, so guests can see the chefs at work.

The American Adventure

Located halfway around the World Showcase Lagoon is the American Adventure. A large colonial-style building is the main structure of this pavilion. Inside, guests are invited to see a twenty-nine-minute attraction called the American Adventure Show, which features Audio-Animatronic characters that bring some of America's heroes and most famous historical figures and entertainers to life. Every American should see the American Adventure Show, so take a break from walking and watch the show. The seats near the front are the best.

Live music is presented at the American Adventure pavilion, which is almost always crowded. Outside of the main pavilion, located in front of the World Showcase Lagoon, the America Gardens Theater offers various concerts and performances that constantly change. Showtimes and details about the various shows are posted in front of the theater, at Guest Relations, and at the Tip Board. The nearby All-American Red, White & Blue gift shop sells items that are patriotic and that represent the country. American flags, clothing, books, and other products are available, along with Coca-Cola merchandise.

⊕ HOT SPOT

Many of the pavilions in this part of Epcot offer food that is totally foreign to most young people. This is the perfect opportunity to encourage them to be adventurous and try something new. If they aren't interested, then stop at the Liberty Inn to find all-American food that your children will recognize and enjoy.

There is no full-service restaurant in this pavilion, but the Liberty Inn offers all-American food like hamburgers, hot dogs, salads, soda, and cookies. Counter service is available, and nearby seating is provided. Lunch, dinner, and snack items are served.

If you're lucky enough to travel to WDW during the Christmas holiday season (late November through late December), you won't want to miss the Candlelight Processional, which is held two or three times per night at the America Gardens Theater. This magical and heartwarming holiday performance lasts about one hour, and it features a 450-voice choir, a fifty-piece orchestra, and a celebrity narrator.

≡ FAST FACT

Some guests that have visited the World Showcase before and are looking for something different to do can travel as a group and "drink around the world." Until recently, you could purchase a native alcoholic beverage at every country except America. The American Pavilion now sells beer.

Japan

The Imperial Palace is the main focal point of this pavilion. Outside, you'll see and hear Japanese music performed, and you might even get to see stilt-walkers dressed like exotic birds perform. Native landscaping is seen around the pavilion. The Bijutsu-Kan Gallery offers an ever-changing exhibit of traditional and more modern Japanese art.

The Mitsukoshi Department Store offers a huge assortment of Japanese products, gifts, and souvenirs offered at a range of prices from extremely affordable to extremely expensive. This is definitely one of the most interesting shops to browse through at Epcot.

One of the very best restaurants in Epcot's World Showcase is Mitsukoshi, a Japanese steak house where your food is prepared by talented chefs right at your table. The Tempura Kiku area of this restaurant serves batter-dipped, deep-fried entrées made from beef, chicken, and seafood. The main dining room offers a full menu of Japanese dishes, all cooked at your table in an extremely entertaining style. At the large tables, you'll probably be seated with strangers as you enjoy this fine-dining experience. Lunch and dinner are served daily. Reservations are strongly suggested.

Yakitori House offers less expensive Japanese cuisine that can be enjoyed for lunch, dinner, or as a snack. Guydon and yakitori are among the main menu selections served here.

Morocco

Inside the Gallery of Arts and History, guests have the opportunity to see authentic Moroccan artwork. Also on hand at the Moroccan National Tourist Office within this pavilion are travel experts who can help you plan your next vacation to their country. Be sure to take a few minutes to watch the slide show that's presented at this office continuously.

If you're in the market for a hard-to-find fez or another article of Moroccan clothing, drop by the Tangier Traders shop. The Marketplace in the Medina shop sells handcrafted baskets and other handmade items. If it can be made out of brass, you'll find it at a shop called the Brass Bazaar. Additional brass items can be purchased at Berber Oasis, a smaller gift shop also found in this pavilion. Kids are sure to find a toy or souvenir at Medina Arts, a shop that sells toys, clothing, and other items featuring characters from Disney's *Aladdin* motion picture.

≡FAST FACT

Morocco is the only pavilion that is not part of the nightly Illumi-Nations show. The buildings in Morocco have great religious significance and are sponsored by a government and not a corporation.

As you dine at Marrakesh, you'll be entertained by belly dancers and live musical performances. The food served is genuine Moroccan cuisine, which includes chicken brochette, couscous, and roast lamb. The live entertainment makes this dining experience extremely memorable and enjoyable. Reservations are strongly recommended. Lunch and dinner are served daily.

France

A re-creation of the Eiffel Tower is the prominent landmark at this pavilion. The main attraction here is the *Impressions de France* movie that offers a comprehensive and visually stunning look at France in eighteen minutes.

Plume et Palette is a beautiful shop that sells cosmetics, fragrances, and bath products imported from France. There's also an area that sells oil paintings and prints by well-known French artists. At La Signature, an assortment of gift items is available, including collectibles and tapestries. The Galerie des Halles also sells an assortment of affordable souvenirs from France, including musical CDs. Posters, prints, and other items imprinted with artwork from famous artists such as Monet and Renoir are available from La Casserole.

🧳 TRAVEL TIP

If you have your cell phone with you it can be fun to call up a relative or friend and say, "Hey, I'm in France! (or any other country)."

If you're in the mood for fine French food for lunch or dinner, make a reservation to eat at Bistro de Paris, a full-service restaurant that's located one flight above Chefs de France. Here, a traditional French bistro menu is served daily. Downstairs at Chefs de France, some of the country's finest chefs are invited to showcase their talent at this posh restaurant. This, however, is one of the most expensive restaurants at Epcot. A special children's menu is available, and lunch or dinner reservations are strongly recommended.

United Kingdom

Guests who visit this pavilion get to enjoy the authentic architecture, landscaping, and shops. There's even a hedge maze that's located just outside of the pavilion's cottage. Meanwhile, at the Crown & Crest, you'll find dart boards, chess sets, and other unique gifts and items. The beautiful chess sets range in price from $250 to $900. Sweaters made of lamb's wool are available at Pringle of Scotland.

═FAST FACT

Between France and the United Kingdom is the back entrance/exit to Epcot called the International Gateway. This waterway and walkway takes you to BoardWalk, Yacht & Beach Club, and the Swan and Dolphin resorts. Another water taxi from those resorts can take you to Disney's MGM Studios.

Lords & Ladies is the home of china products manufactured and sold by Royal Doulton. Figurines and fine china are available at a wide range of prices, but even if you don't want to buy anything, this store is worth visiting just to browse. For handmade products from Wales, visit the Magic of Wales shop. English teas, teapots, biscuits, and fine candies are sold at the Tea Caddy.

When you're ready to eat lunch, dinner, or a snack, check out the menu at Rose & Crown Pub and Dining Room. This authentic English pub offers fish and chips and an assortment of other entrées. Seating in the pub area is available on a first-come-first-served basis; however, reservations are suggested for the dining room.

Canada

If you're traveling around Epcot's World Showcase Lagoon clockwise, then your trip around the world ends at Canada. A seventeen-minute movie, *O Canada!* is shown in Circle-Vision 360 and offers a visual tour of this country. There are no seats in this theater, so be prepared to stand while the movie is shown all around you.

⊕ HOT SPOT

Outside of the Canada pavilion, you're likely to see live performances by Canadian folk dancers and the Caledonia Bagpipe Band.

At the Northwest Mercantile, a selection of Canadian clothing, like lumberjack shirts, as well as other items and handcrafted products, can be purchased. Le Cellier offers a selection of Canadian food in a casual environment that's not too expensive compared to the other restaurants located in the World Showcase pavilions.

Lunch, dinner, and snacks are served in a cafeteria-style setting. For a quick snack, consider stopping at the Refreshment Port. Canadian beer and wine are available, along with frozen yogurt, fresh fruit, and ice cream.

IllumiNations: Reflections of Earth

Ages 2–4:	★★
Ages 5–10:	★★★
Ages 11–15:	★★★
Ages 16–Adult:	★★★

Every evening (just after dark), thousands of people gather around the World Showcase Lagoon for an incredible display of fireworks, lasers, and dancing fountains, all synchronized to music. This thirteen-minute show can be seen from anywhere around the lagoon, but you'll want to stake out your viewing location up to one hour early if the park is extremely crowded. This is one of the most spectacular nighttime shows presented anywhere at WDW, so if you're visiting Epcot, plan on staying into the evening so you don't miss this magical and visually stunning show.

✔ This is a must-see attraction.

🧳 TRAVEL TIP

IllumiNations changes every year, so if you're making a return visit to Epcot, the show you saw during your last visit will be different. Check with Guest Relations or the Tip Board for specific showtimes. You can also call ☎(407) 824-4321.

Tapestry of Dreams Parade

In addition to the nighttime IllumiNations performance, Epcot now has its own parade, which pays tribute to children from around the world, and the dreams and legacy of Walt Disney. This thirty-minute parade features colorful floats, larger-than-life puppets, and 112 cast members who sing, dance, and entertain guests who line the parade route.

Featuring original music, Tapestry of Dreams is presented twice every evening. The parade travels between the Mexico and Morocco pavilions within Epcot's World Showcase. Unlike the parades within the Magic Kingdom and Disney's Animal Kingdom, for example, this one is more adult-oriented, because there's less of an emphasis on the Disney characters. Instead, the large puppets, beautiful floats, and costumed performers are showcased. People of all ages will enjoy this parade.

Leave a Legacy

Epcot offers guests the opportunity to leave their legacy in the form of a digital photo that gets mounted on a series of sculptures located near the main entrance to the park. Guests have an opportunity to purchase "memory tiles" upon which a digital photograph (taken at the park) is etched. One or two images can be included on each tile.

≡FAST FACT

From home, people can view the sculpture and the individual tiles at a specially created Web site (✎*www.disney.go.com/millen niumlegacy*).

The cost of one image is $35. For two images on one tile, the price is $38. With every tile purchased, a verification certificate gets mailed to the purchaser that lists the exact location of the tile on the Legacy Sculpture.

CHAPTER 9

The Disney-MGM Studios

THE DISNEY-MGM STUDIOS THEME PARK offers at least one day's worth of quality entertainment with a Hollywood theme. This chapter describes all of the shows, attractions, rides, restaurants, shops, and guest services available at the Disney-MGM Studios, and will help you plan an exciting visit to this popular WDW Resort theme park.

Park Overview

The Disney-MGM Studios is the home to many highly popular attractions and shows suitable for the entire family. The theme park portion of this complex, where the rides and attractions are located, was inspired by the Golden Age of Hollywood.

The Studios opened to the public in 1989. Since then, millions of tourists, not to mention hundreds of the world's most famous celebrities, have visited this working studio facility/theme park. Even on the busiest of days, you should be able to see most of the shows and attractions, plus experience most (if not all) of the rides and tours that are of interest to you and your family, during one full day at the Disney-MGM Studios.

Getting to the Studios

If you're arriving at the studios by car, you'll need to pay $9 per day for parking. WDW Resort hotel guests park for free. After you park you'll ride a tram to the front entrance of the park. If you are a resort guest at the Dolphin, Swan, Yacht Club, Beach Club, or BoardWalk Inn, you can ride a water taxi directly to the studio's entrance or walk the half mile.

≡FAST FACT

Mickey Mouse would have to stand 350 feet tall to wear the Sorcerer's Hat icon at the center of the Studios. The hat is 22 feet tall.

Guests coming from the Magic Kingdom, Epcot, and all other WDW resorts take the specially marked WDW bus directly to the Studios. Guests traveling to this park from Downtown Disney must take a WDW bus to the Transportation and Ticket Center, and then switch buses to get to the Studios.

Same Day Re-entry

As you leave the Disney-MGM Studios, be sure to have your hand stamped as you exit in order to be granted readmission into the park later that day or evening. In addition to the hand stamp, be sure to retain your ticket stub. The hand stamps are designed to be water-resistant, so don't worry if your hand gets wet if you choose to return to your hotel in the middle of the day to go swimming, and then want to return to Disney-MGM Studios later that evening. Try to refrain, however, from scrubbing your hands clean with soap until your day's visit to the studios is complete.

Hours of Operation

The Disney-MGM Studios are open seven days per week, typically from 9:00 A.M. to 7:00 P.M. During the summertime and on certain holidays and peak periods, the park remains open later. To determine the hours of operation on the date(s) you're planning to visit the park, call (407) 824-4321.

What to Bring

Make sure you wear comfortable shoes! Depending on the weather, you might want to take along a jacket (you can always store it in a locker). Try to avoid carrying too much stuff with you. You'll enjoy your visit more if your hands are as free as possible.

≡ FAST FACT

The nonworking water tower is called the Earffel Tower. It can be seen from all roads near Disney-MGM Studios and from the park. The ears weigh 5,000 pounds and are a size 342-3/8!

Don't forget to bring your camera, along with plenty of film and batteries. The Disney-MGM Studios is a working motion picture and television studio, so you might run into some popular celebrities as well as your favorite Disney characters. Avoid having to purchase high-priced film, batteries, or camera supplies in the park.

The Tip Board

Located at the junction of Hollywood and Sunset Boulevards is the Studios Tip Board. This information board lists the current wait times for all of the major attractions in the Disney-MGM Studios. Stationed at this board is a Disney cast member who is in constant contact with the operators of all of the park's major attractions. Accurate wait times for each ride are posted, so you can better plan your day. Show and parade times are also available at this location. The very best time to visit the park and not have to deal with huge crowds is on Sunday morning.

As a general rule, if you're planning on focusing your attention on experiencing only the Disney-MGM Studios' most popular rides and attractions, it'll take you an average of forty-five minutes per attraction. This, however, depends on how crowded the park is and which attractions and rides you're trying to experience. If you're heading to one popular ride but notice that a line is particularly short for another attraction that you were planning to check out later in the day, adjust your schedule and go where the lines are the shortest.

⊕ HOT SPOT

Oscar's Classic Car Souvenirs, near the park's main entrance, is also the place where you can rent wheelchairs, strollers, or electronic convenience vehicles. Behind this service station, you'll find lockers that can be rented by the day, as well as an ATM, restrooms, a stamp machine, and public telephones.

Choose a Place to Meet

As soon as you arrive at the Studios, choose a place where you'll meet up with the other people in your group if you happen to get separated. Two ideal meeting places are in front of the Mann's Chinese Theater and at the Crossroads to the World (located near the park's main entrance). Cell phones and walkie-talkies work well too.

The Studios' Rides and Attractions

Like all of the Disney theme parks, there's a lot to see and do at the Disney-MGM Studios. Here's a rundown of what you'll discover as you explore this fun-filled "Hollywood"-themed theme park.

Hollywood Boulevard

As soon as you enter the Disney-MGM Studios, you'll find yourself on Hollywood Boulevard, which is lined with a wide assortment of shops. To add to the overall atmosphere of Hollywood in the 1940s, you'll find an assortment of "Streetmosphere" performers who interact with guests while staying in character. Since the shops on Hollywood Boulevard are open thirty minutes after the park's official closing time, save your shopping for later in the day. The daily character parade goes down Hollywood Boulevard. For parade times, visit the Tip Board.

The Twilight Zone: Tower of Terror 4

Ages 2–4:	N.S.
Ages 5–10:	N.S.
Ages 11–15:	★★★
Ages 16–Adult:	★★★

The Hollywood Tower Hotel cost the Walt Disney Company more to build than virtually all of the other WDW Resort hotels, only this one won't ever be used to accommodate living guests. This hotel looks like it's from Hollywood's Golden Age, but that it hasn't been maintained too well over the years. The Hollywood Tower Hotel is where you can experience the Twilight Zone: Tower of Terror 4, which is arguably the most thrilling of thrill rides in all of Walt Disney World.

The attraction starts with a preshow and a brief tour of the hotel. Guests then board the elevator, which is rather unique, because you get to sit down as you ride upward. When you reach one of the top floors, you'll experience some of the most incredible visual special effects you've ever seen. That is, just before you plummet down thirteen floors (157 feet) in what feels like a free fall. The drop lasts about three seconds, but it's very intense. Just when you think the thrill is over after the massive drop, the elevator starts rising upward again, only to drop guests a second time. In fact, there's now a random generator that determines when you drop and how many times the drop occurs during a ride.

To experience Tower of Terror 4, guests must be at least 40 inches tall. This ride is not recommended for anyone with heart or back problems, nor should it be experienced by pregnant women.

Whatever you do, avoid eating before experiencing this ride or you'll be sorry. As you take the thirteen-floor drop, a photo will be taken of you, which can be purchased as a souvenir as you leave the hotel.

✔ This is a must-see attraction.

TRAVEL TIP

The best way to enjoy the Tower of Terror is to raise your arms in the air when dropping. Also, don't be surprised if the person sitting next to you digs her fingernails into your thigh. This normally happens with first-timers.

The Great Movie Ride

Ages 2–4:	★★
Ages 5–10:	★★★
Ages 11–15:	★★★
Ages 16–Adult:	★★★

"Hooray for Hollywood" is the theme of this twenty-two-minute ride that utilizes over fifty Audio-Animatronic characters to re-create scenes from some of the most famous motion pictures of all time. This ride is located inside the Mann's Chinese Theater. As you're waiting to board the ride, once inside the theater, you'll see many authentic props and costumes from classic movies, and then when the ride begins, the movies will come to life before your eyes. The Great Movie Ride is thoroughly entertaining for all ages.

✔ This is a must-see attraction.

Jim Henson's Muppet Vision 3-D

Kermit, Miss Piggy, and all of the classic Muppet characters are

Ages 2–4:	★★★
Ages 5–10:	★★★
Ages 11–15:	★★★
Ages 16–Adult:	★★★

featured in this attraction's twelve-minute preshow that's followed by a comical twelve-minute 3-D movie. Muppet fans of all ages will truly love this attraction.

✔ This is a must-see attraction.

≡FAST FACT

The theater itself looks exactly like the set from *The Muppet Show* television series. You are the audience. During the movie, the theater itself actually becomes part of the show.

Star Tours

Ages 2–4:	N.S.
Ages 5–10:	★★★
Ages 11–15:	★★★
Ages 16–Adult:	★★★

What happens when you combine the creative talent of Disney's Imagineers with the imagination of George Lucas? The result in this case is Star Tours, a ride that's based on the original *Star Wars* movies and features characters like R2-D2 and C3-PO. As an intergalactic tourist, you and thirty-nine other guests will board a StarSpeeder and experience a whirlwind tour of the galaxy. Using flight-simulator technology, the StarSpeeder is on hydraulics and is perfectly synchronized with the movie you'll be watching on the ship's main view screen.

The overall effect is that you'll feel like you're actually traveling at ultrafast speed through space, when, in reality, your StarSpeeder is only a few feet off the ground. Star Tours is a fast-paced and turbulent roller-coaster-like ride with a *Star Wars* twist. Be prepared for a long wait to ride this attraction, but while you're waiting to board the StarSpeeder, you'll be entertained by an elaborate preshow that includes Audio-Animatronic characters from the *Star Wars* movies and video monitors that feature Star Tours travel information.

This ride is suitable for people of all ages, except very young children (under the age of three) and people who suffer from back problems, heart conditions, motion sickness, etc. Once you board the StarSpeeder, stow all of your loose clothing, purse, camera bag, and so on, and fasten your seatbelt. This ride is bumpy, but not scary. The best time to ride this attraction is late in the evening. If the line for this ride doesn't go outside of the building, the wait will be less than twenty minutes.

✔ This is a must-see attraction.

≡FAST FACT

Every year from May to June you can experience Star Wars Weekends at Disney-MGM Studios. You'll get to meet many *Star Wars* celebrities and participate in many activities. An admission ticket to the park is required.

Honey, I Shrunk the Kids Movie Set Adventure

Ages 2–4:	N.S.
Ages 5–10:	★★★
Ages 11–15:	★★★
Ages 16–Adult:	N.S.

This outdoor playground looks like a scene from the popular live-action Disney movie, *Honey, I Shrunk the Kids*, because everything is extremely oversized, making young guests feel incredibly small as they climb, crawl, jump, and slide around. This attraction offers adults a chance to sit down and relax, while the children have fun exploring this playground.

Voyage of the Little Mermaid

Ages 2–4:	★★
Ages 5–10:	★★★
Ages 11–15:	★★★
Ages 16–Adult:	★★★

Here's an exciting opportunity to go under the sea without ever getting wet. Voyage of the Little Mermaid is an extremely innovative live show that features costumed characters and unique life-size puppets, along with black-light special effects. Scenes from the animated Disney movie *The Little Mermaid* are re-created. This is an extremely popular attraction, especially among kids, so be prepared to wait up to one hour to experience this show. Be sure to take advantage of FASTPASS to cut your wait time. Very young children might get scared by some of the special effects used during the seventeen-minute show.

✔ This is a must-see attraction.

⊕ HOT SPOT

Located on the cement ground in front of the Mann's Chinese Theater, the home of the Great Movie Ride, are actual hand imprints, and in some cases, foot imprints, from real-life celebrities who have visited the Disney-MGM Studios since 1989. Spend a few minutes to check out which stars have left their permanent mark imprinted in the sidewalk.

Indiana Jones Epic Stunt Spectacular!

Ages 2–4:	★
Ages 5–10:	★★
Ages 11–15:	★★★
Ages 16–Adult:	★★★

This live-action stunt show was choreographed by Glenn Randall, who was the stunt coordinator for all of the Indiana Jones movies. While you won't see Harrison Ford, you will see talented stunt people re-create scenes from this movie series. Fireworks, explosions, and other special effects are used to add extra drama to this exciting show.

The Indiana Jones Epic Stunt Spectacular is presented several times throughout the day (showtimes are listed in front of the theater and at the Tip Board). About 2,000 people fit into the theater, so if you arrive between fifteen and thirty minutes early, you're virtually guaranteed a seat for this high-action thirty-minute show. A few brave guests are selected at the start of each show to be "extras." Not only do audience members get to see dozens of stunts performed, but they also learn how stunts are actually performed in movies so that nobody gets injured.

Journey to Narnia

Ages 2–4:	N.S.
Ages 5–10:	★★
Ages 11–15:	★★
Ages 16–Adult:	★

This short walk-through experience based on the Disney Pictures and Walden Media motion picture release, *The Chronicles of Narnia: The Lion, the Witch and the Wardrobe*, is a soundstage transformed into a frozen world of Narnia. It's not quite as exciting as the movie, but more educational.

Beauty and the Beast

Ages 2–4:	★★
Ages 5–10:	★★★
Ages 11–15:	★★★
Ages 16–Adult:	★★★

After Disney's *Beauty and the Beast* animated movie was released and became an instant classic, a live adaptation of this movie was created for guests of the Disney-MGM Studios. This thirty-minute live-action performance stars actors and costumed characters. The show re-creates several scenes from the movie.

This show inspired the hit Broadway musical and is presented several times throughout each day. Showtimes are displayed in front of the theater and at the Tip Board. While the theater holds more than 1,500 people, be sure to arrive between fifteen and thirty minutes early to get the best seats (depending on how crowded the Studios are on the day of your visit).

⊕ HOT SPOT

If you arrive at the Beauty and the Beast show early you will be treated to an upbeat, comical, and truly entertaining musical performance by a four-man singing group, called Four for a Dollar.

Fantasmic!

Ages 2–4:	★★
Ages 5–10:	★★★
Ages 11–15:	★★★
Ages 16–Adult:	★★★

Adapted from the highly popular show that was originally created for Disneyland, this nighttime spectacle combines lasers, special effects, walls of water, dancing waters, fiber-optic effects, classic Disney animated movie footage, Disney characters, a cast of over fifty performers, and plenty of Disney music. This is all choreographed perfectly into a twenty-five-minute performance that you'll remember forever. This is perhaps the most spectacular show at the WDW Resort. Fantasmic! should not be missed. Fantasmic! is extremely popular, but the capacity of the outdoor theater is limited. You will need to be at the entrance at the latest thirty minutes ahead of showtime.

To combine a memorable dinner with the memorable performance of Fantasmic! consider taking advantage of the park's "Fantasmic! Dining Experience." After enjoying a full dinner at the Hollywood Brown Derby, Mama Melrose's Ristorante Italiano, or Hollywood & Vine, you'll receive a voucher that guarantees seating for that evening's Fantasmic! performance. The dinner/show combo is priced between $19.99 and $36 per adult and $9.99 for kids (ages three to eleven). Admission to the park is still required and only a limited number of dinner packages are available per day.

✔ This is a must-see attraction.

⊕ HOT SPOT

The Fantasmic! outdoor stadium holds 9,000 people and there is only one public entrance and exit. Every seat is a good seat because the stadium is curved and duplicates the show from all angles. The best place to sit is near the entrance/exit at the top so you can be the first to leave. It has been known for the stadium to take one hour to clear.

Rock 'n' Roller Coaster Starring Aerosmith

Ages 2–4:	N.S.
Ages 5–10:	N.S.
Ages 11–15:	★★★
Ages 16–Adult:	★★★

The latest ride added to the Disney-MGM Studios is a state-of-the-art roller coaster with a musical twist. As you experience this high-speed indoor coaster, 125 speakers will rock your world with Aerosmith music. When this coaster launches, you'll go from zero to 60 miles per hour in under two seconds, but that's just the start of the experience, which offers plenty of unexpected turns, loops, and twists.

The entire experience (including preshow) lasts about ten minutes. Having quickly become one of the most popular attractions at this park, a sixty- to ninety-minute wait for it is typical. To save time, be sure to take advantage of FASTPASS. Riders must be at least 48 inches tall.

⊕ HOT SPOT

The best seats for the Rock 'n' Roller Coaster are the very front row and the very back row. If the line looks too long for people waiting for the front row, then just ask a cast member if you can wait for the very back row.

Mickey's Sorcerer's Hat

Ages 2–4:	N.S.
Ages 5–10:	★
Ages 11–15:	★
Ages 16–Adult:	★★

In December 2001, a giant sorcerer's hat (adapted from the hat Mickey Mouse wore in Fantasia) was built directly in front of the Mann's Chinese Theater to commemorate Walt Disney's hundredth birthday. Using interactive kiosks located behind this giant, 122-foot-tall, 156-ton hat, guests get a peek at events in Disney history. There's also a stage and courtyard area where Disney characters and musical acts appear throughout the day.

Sounds Dangerous—Starring Drew Carey

Ages 2–4:	N.S.
Ages 5–10:	★
Ages 11–15:	★ ★
Ages 16–Adult:	★★

This interactive show stars comedian Drew Carey and showcases how audio special effects are created for television shows and motion pictures. For this presentation, you're invited to a taping of a fictional television series pilot (that stars Drew Carey). The show lasts about twelve minutes and takes place within an indoor theater (the ABC Sound Studio). Keep in mind, a portion of this comedy show, which focuses on audio, is done in complete darkness. While this isn't meant to be scary, it might not be suitable for very young children.

 TRAVEL TIP

If you decide to skip Sounds Dangerous—Starring Drew Carey, at least enter through the glass exit doors (yes, enter through the exit) and you will be in the spill-out area of the attraction. There are several sound booths lined up along the wall each with a red and a green light. Wait for a green light, then enter and listen to this five-minute 3-D sound show. It's totally awesome and not something you'll soon forget.

Disney Stars and Motor Cars Parade

Ages 2–4:	★
Ages 5–10:	★★
Ages 11–15:	★★
Ages 16–Adult:	★★

In this twenty-five-minute daily parade, guests have a chance to see some of Disney's most famous characters as they ride down Hollywood Boulevard. The parade route begins near Star Tours and ends near the Crossroads (at the entrance of the studios). In all, sixty-three Disney characters are featured, along with a handful of Disney-MGM Studios guests who are preselected to participate. By sitting along the curb of Hollywood Boulevard, guests will have a chance to interact with some of the characters, so have your camera ready.

Walt Disney: One Man's Dream

Ages 2–4:	N.S.
Ages 5–10:	★
Ages 11–15:	★
Ages 16–Adult:	★★★

In conjunction with Walt Disney's hundredth birthday celebration, which kicked off in December 2001, the Disney-MGM Studios created a self-paced, walk-through exhibit that showcases the life of Walt Disney and pays tribute to his many achievements. This exhibit contains extensive memorabilia from the Walt Disney archives, much of which has never been displayed to the public before.

According to Disney Imagineer Roger Holzberg, the senior show producer/director of this attraction, "When we were researching the attraction, we found that many of our guests under the age of fifteen did not know Walt Disney was a real person. They thought it was just a company name."

Walt Disney: One Man's Dream features a short film of Walt Disney's life that explores the extraordinary hardships he overcame. "He is an individual, not an icon," added Holzberg. "This tells the story of Walt the man, and we hope that guests will be moved by the scope of his imagination, what he accomplished, and what he inspired."

Anyone who truly appreciates the accomplishments of Walt Disney as a television and motion picture producer, animator, and theme park creator will enjoy this museum-like exhibit, which is not particularly kid oriented. The entire experience lasts about twenty-five minutes and is entirely indoors.

Playhouse Disney—Live on Stage!

Ages 2–4:	★★★
Ages 5–10:	★★★
Ages 11–15:	★
Ages 16–Adult:	★

Designed specifically for the under-ten crowd that watches *Playhouse Disney* on the Disney Channel, this live musical show features characters from Jim Henson's *Bear in the Big Blue House, Rolie Polie Olie, Stanley*, and stars from *The Book of Pooh*. This is a fun twenty-minute show that's colorful, upbeat, and will provide plenty of entertainment for kids (especially those familiar with the characters from the various TV shows on the Disney Channel). If you're traveling with young kids, this adorable show should not be missed!

On days when the park is crowded, be sure to arrive at the theater at least twenty to thirty minutes prior to the posted showtime. To ensure that kids, in particular, get the best view of the action, all audience members sit on a carpeted floor within the air-conditioned theater.

The Osborne Family Spectacle of Lights

Ages 2–4:	★★★
Ages 5–10:	★★★
Ages 11–15:	★★★
Ages 16–Adult:	★★★

Between late November and early January each year, the Disney-MGM Studios celebrate the holiday season by transforming the "back lot" area of the working motion picture studio portion of the theme park into a holiday winter wonderland. Opening every evening after dark, this walk-through attraction is absolutely breathtaking and is suitable for the entire family.

One of the primary focal points of this extravagant light display is a 70-foot-tall Christmas tree that's adorned with over 58,000 lights. In all, however, over 350 miles of Christmas lights are used to create this attraction, which requires 800,000 watts of electricity to bring it to life. As you explore this holiday attraction, be on the lookout for the over forty hidden Mickeys that can be found within the decorative display. Even if you don't celebrate Christmas, this attraction is still worth experiencing.

✔ This is a must-see attraction.

≡FAST FACT

Jennings Osborne, a Little Rock, Arkansas, businessman owned three homes side by side and decorated each house for the holidays. So many neighbors complained about the traffic that it eventually made its way to the Arkansas Supreme Court, which ruled in 1994 that Osborne's holiday houses were a public nuisance. In 1995, the Walt Disney Company brought the Osborne holiday lights to Disney-MGM Studios.

The Disney-MGM Studios Backlot Tour

Ages 2–4:	★
Ages 5–10:	★★
Ages 11–15:	★★★
Ages 16–Adult:	★★★

One of the things that make a trip to the Disney-MGM Studios so special is that you actually have the opportunity to visit a motion picture and television studio where movies and television programs are being produced.

When guests participate in this tour, they'll ride in trams that take them on a thirty-five-minute tour of the Disney-MGM Studios production facilities (a.k.a. the backlot). Although the Disney-MGM Studios are rarely still used to film live-action TV shows and movies, you'll see movie sets, outdoor "facades," as well as soundstages where movies and TV shows are filmed. You'll also see the studio's wardrobe/costume facility, plus get a chance to see costumes from classic movies. Along the tram tour, you can expect a few surprises as well, like the Special Effects Water Tank show. In 2004, this tour began being revamped slightly as the back-lot area gets expanded to include new cityscapes, including Chicago and San Francisco.

Lights, Motors, and Action! Extreme Stunt Show

Ages 2–4:	N.S.
Ages 5–10:	★★
Ages 11–15:	★★★
Ages 16–Adult:	★★★

This high-action edge-of-your-seat outdoor live stadium show features stunt drivers in explosions, falls, high-speed spins, jumps, and more. The stunts use cars, boats, and motorcycles. Anyone afraid of loud noises or fire should sit as far away from the stage as possible or not attend at all. Make sure you mark this one off your list early, because the last show is late afternoon. This is also a FASTPASS attraction.

Dining at the Disney-MGM Studios

The following are the dining locations at the Disney-MGM Studios. For full-service restaurants, especially during peak lunch and dinner hours, be sure to make a reservation in advance. To make a restaurant reservation up to sixty days in advance for any full-service restaurant in the Walt Disney World Resort, call (407) WDW-DINE.

For same-day reservations, visit the restaurant of your choice, or stop at the Tip Board. While several of these restaurants offer somewhat fancy atmospheres and are considered fine-dining experiences, casual attire is acceptable. (After all, you're on vacation at a theme park. Throw on your favorite T-shirt and shorts, but don't forget your wallet.)

The Hollywood Brown Derby

This full-service restaurant is a re-creation of the Brown Derby in Hollywood, where some of Hollywood's biggest and most famous stars used to dine. This is one of the very best restaurants located anywhere in the WDW Resort. While it's rather expensive, it's a wonderful place to enjoy lunch or dinner. Reservations are strongly recommended, and a children's menu is available.

The original Brown Derby is where owner Bob Cobb created the now-popular Cobb Salad in the 1930s. Comprising salad greens, bacon, turkey, tomato, egg, avocado, and blue cheese, this is one of the restaurant's most popular dishes. While the lunch and dinner entrées are incredible, just wait until you see what's offered for dessert. The Hollywood Brown Derby is located in the heart of the Disney-MGM Studios, along Hollywood Boulevard, and like the original restaurant, it is a popular dining location for visiting celebrities and dignitaries.

Mama Melrose's Ristorante Italiano

Open for lunch (and dinner during WDW's busy seasons), this Italian restaurant serves pizzas baked in a wood-burning oven. Seafood, steak, and chicken dishes (grilled on a hardwood charbroiler) are also popular entrées. Although this is one of the Studios' more expensive restaurants, the food is delicious. Reservations are strongly recommended.

50's Prime Time Café

This is the most popular place to eat and requires at least a twenty-four-hour reservation. However, every once in a while you can walk in with minimal wait during nonpeak seasons. This 1950s-style theme restaurant features television monitors on the tables that show black-and-white clips from popular 1950s sitcoms. Instead of serving food on traditional plates, the meals, while cooked fresh, are presented like old-fashioned TV dinners. Hamburgers, turkey burgers, pot roast, roast beef sandwiches, fried chicken, salads, and other staple comfort food items can be found on the menu of this theme restaurant, which will appeal to the entire family. The dessert menu is on a View-Master and there is an attached bar called the Tune-in Lounge. Servers pretend that they are living in the 1950s and liven your dining experience with lots of funny banter. This is one restaurant where you will walk out with a smile on your face.

═FAST FACT

The food here isn't cheap, because you're paying for the atmosphere. However, the food portions are large, so you can share a meal and ask for an extra plate, and a special children's menu is available. Don't forget, reservations are strongly recommended. No reservations are needed for the Tune-in Lounge, which happens to be the only public bar at Disney-MGM Studios.

Sci-Fi Dine-in Theater

This full-service theme restaurant simulates a 1950s drive-in movie theater. Yes! You sit in a convertible car to eat! Fiber-optic special effects are used to simulate stars on the ceiling as guests dine and watch a movie screen that shows continuous science fiction movie trailers and cartoons from the 1950s. Lunch and dinner are served daily, and popcorn is always served as an appetizer. A cocktail menu is also available. Reservations are strongly recommended at least twenty-four hours in advance. If you don't eat here you can still ask to look inside, and they will let you.

Fast Food

If you're not looking for a full-service restaurant, the following options are available for lunch, dinner, and snacks throughout the day. These dining locations are considerably less expensive than the restaurants listed previously.

- **Backlot Express**—A fast and inexpensive dining choice at the Studios is the Backlot Express, which also offers counter service and a Hollywood studio theme. Hamburgers, hot dogs, salads, dessert items, fresh fruit, and soda are among the most popular menu selections. Beer and wine are also available.

- **Commissary**—All of the major Hollywood studios offer a commissary, where actors, actresses, and motion picture or television crews can grab a quick bite to eat on the studio lot. What you will find is fast food. Hamburgers, hot dogs, chicken sandwiches, salads, sodas, bottled water, and ice cream are among the menu options.

- **Dinosaur Gertie's**—This snack shop looks like a giant dinosaur located along Echo Lake. What you'll find here is frozen slush in a variety of flavors—the perfect way for your kids to cool down and get a sugar rush on a hot day.

- **Hollywood & Vine Buffeteria**—Serving breakfast, lunch, and dinner, this cafeteria offers a wide selection of inexpensive menu items. As for the décor, you'll find a huge mural depicting Hollywood landmarks such as several major studios.

- **Min & Bill's Dockside Diner**—Soft-serve ice cream and sandwiches are available at this lakeside diner.

- **Soundstage Restaurant**—This is one of the few places in the Disney-MGM Studios where you're virtually guaranteed to see Disney characters and have a chance to meet them, get autographs, and take pictures. You'll have the opportunity to dine at the all-you-can-eat buffet. Chicken, beef, salads, and seafood dishes are usually among the offerings.

- **Starring Rolls Bakery**—This is the perfect place to stop for breakfast if you're on the go and don't want to waste a minute sitting around eating when you could be experiencing a show, ride, or attraction at the Studios. For lunch, a variety of sandwiches (served on freshly baked croissants) are available.

- **Studio Catering Co.**—Snacks and desserts are the specialty of this eating establishment, which you'll come across at the end of the Studio Backlot Tour tram ride. Beer is available here.

- **Sunset Ranch Market**—This area comprises several food stands along Sunset Boulevard (located on the way to the Tower of Terror). Hot dogs, frozen yogurt, popcorn, assorted fresh fruit, and all sorts of soda, juice, and bottled water are available.

- **Toy Story Pizza Planet**—This themed restaurant will remind guests of Disney's *Toy Story* movie. Individual pizzas are the featured items, although salads, Italian ices, and other snacks are also available.

Shopping at the Studios

While visiting the Studios, chances are you'll want to pick up some souvenirs. Whether you're looking for Disney-themed clothing, collectible Disney animation cells, one-of-a-kind autographed Hollywood memorabilia, or some other gift or souvenir item, chances are you'll find it at one of the shops located within this park. If you're looking for something in particular, but don't know where to find it, call the Disney Merchandise Hotline at (407) 824-5566. A few of the unique gift shops at the Disney-MGM Studios that are worth checking out include:

- **The Darkroom**—In addition to being able to rent video camcorders from this shop, you can also purchase Kodak film, batteries, disposable cameras, and just about any photographic accessory you need. Two-hour photo processing is also available from here, as well as from several other shops within the Studios that have a sign to this effect in the window or on the counter.

- **Mickey's of Hollywood**—Logo-imprinted Mickey Mouse, Walt Disney Studios, and Disney-MGM Studios merchandise and clothing are the main thrust of what's offered at this shop.

- **Planet Hollywood Super Store**—Theme dining Hollywood-style is possible only at Planet Hollywood restaurants. The world's largest Planet Hollywood restaurant can be found at Disney's West Side. For souvenirs from Planet Hollywood, however, drop into this popular shop.

- **Sid Cahuenga's One-of-a-Kind**—Out of all the shops within this park, with the exception of the Animation Gallery, only this one offers extremely interesting and unique non-Disney merchandise. What you'll find here are one-of-a-kind autographed photos, posters, and books, plus items once owned by celebrities.

- **The Writer's Shop**—This small shop is a bookstore where the Disney-MGM Studios often hosts well-known authors for special book-signing events. There's also a gourmet coffee kiosk within the shop.

Disney's Animal Kingdom

BY COMBINING THE TALENTS of zookeepers, wildlife experts, and Disney Imagineers from around the world, Disney's Animal Kingdom has become a unique collection of innovative rides, shows, parades, and attractions that combine the thrill of a Disney theme park with the unpredictable excitement of seeing exotic wild animals up close in re-creations of their natural habitats.

Park Overview

Several years ago, the Walt Disney Company set aside 500 acres of the Walt Disney World Resort to create a totally new type of theme park—one that features a lively cast of animals, but that would be unlike any zoo or wildlife sanctuary. Construction of this theme park began in August 1995. Disney's Animal Kingdom is now larger than the Magic Kingdom, Epcot, and the Disney-MGM Studios, and offers what the company calls "a new species of theme park entertainment."

So, what's Disney's Animal Kingdom all about? It's about seeing the animals that live on our planet in a whole new light and learning about them. It's also about fun, exploration, and excitement.

On April 22, 1998, the hard work and dreams of thousands of Disney Imagineers and cast members came to fruition as Disney's Animal Kingdom opened to the public. Here, guests come face-to-face with more than 1,500 animals (representing more than 250 species) in a theme park that only Disney's Imagineers could conceive. Since its grand opening, this park has continued to expand, with new rides, shows, and attractions that you'll learn about in this chapter.

While guests will see Mickey and his pals in the park, Disney's Animal Kingdom is designed to educate as well as entertain, in an environment that is less commercial than the Magic Kingdom. Messages and lessons about wildlife preservation and conservation are intertwined into virtually every experience that guests have while visiting this exciting theme park.

Area Divisions

Located in the center of this theme park is Safari Village, which contains the Tree of Life (a 145-foot masterpiece with 325 animals carved into its trunk). Just like the Magic Kingdom, Disney's Animal Kingdom is divided into areas, which include Discovery Island, Camp Minnie-Mickey, Africa, the Oasis, Rafiki's Planet Watch, Asia, and DinoLand U.S.A. Each of these areas has a totally different theme, yet all involve interaction with animals that are alive, from the past, or from the imagination of Disney's Imagineers.

Throughout this park, you'll find many rides, shows, and attractions suitable for young kids (under age twelve); however, Camp Minnie-Mickey and, more recently, DinoLand U.S.A. have become the kid-oriented areas of this theme park. So, if you're traveling with kids, be sure to allocate extra time for these two areas.

≡FAST FACT

Disney's Animal Kingdom offers beautiful landscaping that includes 600 species of trees, 350 species of grasses, along with 1,800 species of shrubs, vines, ferns, mosses, epiphytes, and perennials. More than 100,000 trees and more than 4 million individual plants, trees, grasses, and shrubs have been planted on the park's 500 acres.

Animal Care

To ensure that the animals living in this theme park are always given the very best care, the Walt Disney Company has hired hundreds of the most prominent animal specialists, curators, animal keepers, veterinarians, and animal behavioral specialists from over 200 leading zoos, educational institutions, and wild animal parks from around the world.

Depending on when you visit Disney's Animal Kingdom and how crowded the park is, you'll easily be able to spend between one and one- and- a- half days experiencing everything this theme park has to offer.

Animal Viewing

As you plan your time at Disney's Animal Kingdom, pace yourself—lots of walking is required. Since some of the park's most popular attractions involve seeing live animals, keep in mind that many of the animals tend to be more active and visible to the public in the mornings and late afternoons when the temperature is cooler. The majority of the animals are allowed to roam freely in their habitats, so at times they may not be visible to guests, simply because they're napping in the shade. Thus, try to experience the live animal attractions early or late in the day.

The very best time to see the animals, especially the ones in the Kilimanjaro Safaris, is when it's cool, overcast, or raining. Obviously, this isn't ideal for vacationers, but the animals tend to come out and be far more visible and lively.

Virtually all of the live animals you'll be seeing at Disney's Animal Kingdom are wild. They have not been trained or domesticated. They are kept in habitats designed to simulate their natural environments as closely as possible. All of the animals are kept on strict diets in order to keep them healthy. Thus, while as a guest at Disney's Animal Kingdom you can purchase all sorts of food and snacks for yourself, it's critical that you do not share your food or beverages with any of the animals, no matter how tempting it might be to toss a few pieces of popcorn, for example, to one of the animals you encounter.

≡FAST FACT

Animal Kingdom is the largest park at WDW in acreage (over 500); however, it's the smallest in terms of walking space for the two-legged animals (you). You can easily see everything at Animal Kingdom in a day.

Same Day Re-entry

As you leave Disney's Animal Kingdom, be sure to have your hand stamped as you exit in order to be granted readmission into the park later that day or evening. In addition to the hand stamp, be sure to retain your ticket stub. The hand stamps are designed to be water-resistant, so don't worry if your hand gets wet if you choose to return to your hotel in the middle of the day to go swimming, and then want to return to Disney's Animal Kingdom later that evening. Try to refrain, however, from scrubbing your hands clean with soap until your day's visit to Disney's Animal Kingdom is complete.

What to Bring

Make sure you wear comfortable shoes, because you'll be doing a tremendous amount of walking! Much of your time will be spent outdoors while visiting this theme park, so depending on the weather, you might also want to take along a jacket (you can always store it in a locker). Sunglasses, a cap (with a visor), and sunblock are also important items to have with you, especially if the weather is sunny.

Try to avoid carrying too much stuff with you. You'll enjoy your visit more if your hands are as free as possible. Don't forget to bring your camera, along with plenty of film and batteries. Avoid having to purchase high-priced film, batteries, or camera supplies in the park.

In case of rain, plan on getting a bit wet. Wear a raincoat or purchase a Mickey Mouse poncho. Avoid bringing an umbrella into the park. You'll find it frustrating trying to walk around the crowded park with an open umbrella. During a rainstorm, crowds will be smaller; however, some outdoor shows and attractions will be closed or canceled.

The Information Board

Located next to the Creature Comforts shop inside the park is one of the park's Attraction Information Boards. A second board is located outside the Disney Outfitters store, across from the Island Mercantile. These boards list the current wait times for all of the major attractions in Disney's Animal Kingdom, and also list the showtimes for the various parades and stage performances.

Stationed at each board is a Disney cast member who is in constant contact with the operators of all of the park's major attractions. Accurate wait times for each ride and attraction are posted, so you can better plan your day at Disney's Animal Kingdom. If you have any questions about planning your day at the park, the cast members overseeing the Attraction Information Board will be able to provide answers. Other Disney cast members who are always in the know are those roaming the park carrying walkie-talkies.

═FAST FACT

While it's critical that guests refrain from feeding any of the animals that live within Disney's Animal Kingdom (because each animal has a very specialized diet), the team of animal experts that care for the animals feed them over three tons of food per day.

The Disney cast members manning the Information Board will be able to assist you in determining how early you should arrive to the shows and how long you'll have to wait for the various attractions, based on how crowded the park is on the day of your visit.

Transportation

Located just outside the main entrance of Disney's Animal Kingdom is a 6,000-car parking lot. There is a daily parking fee if you're not a guest of a WDW Resort hotel. Guests can also be dropped off and picked up right near the park's main entrance when they use the WDW buses. When using the complimentary bus service, plan on spending thirty to sixty minutes each way getting to and from the park from any location within the WDW Resort complex.

There are no benches, telephones, or restrooms near where you'll wait for the bus (outside of the park's main entrance) to take you back to your hotel or to another Disney theme park, so take advantage of these facilities before leaving the park. You could wind up waiting between twenty and thirty minutes for the right bus to take you where you want to go. The bus stop is, however, covered, so you'll remain pretty sheltered during bad weather.

A faster, but more expensive, mode of transportation for getting to and from Disney's Animal Kingdom is taking a taxi. Guests will, however, ultimately save a tremendous amount of commuting time by renting a car for the duration of their vacation at the WDW Resort. (Renting a car at the Orlando International Airport is cheaper than taking taxis within the WDW Resort and much faster and less frustrating than dealing with the WDW bus.)

Tours

For an additional fee, private and small group tours are available that will give you a special behind-the-scenes look at Disney's Animal Kingdom. These tours are given by people who are extremely knowledgeable about the animals, and are designed for teens and adults. For more information about the tours that are available, call (407) WDW-TOUR. Since the tours are limited to small groups, make your reservations as early as possible.

Mickey's Jammin' Jungle Parade

All of the Disney theme parks are known for their daytime, character-oriented parades. Disney's Animal Kingdom is now the home to Mickey's Jammin' Jungle Parade, a fifteen-minute extravaganza featuring Mickey, Minnie, Rafiki, thirteen other Disney characters, and a cast of over sixty dancers and performers. Complete with an African jungle theme, this parade features original music and a format that encourages guest participation along the parade route. Mickey's Jammin' Jungle Parade is definitely suitable for the entire family.

TRAVEL TIP

For parade times, see the showtime flyer. If you're taking pictures during the parade, remember that Mickey makes an appearance on the last float.

The parade route begins at the Tusker House Gate at Harambe Village, then winds through Disney's Animal Kingdom (around Discovery Island) and returns to the Tusker House Gate. During the parade, it becomes extremely difficult for guests to leave the theme park (because the parade route blocks the entrance/exit), so plan your exit accordingly. Also, be prepared for large groups of people to leave the park immediately after this parade.

The Disney Wildlife Conservation Fund

While many people believe that some of Disney's theme parks and attractions are overly commercial, the underlying theme of the rides, shows, and attractions at Disney's Animal Kingdom is to promote the conservation of animal habitats around the world. The Disney Wildlife Conservation Fund promotes global wildlife conservation by working directly with scientists, educators, and organizations that are committed to preserving Earth's biodiversity.

TRAVEL TIP

To save money when dining at Disney's Animal Kingdom, consider purchasing the "Meal Plus Certificate." Priced at $11.99 (adults) and $5.99 (kids), this certificate can be redeemed at several of the park's dining establishments for one entrée and beverage. You'll also receive coupons that can be redeemed later in the day anywhere in the park for one popcorn or ice cream, plus one bottled soda or water. (When purchased separately, the price of an ice cream is $2.50, a box of popcorn is $2.75, and a bottled soda or water is $2.50.)

The Disney Wildlife Conservation Fund provides financial support and resources to over 200 programs in over twenty-four different countries. To help raise money and awareness for this fund, each of the gift shops located in Disney's Animal Kingdom encourages guests to make a $1 donation to the fund when they make a purchase. All of the contributions are combined with the funds of the Walt Disney Company Foundation and are distributed to the wildlife conservation programs that the Disney Wildlife Conservation Fund supports. To obtain a list of these organizations, write to: The Disney Wildlife Conservation Fund c/o Conservation Initiatives, Walt Disney World Co., P.O. Box 10000, Lake Buena Vista, Florida 32830.

FAST FACT

Walt Disney's love for animals began when he was four years old. His family moved from Chicago to a 45-acre farm in Marceline, Missouri. Growing up, Walt helped to care for the animals on the farm and learned how to draw them.

The Oasis

The Oasis is a park area that separates Entrance Plaza from the rest of the Animal Kingdom. As you walk through this area, you'll see exotic plants as well as colorful birds in the trees. It's about a three-minute walk from the main entrance to Discovery Island.

Discovery Island

This island is the hub from which you'll depart on your animal-based adventures. The centerpiece of this island is the Tree of Life, which houses a theater where you can see the 3-D movie *It's Tough to Be a Bug!* On this island, you'll experience live entertainment, see exotic birds and wildlife, and get a preview of what this park is all about.

The Tree of Life

Not only is the Tree of Life the centerpiece of Disney's Animal Kingdom, but it's also a stunning work of art. A picture of the people you're traveling with standing in front of this tree will make the perfect addition to your vacation photo album.

Here's the scoop on this man-made masterpiece:

- **Animal Carvings:** 325 animals
- **Sculptors:** Zsolt Hormay and a team of three Native American artists, plus artists from France, Ireland, Indianapolis, and Central Florida spent eighteen months creating the carvings on the Tree of Life
- **Height:** 145 feet (14 stories tall)
- **Number of Branches:** 8,000
- **Number of Leaves:** 103,000
- **Trunk Width:** 50 feet
- **Width at Root Base:** 170 feet

Pathways have been created throughout Safari Village so guests can wander around and enjoy the landscaping and wildlife.

It's Tough to Be a Bug!

Ages 2–4:	★
Ages 5–10:	★★
Ages 11–15:	★★★
Ages 16–Adult:	★★★

For a reminder of the rating system, see page xiv.

When you enter the theater (located in the trunk of the Tree of Life), you become an honorary bug and begin to see the world from a bug's point of view. Not only is this a 3-D movie with incredibly life-like special effects, but the entire theater becomes part of the adventure, so expect to see, hear, and feel what's happening. Remember, the best seats are in the sixth or seventh row close to the center. As you enter the theater, you'll be given a pair of 3-D glasses. Don't put the glasses over your eyes until you're seated and the Audio-Animatronic character who hosts the show (a bug, of course) tells you to put on the glasses.

⊕ HOT SPOT

Throughout the day, bands and other forms of live entertainment perform at various locations around Safari Village. Kick back, relax, and enjoy the show!

The theater holds 430 guests and shows are presented continuously throughout the day. This is, however, one of the most popular attractions in the park, so be prepared to wait in line. *It's Tough to Be a Bug!* appeals to people of all ages, whether they like real-life bugs or not. Like all of the attractions at Disney's Animal Kingdom, this one has a positive message. Let's just say you'll think twice before zapping a bug with a can of bug spray or a fly swatter when you get home. Because this 3-D movie takes place within a custom-built theater that's interactive, young children (under the age of eight) may get frightened by some of the special effects.

✔ This is a must-see attraction.

Africa

Just in case you haven't yet traveled to Africa and experienced a real-life safari, Disney has brought Africa to Orlando. Everyone from the performers to the cast members will be dressed in African fashions, while the architecture and atmosphere in this area of the park are all authentically African.

This area is designed to replicate a port in East Africa. The restaurants, shops, and entertainment all help guests feel like they've traveled across the world.

Kilimanjaro Safaris

Ages 2–4:	★★
Ages 5–10:	★★★
Ages 11–15:	★★★
Ages 16–Adult:	★★★

You came to Disney's Animal Kingdom to see animals, and that's exactly what you'll see when you experience this safari ride. You'll ride on a thirty-two-passenger camouflage safari truck with a tour guide as this true-life adventure unfolds on more than 100 acres of savanna, rivers, and rocky hills. Antelope, giraffes, zebras, baboons, rhinos, elephants, crocodiles, lions, hippos, and other animals roam freely. As a result, what you see and where and when you see it will be different every time you experience this tour.

The best time to experience Kilimanjaro Safaris is in the morning or late afternoon, because that's when the animals are most active. During the hottest times of the day, many of the animals take naps in the shade. As you see the animals, the tour guide talks about animal poachers and how some species of animals are becoming extinct. Throughout this ride, keep your camera ready. There's no telling when a perfect photo opportunity will happen.

≡FAST FACT

To save time waiting in line for Kilimanjaro Safaris, be sure to take advantage of FASTPASS.

Throughout the safari, you'll see many different animals, so don't use up all of your film early on. Kilimanjaro Safaris will appeal to people of all ages and is one of this park's very best and most popular attractions. It shouldn't be missed! Each time you visit this safari, your experience will be different, because you'll see different animals and sites. Thus, if you have time to experience the Kilimanjaro Safaris twice during your visit, it's well worth it.

✔ This is a must-see attraction.

Pangani Forest Exploration Trail

Ages 2–4:	★★
Ages 5–10:	★★★
Ages 11–15:	★★★
Ages 16–Adult:	★★★

Take a walking tour through a park-like environment and see a troop of gorillas, colorful African birds, and even a few hippos. You can walk through this area at your own pace, so the lines are usually minimal. On hand near each of the exhibits are experts who will answer questions about the animals. About halfway through this exhibit is a small building that contains computers that guests can use to learn more about naked mole rats (also on exhibit within this building). As you make your way through the Pangani Forest Exploration Trail, be sure to look up into the trees to see about thirty-five different species of exotic birds.

Wildlife Express to Conservation Station

Ages 2–4:	★
Ages 5–10:	★★
Ages 11–15:	★★★
Ages 16–Adult:	★★★

A short train ride takes you partway through the 100-acre savanna, where you'll catch glimpses of some of the same animals you'll see on the Kilimanjaro Safaris. You'll also see some of the buildings where the animals are kept at night. Your destination is Disney's Conservation Station, where animals are cared for. As you ride the train, keep your camera handy. There are some excellent photo opportunities along the way.

⊕ HOT SPOT

Disney "Streetmosphere" performers take on the roles of Harambe citizens who are very pleased to have you as a guest in their African village. Guests are invited to interact with the citizens of Harambe while enjoying the live musical performances from an African contemporary band.

There may be a wait to board and ride the train to and from Conservation Station, but once you're there, you can roam freely and see things at your own pace. Thus, the waits to see the various attractions and exhibits at Conservation Station are kept to a minimum. The round-trip train ride to and from the station is 1.2 miles long.

DinoLand U.S.A.

This area of Disney's Animal Kingdom is somewhat kid-oriented; however, it's here that you'll find the most exciting thrill ride in the park, which is far more suitable for teens and adults than it is for young kids. In this area, you'll also see life-size replicas of dinosaur skeletons and discover how fossils are found and prepared for display.

Anyone who is fascinated by dinosaurs will want to explore DinoLand U.S.A., which is sponsored by McDonald's. In this case, you'll see some innovative, educational, and highly entertaining attractions, shows, exhibits, and rides. The best time to check out this area is in the morning when the park opens.

DINOSAUR!

Ages 2–4:	N.S.
Ages 5–10:	★★
Ages 11–15:	★★★
Ages 16–Adult:	★★★

This is a highly turbulent and extremely loud ride that takes you back in time to see a group of life-size, very realistic, Audio-Animatronic dinos. After watching a preshow movie, you'll climb aboard a twelve-person vehicle that'll transport you back to prehistoric times. Much of the ride itself takes place in dark surroundings as the vehicles follow an extremely bumpy track and travel at high speeds. Thus, young children may find it scary and senior citizens may find it too jerky. As for everyone else, this is an awesome ride with spectacular special effects.

For the most thrilling ride, as you climb aboard your vehicle, try to grab a seat that's in the back row and on the left side of the vehicle. Be sure to safely stow loose items like hats, purses, and cameras in the seat pockets in front of you before the ride begins.

The Boneyard

Ages 2–4:	★★★
Ages 5–10:	★★★
Ages 11–15:	★★
Ages 16–Adult:	N.S.

Designed for young people, the Boneyard offers a preview of what it's like to be an archeologist or paleontologist. Best described as a huge sandbox, in this attraction, young guests get to dig for dino bones.

Cretaceous Trail

Guests of all ages can take a walking tour (at their own pace) and explore an outdoor exhibit of plants and animals that have survived on this planet since the days of the dinosaurs.

TriceraTop Spin

Ages 2–4:	★★
Ages 5–10:	★★★
Ages 11–15:	★★★
Ages 16–Adult:	★

Up to four guests ride in triceratops-shaped vehicles that rise and tilt as they spin around a giant top while cartoon comets whiz past and playful dinosaurs pop up. This ride is very much like Dumbo the Flying Elephant (a popular kids' ride found within the Magic Kingdom's Fantasyland); however, instead of being shaped like an elephant, the vehicles resemble dinosaurs.

Primeval Whirl

Ages 2–4:	N.S.
Ages 5–10:	★★★
Ages 11–15:	★★★
Ages 16–Adult:	★★★

This kid-oriented ride has side-by-side roller coasters that are mirrors of each other and feature free-spinning cars that travel along a twisting track of tight loops and short drops. It's designed to offer a mild thrill-ride experience for children, but adults love this ride too. Riders must be at least 48 inches tall. To save time, take advantage of FASTPASS to experience this popular ride.

✔ This is a must-see attraction.

Fossil Fun Games

The Fossil Fun Games area contains TriceraTop Spin and Primeval Whirl! in addition to a handful of classic carnival games (all of which have a dinosaur twist). Young players can win prizes for playing the carnival games, but there is an additional charge to participate.

Camp Minnie-Mickey

Disney's Animal Kingdom is the largest Disney theme park at the WDW Resort in Orlando, yet it's only in this area of the park where you'll get to meet some of the popular Disney characters, like Mickey and Minnie (dressed in safari attire). This area of the park is also where you'll see several different live shows.

Character Meet-and-Greet Areas

Located across from where the "Festival of the Lion King" stage show is presented are several trails that lead to secluded character meeting areas. Get your camera ready, because throughout the day, this is where you and your kids will get to meet Mickey Mouse and his pals up close and in person. Make sure your kids have their autograph books with them, since young people enjoy collecting the signatures of the Disney characters. (Official Disney autograph books are sold at many of the gift shops for about $6.)

"Festival of the Lion King"

Ages 2–4:	★★★
Ages 5–10:	★★★
Ages 11–15:	★★★
Ages 16–Adult:	★★★

Out of all the shows and parades featured at Disney's Animal Kingdom and the other Disney theme parks, this one is the best! This live show is presented several times throughout the day, and it is one of the most popular attractions at the park for people of all ages (although kids in particular will love this thirty-minute musical show).

"Festival of the Lion King" features human actors along with costumed characters and Audio-Animatronic characters, and includes nonstop singing and dancing. Several of the popular songs from Disney's *The Lion King* are performed live; however, new music has also been incorporated into this show, which is very different from the animated movie, *The Legend of the Lion King* Audio-Animatronic puppet show presented at the Magic Kingdom, and "The Lion King: The Broadway Show" (at the New Amsterdam Theatre on Broadway in New York City).

✔ This is a must-see attraction.

⊕ HOT SPOT

This show is "in the round," which makes all seats good seats. However if you want the very best seats possible, sit in the front and at the end of the row, because "end of the row" seats will be close to large sets used for the show.

"Pocahontas and Her Forest Friends"

Ages 2–4:	★★★
Ages 5–10:	★★★
Ages 11–15:	★★
Ages 16–Adult:	★

Unlike "Festival of the Lion King," which features a large cast of characters, this show stars a human actress who portrays Pocahontas; a life-size Audio-Animatronic tree (Grandmother Willow);

and several real-life animals. The show, designed primarily for young guests, talks about the importance of preserving the planet's forests and runs about twelve minutes. It is presented throughout the day in an outdoor theater that holds 350 guests. Be sure to arrive at the theater between thirty and forty-five minutes prior to the posted showtime in order to ensure yourself a seat for the performance of your choice. No food or beverages are allowed in the theater.

Rafiki's Planet Watch

Especially for young people (age fifteen and under) this area of Disney's Animal Kingdom will encourage education and exploration. Ages sixteen and over should spend their time seeing other parts of the park. The focus is on conservation and protecting our planet and its wildlife.

The Conservation Station

This facility combines hands-on displays, live animal displays, and a chance to see some of the park's veterinary facilities, animal nurseries, and even where some of the food for the animals in the park gets prepared. Upon arriving at Conservation Station, guests can roam freely and see everything at their own pace. Plenty of animal experts are on hand to answer questions and conduct various types of demonstrations.

≡FAST FACT

This is one of the most educational areas of Disney's Animal Kingdom. Some of the live animals you'll see include aardvarks, chinchillas, a miniature donkey, great horned owls, porcupines, guinea pigs, and a rock hyrax. Young guests can also pet some of the animals; however, feeding them is strictly prohibited.

Affection Section

Ages 2–4:	★★
Ages 5–10:	★★★
Ages 11–15:	★★
Ages 16–Adult:	★

Designed for young children, Affection Section is a petting zoo where guests can get up close to animals, pet them, and have pictures taken with them. Guests are welcome to spend as much time as they'd like in this area and proceed at their own pace. Kids who will be interacting with the animals are encouraged to wash their hands both prior to and after touching the animals. For parents, this area offers wonderful photo opportunities.

Look Backstage!

Ages 2–4:	★
Ages 5–10:	★★
Ages 11–15:	★★
Ages 16–Adult:	★★

Inside the Hall of Animal Care, guests get to see many animal experts, including vets, researchers, and keepers, work with live animals. This is an educational area where the animals are the stars. Animal experts are always on hand to answer questions. One of the favorite parts of this exhibit is the baby mammal nurseries.

There are interactive exhibits that allow guests of all ages to use touch-screen computers to learn more about animals and their habitats.

Asia

This area of Disney's Animal Kingdom features one of the most awaited thriller rides in the park—Expedition Everest.

Expedition Everest—The Legend of Forbidden Mountain

Ages 2–4:	★
Ages 5–10:	★★
Ages 11–15:	★★★
Ages 16–Adult:	★★★

While not as intense as a typical roller coaster, this high-speed train ride takes you to the top of Mount Everest, then sends you rolling backward in and out of the mountain. Inside of the mountain you come across the Yeti (an Asian abominable snowman) and make your escape just in time.

✔ This is a must-see attraction.

TRAVEL TIP

Expedition Everest is in the "right" back corner of the park and the Kilimanjaro Safaris is in the "left" back corner of the park. To mark both these off your list early, send your party to the Safari line while you get a FASTPASS for everyone at Expedition Everest. Then head over to the Safari tour line, find your party, and afterward you can walk to the front of the line at Expedition Everest.

"Wonder" at Caravan Stage

Ages 2–4:	★
Ages 5–10:	★★★
Ages 11–15:	★★★
Ages 16–Adult:	★★

Presented several times throughout the day, this live show features human bird handlers and a cast of over twenty species of trained exotic birds from around the world, some of which fly out into the audience. The Caravan Stage is an outdoor theater that holds about 1,250 guests. No food or beverages are allowed in the theater. Be sure to arrive between twenty and thirty minutes prior to a posted showtime to guarantee yourself a seat for the performance of your choice.

This show presents a story about a character named Luke who is in search of lost treasures. Kids especially will enjoy this show, although it is entertaining for people of all ages. The show itself lasts about twenty-five minutes.

Kali River Rapids: A Whitewater Adventure

Ages 2–4:	N.S.
Ages 5–10:	★★★
Ages 11–15:	★★★
Ages 16–Adult:	★★★

In addition to Expedition Everest and DINOSAUR! Kali River Rapids is another thrill ride that's designed for teens and adults. Guests ride in six-passenger rubber rafts and slide down a raging and winding river through rapids and waterfalls. This is definitely one of the most popular attractions at Disney's Animal Kingdom, so be prepared to wait in line to experience it. Also, be prepared to get soaked! (If you're carrying items that aren't waterproof, be sure to store them in lockers, leave them with someone not riding this attraction, or use the watertight storage compartment on the raft.) Guests must be at least 40 inches tall to experience this rather turbulent ride.

 TRAVEL TIP

To save time waiting in line for Kali River Rapids, be sure to take advantage of FASTPASS. If you have one of the Disney ponchos, be sure to wear it on this ride to help you stay dry. As a bystander, it's possible to shoot water at guests experiencing the ride.

"Finding Nemo—The Musical"

Ages 2–4:	★
Ages 5–10:	★★★
Ages 11–15:	★★★
Ages 16–Adult:	★★★

This show is similar to the black light show, "Voyage of the Little Mermaid," at Disney-MGM Studios, but with Nemo and friends. However, "Finding Nemo—The Musical" is on a much larger scale. This is the first time Disney has taken a nonmusical movie and spun it off into a musical show, so all the songs are new to long-time lovers of this charming movie.

✔ This is a must see attraction.

Maharajah Jungle Trek

Here's an opportunity to wander down jungle paths, explore temple ruins, and see some of the world's most exotic and powerful animals—Bengal tigers, Komodo monitor dragons, gibbons, and an assortment of other wild animals that are native to Asia. There are some excellent photo opportunities along this trail.

Shopping at the Animal Kingdom

Like all of the Disney theme parks, you'll find many gift shops and souvenir kiosks scattered throughout Disney's Animal Kingdom. Sure, you'll find a wide assortment of Disney's Animal Kingdom logo merchandise, along with plenty of T-shirts, plush toys, and other items featuring Mickey dressed in a safari outfit, but you'll also find a great assortment of non-Disney-based items that make excellent souvenirs or great gifts.

All of the gift shops accept cash, credit cards, checks, traveler's checks, and Disney Dollars, along with your hotel room charge card (your room key, if you're staying at a Disney Resort hotel). The souvenir kiosks and carts accept cash, checks, and traveler's checks only.

Keep in mind that much of the merchandise sold at these shops is available only within this park and can't be purchased at the shops in Downtown Disney, from the Disney Stores, or through the Disney Catalog. You can, however, purchase most items sold exclusively at the park by calling (407) 363-6200 during business hours. You must, however, know exactly what item(s) you want to purchase and be willing to pay by credit card.

When you make a purchase, you can take your merchandise with you (and carry it around the park), arrange to have it delivered to the park's exit so that you can pick up your purchases on your way out, arrange to have the purchase delivered to your WDW Resort hotel, or, for an additional fee, you can have your purchases shipped anywhere in the world. If you arrange to have your packages delivered to the park's exit, keep in mind that on busy days, it could take up to ninety minutes for your packages to arrive, so plan accordingly. Likewise, if you're having packages shipped, even if you pay FedEx charges, it might take up to several weeks for your purchases to actually get shipped.

Dining at the Animal Kingdom

Like all of the Disney theme parks, Disney's Animal Kingdom offers a selection of fast-food and full-service dining establishments that serve everything from snack foods to full multicourse meals. No matter where you eat within the park, it's not going to be cheap, but if you're hungry, you'll find many different food and drink choices available. Chocolate-covered frozen bananas, one of Disneyland's most popular treats (previously unavailable at the WDW theme parks), are now available from many of the ice-cream carts throughout Disney's Animal Kingdom.

If you're looking for an animal-themed dining experience where you're surrounded by waterfalls, tropical plants, and an exciting atmosphere for lunch or dinner, you'll want to experience the Rainforest Café, located in Entrance Plaza. A second Rainforest Café is located within Downtown Disney.

CHAPTER 11

Disney's Water Parks

FOR PEOPLE WHO ENJOY the water, the WDW Resort offers two full-size water parks that contain various kid- and family-oriented activities that are water based. So, if visiting one or more of these water parks is on your vacation itinerary, plan on packing bathing suits, plenty of sunblock, and beach shoes.

Water Park Information

If you're staying at one of the Disney resorts, you're entitled to take advantage of the swimming pools and beaches at any of Disney's resorts. Many of the resorts offer multiple pools, whirlpools, water slides, and kid-oriented areas. The WDW Resort also offers two exciting water parks—Blizzard Beach and Typhoon Lagoon—that have become favorite attractions of families traveling with kids.

Families can easily spend at least one full day at Blizzard Beach or Typhoon Lagoon. These parks are always busiest in the mornings, so if you have a multiday Park Hopper Plus Pass, plan on arriving around lunchtime to avoid the heavy morning crowds. Spend the morning at the Magic Kingdom, Epcot, the Disney-MGM Studios, or Disney's Animal Kingdom, then cool off at one of the refreshingly wet and wildly exciting water parks.

For female guests, wearing a one-piece bathing suit is highly recommended, due to the "rough water" and "waves" you'll be encountering.

These water parks offer family-oriented entertainment with kids and teens in mind.

═FAST FACT

Being able to swim is a prerequisite for some, but not all, of these water-based attractions. Keep in mind, Disney's water parks are either open seasonally or have limited hours during off-peak times of the year.

Hours of Operation

All of these water parks are somewhat seasonal and are open during nice weather only. Typically, the hours of operation are between 10:00 A.M. and 5:00 P.M. (with extended hours during the peak summer months). Call (407) 824-4321 to ensure that the water parks will be open during your visit and to confirm exact operating hours. All of the water parks can be reached using the WDW Transportation bus system.

TRAVEL TIP

Disney's Winter Summerland Miniature Golf is located near Blizzard Beach. Families can experience this eighteen-hole miniature golf course with a winter theme for $9.76 per adult and $7.78 per child. If you play a second round of golf on the same day, the second round is half off. You can also purchase money-saving combo tickets for Blizzard Beach and Disney's Winter Summerland Miniature Golf.

Guest Services

At all of the water parks, showers and restrooms are available. Lockers may be rented on a daily basis. Life jackets are available for free, but a $25 refundable deposit is required. Towels can be rented at the various water parks for $1 each, or you can bring your own from your hotel room (but you must also return them to your hotel room at the end of the day).

Admission to the Water Parks

Admission to the three Disney water parks is included in the price of the multiday Park Hopper Plus tickets. You can, however, also purchase one-day admission tickets or annual passes for each of the water parks separately. See Chapter 3 for details. As you'll soon discover, each of the water parks has a totally different theme and a different set of activities and attractions.

Blizzard Beach

Blizzard Beach opened in 1995 and has a winter, ski-slope theme. If a 66-acre ski slope existed in the middle of Orlando, what would happen if all of a sudden the weather went from below freezing to the mid-80s and all of the snow on the mountain started to melt? That's the premise for many of the attractions at Blizzard Beach, which features some of the world's fastest water slides. The attractions include:

- **Chair Lift**—Soar over the face of Mount Gushmore.
- **Cross Country Creek**—If high-speed, turbulent tube rides aren't your thing, you can relax and enjoy a one-mile lazy tube ride around the entire Blizzard Beach park.
- **Downhill Double Dipper**—Ride along a twin tube run and race against others as you travel at speeds of up to 25 miles per hour.
- **Melt-away Bay**—Take a dip in a one-acre wave pool.
- **Run-off Rapids**—Ride a tube along flume runs filled with wet and wild surprises.
- **Ski Patrol Training Camp**—This area of Blizzard Beach is designed specifically for preteens.
- **Slush Gusher**—This is a fast-paced and exciting slide experience that sends guests down through a snow-banked gully.

- **Snow Stormers**—Experience a toboggan flume ride, water-style.
- **Summit Plummet**—Take a plunge down the world's tallest free-fall speed slide. This is a 120-foot, nearly vertical drop that allows guests to reach speeds of up to 50 miles per hour.
- **Teamboat Springs**—This is the longest and most exciting man-made family white-water raft ride in the world. Groups of people travel down 1,200 feet of twisting rapids while riding in six-passenger tube rafts.
- **Tike's Peak**—This kid-oriented area of Blizzard Beach offers thrill rides that younger kids will enjoy.
- **Toboggan Racer**—Ride on foam toboggan-like sleds along an eight-lane run that goes down a water-slick mountain.

Typhoon Lagoon

When visiting Typhoon Lagoon, guests are asked to imagine a small resort village that just got hit by a typhoon. While if this happened in real life it would be a disaster, when it's done Disney-style, the result is a 56-acre water park that offers a splashing good time.

The main Typhoon Lagoon swimming area is a massive wave pool that contains almost 3 million gallons of water. Along the coast of this pool is a sandy white beach. Meanwhile, Castaway Creek is a 2,100-foot-long river that allows guests to enjoy a fun-filled tubing ride that takes them through a series of themed areas.

TRAVEL TIP

Visiting any of Disney's water parks in the summer can be frustrating sometimes because it's the rainy season in Florida. As soon as lightning is seen by a lifeguard, everyone must be out of the water. Most people leave not knowing that most afternoon showers pass over quickly.

Gangplank Falls, Keelhaul Falls, and Mayday Falls are the thrill rides offered at Typhoon Lagoon. Guests ride on various types of tubes as they plummet down waterfalls and other white-water terrain.

Water slides at Typhoon Lagoon provide for extremely wet and fast-paced experiences that nobody who rides them will soon forget. Humunga Kowabunga is a 214-foot slide that includes a 51-foot drop, allowing guests to travel upward of 30 miles per hour. The Storm Slides are a bit tamer, but not much. These fiberglass slides are 300 feet long and allow guests to slide down at 20 miles per hour.

⊕ HOT SPOT

Surfers (or wanna-be surfers) can obtain top-notch instruction and then experience two and a half hours of surfing at Typhoon Lagoon before the park opens to the general public. The fee (which includes the instruction) is $125 per person. Reservations are required for this Surfer's Secret package. Call ✆(407) WDW-PLAY.

For some snorkeling fun, check out Shark Reef (snorkeling equipment is provided) and explore a man-made coral reef where you'll come face-to-face with friendly leopard, nurse, and bonnethead sharks, plus schools of exotic and colorful fish.

Ketchakiddee Creek is a water park unto itself, but it's designed only for people under four feet tall.

CHAPTER 12

Disney Nightlife

SO, WHAT'S THERE TO DO AFTER DARK at the WDW Resort? Well, for adults, there is an abundance of activities, clubs, shops, and restaurants within Downtown Disney. There's also Disney's Board-Walk Inn area, which offers an exciting nightlife for adult vacationers.

Nighttime Entertainment Overview

Downtown Disney has three unique areas: Pleasure Island (in the middle), the Marketplace, and Disney's West Side. During the day the Marketplace and the West Side are open for shopping and dining. Some entertainment can be found as well. Every night, Pleasure Island opens their nightclubs for a nighttime experience. The West Side is a great nighttime experience that's free, but it costs to enter Pleasure Island to club hop.

While both Downtown Disney and Disney's BoardWalk Inn offer some family-oriented activities, several of the nightclubs are restricted to those over twenty-one years of age, since alcoholic beverages are served. After spending an exciting day at the park with the family, you might consider leaving your young kids with a babysitter and experiencing Disney's nightlife. (See Chapter 3 for child care options.)

If you're visiting the WDW Resort for multiple nights, plan on spending at least one night at Pleasure Island and at least one additional evening/night exploring everything that the Marketplace and Disney's West Side have to offer.

Getting to Downtown Disney

Plenty of free parking is available in front of Disney's West Side, Pleasure Island, and the Marketplace. Valet parking (daily between 5:30 P.M. and 2:00 A.M.) is also available for $7 (free to guests with physical disabilities). Free valet parking is also provided to WDW Resort hotel guests. From anywhere in the WDW Resort, follow the signs to Downtown Disney/Pleasure Island.

Buses run constantly to and from Disney's resort hotels and theme parks to Pleasure Island, the Marketplace, and Disney's West Side areas.

If you're staying at Port Orleans, Old Key West Resort, or Saratoga Springs Resort & Spa, complimentary boat launches are available that drop off and pick up passengers from the docks located at the Marketplace near the Rainforest Café.

For a fee, taxi service is available to take you back to your hotel or anywhere in the Orlando area. Taxis can be hailed at any of the exits of the Downtown Disney area. This, however, is a costly option.

Admission Information and Prices

While there is no charge to shop and explore the Marketplace or Disney's West Side, there is an admission charge to enter Pleasure Island after 7:00 P.M. This admission fee gives you unlimited access (for the night) to all of the area's nightclubs, including:

- Adventurers Club
- BET SoundStage Club
- Comedy Warehouse
- 8Trax
- Mannequins Dance Palace
- Motion
- Pleasure Island Jazz Company
- Rock 'n' Roll Beach Club

You'll also get to see the live entertainment presented outside at the West End Stage. Drinks and food are not included in the admission price. Adult admission to Pleasure Island after 7:00 P.M. is $20.95 per night. An annual pass to Pleasure Island costs $64.95. Admission to Pleasure Island is included with a multiday Park Hopper Plus pass and the WDW Premium Annual Pass.

 TRAVEL TIP

If you're spending three or more days (and nights) at the WDW Resort and plan on returning to Pleasure Island during each of those nights, consider purchasing an annual pass in order to save yourself some cash. A special promotion is also sometimes offered where guests can upgrade their one-night admission ticket to a six-consecutive-night admission ticket for $5 more than the one-day admission price.

People under the age of eighteen will not be permitted into Pleasure Island after 7:00 P.M. unless accompanied by a parent or guardian. No alcoholic beverages will be served to anyone under the age of twenty-one. People under the age of twenty-one will not be admitted into Mannequins Dance Palace (and some of the other clubs) under any circumstances. Be prepared to show a valid passport, U.S. (or foreign) driver's license with a photo, or a U.S. military ID to be served alcohol and to be admitted into the adults-only clubs.

Guest Services

A Guest Services office is available at the Marketplace and also inside the AMC 24 Theater building. At various locations within the Downtown Disney area you'll find ATM machines, restrooms (containing baby-changing facilities), and public telephones. If any type of first aid is required, contact any Disney cast member for assistance. For additional information about the Pleasure Island, Disney's West Side, and the Downtown Disney area, call (407) 934-7781.

Dining Reservations

Reservations are recommended for many of the full-service restaurants located in Pleasure Island, the Marketplace, and Disney's West Side. Check with the restaurant of your choice directly, or call (407) WDW-DINE. Without a reservation, be prepared to wait up to two hours to be seated. Most of the full-service restaurants will give you a beeper, allowing you to walk around the area and shop until your table is ready. Reservations for the Rainforest Café at Downtown Disney must be made in person.

Pleasure Island, the Marketplace, and Downtown Disney West Side are all vacation areas, so you're not expected to dress up in formal attire to dine or go dancing; however, some type of shirt and shoes must be worn at all times.

Disney's West Side

There is no charge to visit Disney's West Side. However, there is an admission fee to several of the shows, movies, and attractions. The shops in this area open at 11:00 A.M. daily and remain open until 11:00 P.M. Many of the restaurants serve until midnight.

AMC Theaters

The largest movie theater complex in the Southeast, the AMC 24 Theaters offers twenty-four screens with stadium seating and balconies, all showing the hottest new movies in theaters with state-of-the-art sound systems.

Bongos Cuban Café

Gloria Estefan and husband, Emilio, are the owners of this 550-seat family restaurant, which serves authentic Cuban cuisine in a two-story building that's decorated with colorful hand-painted mosaic murals that depict Old World Cuba in the 1940s and 1950s. Seating is available both inside and outside, and live entertainment is presented throughout the night. The main performer each night is Desi Arnaz (well, he's an incredibly talented impersonator who looks and sounds just like the real Desi).

Like all of the full-service restaurants located at the WDW Resort, this one isn't cheap, but the food is delicious! In a typical night, Bongos Cuban Café serves up to 3,000 people. If you're planning to drop in to enjoy the restaurant's three fully stocked bars, plan on paying a $15 cover charge, which includes one drink and plenty of live entertainment and dancing. This is also the best place to get a real mojito made with fresh lime.

⊕ HOT SPOT

Designer sunglasses and prescription eyewear are available at Celebrity Eyeworks Studio. Included in this shop's inventory are replicas of sunglasses worn in recent hit films.

Bongos Cuban Café is open daily from 11:00 A.M. to 2:00 A.M. "We specifically created Bongos Cuban Café for the entire family so they may enjoy the festive Cuba that once was—and will be again," said Emilio Estefan.

Cirque du Soleil: La Nouba

This is the best show in all of Orlando, hands down. Within the 70,000-square-foot, custom-designed, state-of-the-art theater that's located at the end of Disney's West Side is the permanent U.S. home of Cirque du Soleil. This theater holds 1,650 guests per performance and was designed to actually be part of the show itself.

Cirque du Soleil is a nontraditional French-Canadian circus that includes specialty acts the likes of which you've probably never seen before. Circus acts are mixed with special effects, colorful and unusual costumes, and wonderful music. This is a wonderful, memorable, and breathtaking show for people of all ages. Children are always intrigued and can't stop clapping, especially when the Chinese yo-yo girls hit the stage.

Two performances are held Tuesday through Saturday evenings at 6:00 P.M. and 9:00 P.M. (There are no performances on Sunday or Monday nights.) The show lasts about ninety minutes and contains no intermission. Ticket prices are $80 to $100 for adults, and $70 to $90 for children, ages three to nine. Tickets can be purchased at the box office located within the theater itself, or by calling (407) 939-7600. This is a popular show, so once you know your travel schedule, reserve your tickets as far in advance as possible, especially during peak travel times. Once you make your reservations for the show, you can make reservations to have dinner before (or after) at Downtown Disney. For more information about this highly unique show, visit the Cirque du Soleil Web site at *www.cirquedusoleil.com.*

≡FAST FACT

The more expensive tickets at Cirque du Soleil are not necessarily the best seats. Keep in mind that if you are at the front of the theater, you will be looking up most of the show. Choose midpriced tickets to save your neck and pocketbook.

DisneyQuest

This interactive, five-story, high-tech attraction provides fun and exciting entertainment and dining opportunities for the whole family. When guests step into this flashy-looking 100,000-square-foot pavilion, they're taken on a virtual journey to places that could only be dreamed of.

Combining video games, virtual reality, motion simulator rides, and other high-tech forms of entertainment, DisneyQuest is an indoor theme park unto itself that will appeal mainly to teenagers and younger kids. Make sure you don't miss Pirates of the Caribbean and CyberSpace Mountain, where you design your own roller coaster on a computer and then ride it in a simulator.

📁 TRAVEL TIP

DisneyQuest is a little loud, so adults usually like to escape to the Cheesecake Factory on the fourth floor, where there is adorable Alice in Wonderland seating with computers and Internet access. Another adult spot is the old-school video game area.

Admission to DisneyQuest is included with a multiday Park Hopper Plus Pass or the WDW Premium Annual Pass. Otherwise, there's a per-day entrance fee of $35 (adults) and $30 (children). An annual pass for DisneyQuest can be purchased for $89 (adults) or $73 (children).

Disney's Candy Cauldron

If you're in the mood to sample a wide range of candy and other treats that are guaranteed to satisfy your sweet tooth, drop in to this shop for the perfect snack or after-lunch/dinner dessert.

⊕ HOT SPOT

Cappuccino, espresso, smoothies, juice, and an assortment of other drinks and yummy desserts are available at Forty Thirst Street between 7:00 A.M. and 2:00 A.M. daily.

Guitar Gallery

This is a music shop for serious guitarists and amateur musicians alike. Guitar Gallery offers a wide selection of guitars and accessories from all major manufacturers. You'll also find very rare instruments of interest to serious collectors.

House of Blues

As you've probably guessed, the Downtown Disney complex is a mecca of themed restaurants. House of Blues serves lunch and dinner daily, between 11:00 A.M. and 2:00 A.M. in the dining room. The BB Blues Bar offers live entertainment and a fully stocked bar that's open every evening.

There's also an official House of Blues merchandise shop attached to the restaurant. In the dining room, authentic Mississippi Delta cooking is served as live blues, R & B, jazz, country, and gospel music are performed nightly. Specialties of the house include jambalaya, étouffée, gumbo, and bread pudding. There is also a Sunday Gospel Brunch every Sunday.

The restaurant's concert hall features regular performances by big-name recording artists, so be sure to check the schedule to see who's performing during your stay at the WDW Resort. For concert information, call (407) 934-2222, or visit the House of Blues Web site at *www.hob.com.*

Hoypoloi

This gallery/gift shop offers a large assortment of highly unusual non-Disney gift items, jewelry, and art. Tabletop fountains, wind chimes, mini Zen gardens, and other tastefully displayed items make this an extremely interesting store to browse through, especially for adults.

Magic Masters

Want to amaze and astound your friends and family members? Learn how to perform magic tricks just like a professional magician. This store is staffed by highly skilled magicians who offer demonstrations and perform short magic shows. Even if you don't plan on shopping here, it's a great place to visit for a few minutes if you want to enjoy watching magic tricks and illusions performed right before your eyes.

Magnetron

Magnets, magnets, and more magnets, of every shape, size, and color, are what you'll find at this small shop. Whether you're a collector or someone looking for a new magnet for your refrigerator, you'll find it here. Even the salespeople have magnetic personalities.

≡ FAST FACT

Mickey's Groove is a Disney-owned shop offering an assortment of Disney-themed merchandise, including apparel.

Planet Hollywood

As you approach Disney's West Side, you can't miss seeing Planet Hollywood, the giant globe-shaped restaurant that's jam-packed with Hollywood memorabilia, movie props, posters, photos, costumes, and giant monitors that constantly show music videos and movie clips.

Menu entrées range in price from about $10 to $25 each, and include salads, pizzas, burgers, steaks, pastas, and a wide assortment of desserts. Planet Hollywood also offers a fully stocked bar and non-stop entertainment. The Crunch Chicken appetizer is awesome! This is a great place to go for lunch, dinner, or a late-night dessert.

Dining at Planet Hollywood is an interactive and highly entertaining experience, so be sure to bring your camera. Also, don't be surprised if you run into a popular celebrity or pop star dining right along with you.

Planet Hollywood on Location

In addition to being the home of the world's largest Planet Hollywood restaurant, Disney's West Side also features two Planet Hollywood merchandise shops. This is where you can pick up official Planet Hollywood Orlando and Planet Hollywood America apparel, toys, and other merchandise with the Planet Hollywood logo. You'll discover that some of the limited-edition clothing is endorsed by big-name recording artists and pop groups. To see a preview of the merchandise, visit *www.planethollywood.com*.

⊕ HOT SPOT

Hand-rolled fresh cigars and other smoking accessories are available at Sosa Family Cigars. You'll find a knowledgeable staff on hand to answer your questions and make recommendations.

Starabilias

This unusual antique and collectibles showroom and store allows you to take home valuable pieces of authentic pop culture and history. Whether or not you consider yourself a collector, Starabilias is a fun place for adults and teens to explore.

Here, you'll find genuine items such as an antique Coca-Cola vending machine (which can be yours for $8,995), a 1930s Texaco gas pump (suggested retail price $10,000), and a Ty Cobb–autographed baseball bat (which you can own for $10,000). A wide range of autographed memorabilia from politicians, recording artists, Hollywood's superstars, and historical figures is available.

The inventory of this store changes regularly. In addition to high-priced collectibles, you'll also find a selection of inexpensive toys and collectibles. For a preview of the items you'll find at Starabilias, or to place an order online, you can visit the company's Web site at *www* *.starabilias.com*.

Virgin Megastore

Three massive floors in this store offer thousands upon thousands of music CDs, cassettes, videos, laser discs, DVD movies, computer games, video games, magazines, music accessories, and books. There's even a Virgin Megastore café located on the top floor. Throughout this store, you'll find CD-listening stations, computers to try out the hottest new games, and over twenty video/laser stations for previewing movies. Live musical performances, author appearances, and other special events are held regularly at this store.

Wolfgang Puck Café

Spago's is a premier restaurant in Hollywood where the biggest stars go for dinner and to be seen. Owner/chef Wolfgang Puck has also created the California Pizza Kitchen (CPK) restaurants (now located throughout the country), as well as the Wolfgang Puck Cafés. This chain can best be described as an overpriced, albeit extremely trendy, CPK restaurant. Pizzas and California cuisine are what's offered on the menu. A basic four-cheese 10-inch pizza (which will feed one or two people max) is priced at $9.95. Reservations are strongly recommended, so call (407) 939-3463.

Pleasure Island

Most people think of Pleasure Island as a Magic Kingdom for adults who enjoy dancing, drinking, and having fun. Whether you like disco dancing or dancing to the latest hits, there's a dance club at Pleasure Island that'll appeal to you.

There are also clubs that allow you to enjoy comedy shows, live jazz performances, and rhythm and blues music. One flat nightly admission fee gives you unlimited access to all of the clubs within Pleasure Island. (All food and drinks are extra.) In addition to the various nightclubs, Pleasure Island offers carnival-like games and several unique shops, not to mention a nonstop street-party atmosphere that doesn't end until 1:00 A.M. or 2:00 A.M. (depending on the season). Pleasure Island offers "the largest nightly street party on the planet."

≡FAST FACT

From it's opening in 1989, Pleasure Island had an outdoor New Year's Eve celebration each night complete with a short fireworks show and dancers at exactly midnight. As of January 1, 2006, this celebration was canceled.

8Trax

Disco is back and at 8Trax, you can boogie down to the hottest hits from the 1970s. Disco lights surround the dance floor and fully stocked bar. There are also video monitors located throughout the club that continuously show classic music videos from the disco era. There's always a party atmosphere here as you're taken back in time.

 TRAVEL TIP

Drinks at Pleasure Island can be pricey. It's best not to order the "specialty drinks" in novelty plastic ware because by Disney policy, bartenders are only allowed to use a certain amount of alcohol per serving. It's best to order a double tall of a standard cocktail, like a rum and Coke or a vodka and cranberry, because a double only costs $2 more. So, if a rum and Coke costs $5, then a double rum and Coke will cost only $7, therefore saving you $3 a drink. Ask for plastic, so you can travel with it.

Adventurers Club

Modeled after an adventurers club from the 1930s, this club features live stage shows and actors who roam around (in character) and mingle with the crowds. It would not be unusual if Graves the butler greets you at the door or you see a French maid dusting the entrance. Masks talk on the wall, there's a floating genie head, elephant feet barstools move up and down at the bar, and the décor of this club is rather unusual. There are several shows in the library, but the one not to miss is the Balderdash Cup Competition. It's quite humorous. Full bar service is available.

The Comedy Warehouse

One of the funniest thirty to forty minutes you'll spend at the WDW Resort will be at the Comedy Warehouse, where a troupe of five improvisational comedians and a piano/keyboards player perform five off-the-wall shows per night. Since this is improvisational comedy, the show is totally based around comments and suggestions from the audience. The more creative the audience's input is, the funnier the show itself will be.

⊕ HOT SPOT

If you don't want to be "part of the show" at the Comedy Warehouse, don't sit by one of the wall phones found at the end of the rows. However, if you do want the chance to participate, then go for it!

The Comedy Warehouse holds 250 guests and seating is on a first-come basis, so arrive at least thirty minutes prior to showtime to ensure you'll get a seat. (If Pleasure Island is extremely crowded, arrive forty-five minutes to one hour early.) All seating is on bar stools, except for a few small tables in front near the stage. Shows earlier in the evening tend to be less crowded than the ones presented between 11:00 P.M. and 1:00 A.M.

Hub Video Stage

Located opposite the DJ tower is this small stage, featuring a large video wall, where music videos are played in conjunction with the music that's heard throughout the outdoor area of Pleasure Island. Live performances are also presented here.

Island Depot

Stroller and wheelchair rentals, along with the Pleasure Island lost and found, are located near the Rock 'n' Roll Beach Club building. You can also purchase a selection of official Pleasure Island merchandise at the shop in this building. An ATM is nearby.

Mannequins Dance Palace

This is Pleasure Island's premier dance club. It features a giant rotating dance floor, a state-of-the-art lighting and sound system, live

DJs, and plenty of nonstop popular dance and trance music. The club was recently renovated to maintain its cutting-edge atmosphere. You must be twenty-one years or older to enter Mannequins, which offers a fully stocked bar and small cocktail tables. Throughout the night, Pleasure Island's Explosion Dancers perform.

Motion

Pleasure Island's newest club offers nonstop top-forty music. This club features a casual party atmosphere and live DJs. Local Orlando residents, off-duty Disney cast members, and tourists alike gather here for great nighttime entertainment. While Mannequins Dance Palace appeals to a slightly older crowd (twenty-one-plus), those over eighteen will find that this club offers a great atmosphere for socializing and dancing.

Portobello Yacht Club

For a fine-dining experience, Portobello Yacht Club is one of the few nontrendy, nonthemed restaurants located in the Downtown Disney area. While the food is a bit pricey (between $21 and $35 per person), what you'll find here is award-winning Northern Italian cuisine that includes seafood, pasta, and chicken dishes, along with pizzas baked in a wood-burning oven and some incredible desserts. Lunch is served starting at 11:30 A.M., and dinner is served until midnight daily.

Ragland Road Irish Pub and Restaurant

Ragland Road feels like an authentic Irish pub. There is live music nightly and a wonderful Irish menu with a modern twist. Lunch entrée's start around $11 and Dinner entrée's start around $16. Lunch is served starting at 11:30 A.M., and dinner is served until midnight daily. You'll find Ragland Road directly across from Mannequins Dance Palace.

⊕ HOT SPOT

A variety of carnival-like games are offered at Pleasure Island near Motion. Large plush toys are awarded as prizes. There's an additional fee to try your luck or show off your skills at these games.

Rock 'n' Roll Beach Club

Nonstop rock 'n' roll music from the past and present is played continuously throughout the evening and late into the night. This club has a beach-party theme and features a mix of live performances and talented DJs who keep cranking out the music. Snacks and full bar service are available.

The Marketplace

This entire shopping area is dedicated to everything Disney, but there are also plenty of shops that offer unique non-Disney merchandise. It's easy to spend an evening here browsing, shopping, and enjoying the festive atmosphere, whether or not you plan on making purchases.

≡ FAST FACT

Disney animation cells, collectible figurines, and Disney poster art-work is sold at the Suspended Animation gallery. Some of the stuff sold here is rather expensive, but it's fun to browse, especially if you enjoy Disney's classic animated movies. A limited number of auto-graphed animation cells are also available.

In addition to the shops, restaurants, and activities available at the Marketplace, there are also dozens of kiosks that sell unique hand-crafted souvenirs and snacks. The Marketplace is open daily from 9:30 A.M. to 11:00 P.M. Most of the full-service restaurants open at 10:30 A.M. and serve until 11:00 P.M.

Art of Disney

This is an upscale gallery that sells high-priced Disney anima-tion and artwork. Some of the pieces on display here are absolutely stunning. Less expensive Disney posters and figurines issued by the Walt Disney Collector's Society are also available. This store gives out prizes if you can answer the question of the day, so make sure to ask.

⊕ HOT SPOT

Ask one of the cast members in a Disney-owned store for a kids sticker hunt book. Fifteen stores each have a sticker that kids can collect and put into their book. It makes shopping easier when they have an activity to do.

Boating at Cap'N Jack's Marina

During the day, a selection of boats can be rented here by the half-hour or by the hour. Guests must be twelve years of age or older and as least 5 feet tall to rent a boat. Water sprites, canopy boats, and pon-toon boats are available. For more information, call (407) 828-2204.

Cap'N Jack's Oyster Bar Restaurant

Located along the coast of Buena Vista Lagoon, this restaurant features seafood dishes, including shrimp, clam chowder, and oys-ters, served daily between 11:30 A.M. and 10:30 P.M. Several nonseafood dishes are also available, although if you're not looking for seafood, there are plenty of other dining options available to you elsewhere.

Disney at Home

Here's your opportunity to take some of the magic of Walt Disney World home with you. Disney-themed furniture, kitchen accessories, bathroom fixtures, and household accessories (even bed sheets and pillowcases) are sold here.

Mickey's Mart

Near Disney at Home is Mickey's Mart. They have merchandise priced $10 and under, so make sure that you check them out!

⊕ HOT SPOT

Three hundred and sixty-five days a year, it's always the Christmas holiday season in Disney's Days of Christmas, a lovely shop that sells Christmas tree ornaments and other Disney-themed holiday merchandise like animated Disney character statues.

Bibbidi Bobbidi Boutique

As discussed in Chapter 4, the Bibbidi Bobbidi Boutique turns little girls ages three and up into Princesses, and little boys into "Cool Dudes" with the help of a "Fairy Godmother-in-Training."

A Coach Package includes hairstyling and shimmering makeup for $35. The Crown Package includes hairstyling, shimmering makeup, and nails for $45. And the Castle Package includes the Crown Package plus a complete costume of your choice with accessories for $175.

Call (407) 939-7895 to make a reservation.

Eurospain

Lovely handmade glass and crystal merchandise is sold here, and not all of it has a Disney theme. This is a beautiful shop to browse through, but keep a close eye on your kids. The items on display here are extremely fragile. Many of the gift items can be engraved while you wait. In the center of this shop is an area where a glass blower demonstrates how some of the products in this shop are made.

Fulton's Crab House

Lunch and dinner are served daily. This is the place to eat if you're looking for an upscale environment and fresh seafood from around the world. The food here is rather expensive, but delicious. You and your children can also join popular Disney characters at Fulton's Crab House for breakfast every morning between 8:00 A.M. and 10:00 A.M. Lunch is served from noon to 5:00 P.M. Dinner is served from 5:00 P.M. until midnight.

Ghirardelli Soda Fountain & Chocolate Shop

This ice-cream parlor serves a tasty selection of shakes, ice-cream sundaes, and chocolates. It's the perfect place to drop in for a midday (or midnight) snack, especially if you're in the mood for something sweet. Indoor and nearby outdoor tables are available.

Gourmet Pantry

You'll find all sorts of kitchen goodies here, most with a Disney theme. Cookbooks, aprons, Mickey Mouse cutting boards, coffee mugs, dinner plates, pot holders, and even Mickey Mouse–shaped ice trays can be purchased here. If you want to make Mickey Mouse–shaped sandwiches (like grilled cheese) at home, the Mickey and Minnie Sandwich Maker costs $59.95. This shop also offers a full deli and bakery where you can grab a snack and eat on the go as you shop.

LEGO Imagination Center

This colorful LEGO superstore and activity center is like a magnet for young people. Throughout the store (and outside) are giant statues made from LEGOs. In the courtyard that's just outside this shop, kids can walk up to the various kiosks and build their own LEGO creations. The LEGO playground is a great place for young people to hang out and have a blast (as long as they're supervised by a parent or guardian). This is one of the coolest shops/activities for kids in the Downtown Disney area. Here you can purchase virtually every LEGO play set currently available, plus LEGO-themed clothing and souvenirs.

McDonald's

It took the McDonald's Corporation over twenty-five years, but it finally succeeded in opening a McDonald's restaurant on Disney property. This inexpensive fast-food establishment offers a large play area for kids, plus a full menu of McDonald's favorites, like Big Macs, Chicken McNuggets, French fries, and Happy Meals. The Golden Arches are located in the heart of the Marketplace. There's virtually always a crowd here, so expect a slight wait to order your food.

≡FAST FACT

Only two restaurants at Downtown Disney do not take reservations and they are the Rainforest Café and Cap'N Jack's Oyster Bar Restaurant.

The Rainforest Café

Why travel to a tropical rain forest when you can enjoy a wild meal in a rain forest setting, complete with live wildlife and Audio-Animatronic creatures! Inside the restaurant you'll find huge saltwater fish tanks. Lunch and dinner are served daily (between 10:30 A.M. and 11:00 P.M.).

This is an extremely popular restaurant at the Marketplace, so be prepared to add your name to the waiting list and then have plenty of time to shop before your table becomes available. The prices here are reasonable, and a wide assortment of American cuisine and seafood is offered. This is a wonderful family-oriented restaurant that's unique and offers a very different dining experience from the many themed restaurants located nearby.

Sand Street Station

This is an outdoor playground area for young people. While this is an area in which kids can climb, run around, and have fun, they should never be left unsupervised, here or anywhere else within the WDW Resort.

Studio M

In case you were wondering what the "M" stands for, simply step foot into this shop and there will be no doubt in your mind. Studio M is divided up into small areas, each offering something unique, like Disney-themed airbrushed T-shirts created while you wait by robots (priced between $23 and $42).

You can also pick up a Mickey Mouse mug with your name on it, or meet and greet Mickey Mouse in person and have your photo taken with him. The cost of the Mickey photo session is $29.95 and includes one 8" × 10", two 4" × 5", and four wallet-size color photos of you (or your kids) and Disney's main mouse.

Team Mickey's Athletic Club

All sorts of Disney-themed sports-related apparel and sporting equipment is for sale at this shop. Mickey Mouse tennis balls, Disney-character golf balls, and Disney-themed golf bags from Belding Sports (ranging in price from $210 to $285) are among the most popular items.

 TRAVEL TIP

When visiting the Marketplace, let kids wear swimsuits under their clothes because there is a big fountain area where they can play. Shaded benches are provided for the adults.

Wolfgang Puck Express

This is fast food, Wolfgang Puck–style. The prices here are lower than at the Wolfgang Puck Café located at Disney's West Side. Lunch and dinner are served daily. Outdoor, but covered, seating is available. Gourmet pizzas are the specialty here, although salads, sandwiches, and baked goods are also available. While this is fast food, the prices aren't too cheap. McDonald's might not be as tasty, but it's a far less expensive fast-food alternative.

World of Disney

The world's largest Disney Store features all sorts of Disney clothing, toys, gifts, souvenirs, plush toys, collectibles, kitchen items, and other Disney-character-based products. This store is divided into twelve different (and very large) rooms. In the center of the store there's an information booth manned by Disney cast members who can help you locate any type of Disney merchandise available anywhere at the WDW Resort, the Disney stores, and the Disney catalog.

Once upon a Toy

This is an interactive toy shop featuring Walt Disney World attraction toys and Hasbro games that have a Disney twist.

Disney's Wonderful World of Memories

Here you'll find a large selection of picture frames, photo albums, and scrapbooking supplies, all with a Disney theme. Also available are Disney books, stationery, pens, and postcards, plus several stations where guests can create scrapbook pages and postcards.

Earl of Sandwich

This gourmet sandwich shop is located in the heart of Downtown Disney. It's a great place to stop for lunch or dinner.

Disney's BoardWalk

Located a short walk from Epcot (and several of the WDW Resort hotels), Disney's BoardWalk Inn offers another alternative for adult-oriented evening and nighttime entertainment. There is no admission charge to enter the BoardWalk area, although several of the clubs have a small cover charge.

This half-mile stretch of nightclubs, restaurants, shops, and activities is located along Crescent Lake and is modeled after the boardwalks of the 1920s and 1930s. While the shops and restaurants in this area are open during the day, Disney's BoardWalk is most enjoyable after dark, when you can experience the lights and festive atmosphere. If you happen to be a guest at Disney's BoardWalk Villas hotel, then the excitement of Disney's BoardWalk will happen all around you.

An ATM is located in the main courtyard area of the BoardWalk, behind the hotel (near Wyland Galleries). For additional information about Disney's BoardWalk, call (407) 939-5100. Don't forget to bring your passport, U.S. (or foreign) driver's license with photo, or U.S. military ID in order to show proof of age, required for entry into some of the clubs. The hours of operation for each of the restaurants and clubs listed are subject to change based on the season.

⊕ HOT SPOT

Listen to a ten-piece swing band perform hits from the 1940s, and strut your stuff on the ballroom dance floor of the Atlantic Dance Club. You must be twenty-one years old or older to get into this club. There is an admission charge of $5, and special events are held here on holidays.

Big River Grille & Brewing Works

Lunch and dinner entrées (ranging in price from $12.95 to $15.95), along with sandwiches, appetizers, salads, and desserts, are available, but the main draw of this dining establishment is the assortment of specialty beers that are served. Operating hours are from 10:00 A.M. to 2:00 A.M. daily.

BoardWalk Bakery

An assortment of freshly baked goodies is available here, along with cappuccino and espresso. All items are served to go, but if you choose, you can hang out and watch the bakers at work in the kitchen.

Disney Vacation Club Information Center

In case you're interested in learning about the Disney Vacation Club time-sharing facilities offered at the WDW Resort, you can drop into this information office to schedule an appointment or obtain literature. Time-share vacation opportunities are extremely popular in the Orlando area, so be prepared to hear a sales pitch.

The ESPN Club

Sports fans will feel like they're in heaven when they step foot into this giant sports bar, which offers dozens of sporting events shown on monitors throughout the club. Live ESPN radio and television broadcasts originate from here, so guests often get to meet their favorite ESPN personalities and sportscasters. A full and pretty inexpensive menu and bar service are available. Food entrées range in price from $7.95 to under $15, and include burgers, hot dogs, tuna salad, and Caesar salad.

There's no admission charge to hang out at the ESPN club. Operating hours are from 11:00 A.M. to 2:00 A.M. If there's a big sporting event taking place, like the Super Bowl or World Series, this club will be packed with sports fans. This club is, however, packed pretty much every evening and night.

After hanging out at the ESPN Club, you can purchase official ESPN merchandise at the nearby shop. Glasses, sports clothing, and caps with the ESPN logo are among the offerings.

≡FAST FACT

Open daily for dinner only, the Flying Fish Café serves fine American cuisine including seafood and steak entrées. This is the most classy and expensive restaurant in the BoardWalk area. Reservations are recommended. Call ✆(407) WDW-DINE.

Jellyrolls

If you're in the mood for some lighthearted musical entertainment, often with a comedy twist, drop into Jellyrolls. This is a dueling piano bar, where two extremely talented singers/musicians entertain guests simultaneously in a casual and cozy bar atmosphere. The performers change every hour or so, and each pair has its own repertoire of music. Of course, audience participation is expected, so be prepared to sing and clap along, plus request your favorite songs.

To ensure that the performers will honor your song request, write it down on a cocktail napkin and take it up onto the small stage, accompanied by a tip. Even if you don't drink, you'll easily be able to spend a very enjoyable hour or two watching the performances. There's a small admission fee ($5 or less) to enter Jellyrolls, and the drink prices are reasonable.

You must be twenty-one years old or older to be admitted into this piano bar. If you do nothing else during your visit to the Board-Walk, drop into Jellyrolls to experience the live entertainment. Of course, Jellyrolls T-shirts and other souvenirs are available near the exit.

Leaping Horse Libations

Open from 11:00 A.M. until dusk, this poolside bar offers a small menu of inexpensive food items. Relax by the pool and enjoy your favorite alcoholic or nonalcoholic beverage, along with a burger, hot dog, French fries, or ice cream. This area is mainly for guests of the BoardWalk Inn hotel, but it's open to everyone.

Seashore Sweets

Styled after an old-fashioned sweet shop, you'll find a delicious assortment of cookies, candies, taffy, hand-dipped gelato, and flavored coffees served here between 11:00 A.M. and 2:00 A.M. A limited number of small tables are available.

⊕ HOT SPOT

Men's and women's fashions, resort apparel, and swimwear are sold at Thimbles and Threads, and not all of the clothing has a Disney character imprinted on it.

Wyland Galleries

Wyland is a world-renowned artist who specializes in painting and drawing dolphins, whales, and other sea life. You can see (and purchase) his work at this stunning gallery located in the heart of Disney's BoardWalk. The art on display is beautiful, so be sure to drop in to browse. Another Wyland Gallery is located in Celebration, Florida (the city that Disney built). If you can't afford the actual artwork, postcards, posters, books, and other merchandise featuring Wyland's work are also on sale.

Souvenir Kiosks

Along with the shops, throughout the BoardWalk area you'll encounter many souvenir kiosks that offer a variety of unique products and services, such as face painting (a favorite among kids). There's also a hair-wrap kiosk (also popular among young girls). At the Design Your Own Cap kiosk, you can have a baseball cap embroidered with a name or design, while you wait. Another interesting souvenir is your hand in wax, which is created by dipping your hand in hot wax. There's usually a small crowd around this kiosk because watching the hand-dipping process is somewhat interesting. A box for your wax creation is provided for easy transport home.

CHAPTER 13

A High Seas Adventure

THE MAGIC AND WONDER of a Walt Disney World vacation no longer has to end in Orlando. Disney's Imagineers have dreamed up a way for people of all ages, traveling with or without children, to enjoy a cruise to the Bahamas that's unlike what any other cruise line has to offer.

Disney Cruise Lines

Disney Cruise Lines features two state-of-the-art ships, offering three-, four-, seven-, and ten-night cruises from Cape Canaveral (located near Orlando) to destinations like Key West, Saint Martin, Saint Lucia, Antigua, Saint Thomas, San Juan, Grand Cayman, Cozumel, Nassau, Grand Bahama Island, and Disney's own private island, called Castaway Cay. While these may sound like fun-filled and exotic destinations (which they are), getting there is more than half the fun. The Disney Cruise Line ships offer all kinds of activities and world-class service that will make your cruise a vacation you'll remember for a lifetime. In most cases, you can combine your Disney cruise with a several-day visit to the WDW Resort, thus creating the ultimate all-inclusive Disney vacation package.

The vacations available through Disney Cruise Lines are offered at a variety of prices (with special package deals always being made available through travel agents, online travel services, and directly through Disney Cruise Lines). Since this is a family-oriented cruise ship, accommodations and itineraries are available that cater to guests of all ages.

When you board either the *Disney Magic* or the *Disney Wonder,* you will find in your cabin a daily itinerary for what's happening aboard the ship. Each evening, the next day's itinerary will be delivered to your cabin.

≡ FAST FACT

If you're leaving from the WDW Resort to the cruise ship, your baggage will be picked up at your hotel early in the morning on your day of departure and delivered directly to your stateroom aboard the ship. The bus ride from the WDW Resort to Cape Canaveral is about one hour and fifteen minutes. During the bus ride, an entertaining video will introduce you to shipboard activities and prepare you for your high-seas journey.

Meet Disney Characters

What would a Disney vacation be without seeing Mickey, Minnie, and the other Disney characters? Well, while sailing aboard either of Disney's cruise ships, you'll meet up with your favorite Disney characters many times. Plenty of photo opportunities are available. The majority of character appearances are preplanned and listed with your itinerary.

Extra Charges

While the majority of activities and the dining are all included within your cruise package, alcoholic beverages, bottled water, and soft drinks cost extra. (Soda and water are served free of charge within the dining rooms, however.) There's also a charge to play bingo onboard (because cash prizes are awarded), and separate charges apply for land-based excursions and tours when the ship stops at the various ports of call. All charges can be billed to your room (just like at the WDW Resort), so unless you leave the ship, there's no need to carry cash.

Castaway Cay

One of the highlights of a Disney Cruise Line vacation is the stop the ship makes at Disney's Castaway Cay, a 1,000-acre private island in the Abacos. During the one-day stop at this private tropical island paradise, guests enjoy an authentic island experience that features the Bahamas' best attributes, such as a half-mile-long beach area and a wide range of water sports and activities for families.

 TRAVEL TIP

Kids and teens in particular will enjoy having their hair braided with beads while on the island (for an additional fee). If you want to have this done, don't wait until the end of the day. The line gets long in the afternoon, and the braiders stop taking new people about one hour before the ship's scheduled departure.

There's also a secluded mile-long pristine beach that provides the ideal place to relax and unwind, plus an adults-only beach, where older people can go to enjoy quiet time. Snorkeling, sailboat and kayak rentals, bike riding, massages on the beach, and live entertainment are among the ways guests spend their time on the island.

The *Magic* and the *Wonder*

If you and your family have already experienced a Disney World vacation and you're looking for something new, different, but equally exciting, set sail aboard the *Disney Magic* or *Disney Wonder* cruise ships.

Disney Cruise Line's first ship, *Disney Magic*, began service in mid-1998, with its cruises leaving from the $27 million glass-towered

Disney terminal in Port Canaveral, Florida. On August 15, 1999, *Disney Wonder* made its maiden voyage. Both ships are similar and hold between 1,760 and 2,400 guests per voyage.

Both *Disney Magic* and *Disney Wonder* are 85,000-ton ships that were built at the Fincantieri Shipyards in Ancona and Marghera, Italy. Each ship was designed to cater to the vacation demands of four distinct audiences: kids, teens, families, and adults. Instead of relying on ship designers from Fincantieri Shipyards to design and then build the two ships, Disney tapped the talent of its own Imagineers, giving them the task of creating a totally unique cruise ship design that would result in guests' experiencing a cruise vacation that only Disney could offer. The result is that *Disney Magic* and *Disney Wonder* are among the most technologically advanced ships afloat.

⊕ HOT SPOT

If you're interested in experiencing the many different treatments and massages available within the onboard day spa, be sure to make your appointment within several hours of first boarding the ship. Appointments for massages, facials, and other treatments fill up immediately. These services cost extra—however, the facilities are equivalent to what you'd find at a world-class day spa on land.

The ships offer 875 staterooms (73 percent of which offer outside views) featuring more space and attention to detail than most other cruise ships in existence. Even the smallest of the ship's staterooms will easily accommodate three guests, with many staterooms designed for families of up to six people (using bunk beds). The staterooms aboard both the *Magic* and the *Wonder* are 25 percent larger than the current industry average and have been designed to offer more storage and usable space than any other cruise ship accommodations. Many of the staterooms also feature a bathroom-and-a-half, featuring separate bath facilities. About 44 percent of the staterooms feature private verandas.

Pricing Your Vacation

The pricing structure for the various cruise packages is divided up much like that of the Walt Disney World Resort hotels. For example, *Disney Magic* offers twelve different stateroom categories to make it easy to choose the perfect accommodations for your family or traveling companions.

Disney Cruise Line's vacation packages include airfare from major U.S. cities. Based on the package you choose, the package might also include three or four days' worth of hotel accommodations, plus unlimited admission to the WDW Resort's theme parks and other land-based recreational activities, such as ninety-nine holes of golf (on six courses).

TRAVEL TIP

Some of the land-based excursions have limited space available and fill up quickly (in some cases, before the ship ever sets sail). You can book your shore excursions up to sixty days prior to sailing by calling ✆(877) 566-0968. A listing of available excursions is provided when you make your cruise reservation or online at ✍*www.disneycruise* *.com*. These excursions cost extra, but add a lot to the overall vacation experience.

Prices for the seven-night theme park/cruise vacation packages range from $939 per person (based on double occupancy) to as high as $5,399 per person (for a royal suite), depending on the level of hotel and stateroom accommodations guests desire. Three-night cruise-only vacation packages start at $429 per person (based on double occupancy) and go as high as $2,999 per person (for a royal suite). The four-night cruise-only packages average between $100 and $200 higher per person than the three-night packages. When traveling with at least one adult, kids and teens receive highly discounted rates. $149–$189 for children under age 3, $229–$2,199 for ages 3–12, and $279–$2,199 for ages above 12. Using an online service, such as Travelocity.com or Hotwire.com, discounted rates for nonpeak travel periods can be found for Disney Cruise Lines.

For additional information about Disney Cruise Lines, to request a free vacation-planning brochure, or to make a reservation, call (888) DCL-2500, visit any travel agent, or check out the Disney Cruise Line's Web site at *www.disneycruise.com*. Be sure to inquire about early-booking discounts that could save you hundreds of dollars per stateroom for some of the cruises scheduled to take place during nonholiday periods. Special honeymoon packages are also available.

Children's Space

In order to cater to the unique needs of young guests, 15,000 square feet of the ship have been set aside as dedicated children's space. The kid- and teen-oriented areas of the ship are staffed by more than forty professional counselors, who personalize each guest's experience. Kids and teens are encouraged to participate in a wide range of organized camplike activities.

Adult Activities

While the children are enjoying the personalized attention and the dozens of activities designed specifically for them, parents and adults traveling without children will be able to enjoy the ship's adults-only areas, including a nighttime entertainment complex that offers three themed nightclubs and shopping. There's a rock 'n' roll club, a comedy club, and a piano/cappuccino club. A special adults-only alternative restaurant, a separate adults-only swimming pool, and a fully equipped day spa facility (offering the most modern exercise equipment and spa treatments, as well as educational and enrichment programs) are offered.

≡ FAST FACT

Every night, a different Broadway-style show is presented that's suitable for the entire family. In 2003, "The Golden Mickeys" show made its debut aboard both of Disney Cruise Lines' ships. This is a salute to Walt Disney and his legacy of animation magic that includes theatrical song and dance, animated film, video, and special effects.

When parents want to leave their children and experience the nightlife aboard the ship, private baby-sitting service is available (for an additional fee). No matter what time it is, day or night, unlimited room service is available (and all food is included in the cruise package).

Family Time

During times when parents and children want to spend time together, many family-oriented activities are also available on Disney Cruise Lines' ships. Each ship offers three family-oriented restaurants, snack bars, a buffet, and multiple bars. Each night, guests experience a different restaurant with a different theme, but the entire staff remains the same, so your waiter will quickly get to know your personal preferences and accommodate your every need.

Of course, since the Walt Disney Company specializes in family-oriented entertainment, there is no shortage of Disney-style entertainment aboard the cruise ship. There's a 1,040-seat theater that features one of the most sophisticated show settings in the world. This theater is the home of three different Broadway-style shows. Each evening, the cruise line offers a uniquely themed production, including

Disney classics and newly created shows that combine storytelling and music.

☰FAST FACT

Throughout the year, Disney Cruise Lines hosts special theme cruises, with celebrity guests making appearances, performing concerts, conducting workshops, and interacting with guests.

Throughout each day, the Buena Vista Theater (a 270-seat full-screen cinema with state-of-the-art Dolby sound) shows a variety of Disney's animated classics and first-run movie releases. For less-formal entertainment, the ships offer multiple lounges and the ESPN Sports Club. In this sports club, multiple screens continuously broadcast all of the latest sports news and events from around the world.

Dining Experiences

Out of all the dining experiences on the ships, the Animator's Palate offers the most unique one. When guests first enter this dining room, everything is in black and white. As guests dine on California cuisine, the entire room begins to change—colors begin to appear on the walls, on the ceiling, and at each table. As the meal proceeds, the entire restaurant undergoes a complete transformation that's synchronized with light and sound. At the end of the meal, diners are treated to an appearance from a few surprise guests who participate in a musical finale.

The Palo (which requires separate reservations) definitely offers the most spectacular view aboard the ship, not to mention incredible food, mouthwatering desserts, and an impressive wine list. If you're celebrating a special occasion, want to enjoy a romantic dinner, or just want to relax and experience an awesome dining experience, make plans to dine at this onboard restaurant at least one evening. As a guest aboard Disney Cruise Lines, you'll automatically be invited to dine at the ships' regular restaurants. A reservation for Palo must be requested.

Guest Services

As if having the facilities and built-in entertainment venues and offering countless activities isn't enough, each ship is operated by a crew of almost 1,000 people (representing over fifty countries) who are totally dedicated to providing superior Disney-style service to all guests.

Other services aboard the ships include complete photographic services, complete laundry and dry-cleaning services, satellite telephone service, modern medical facilities, a twenty-four-hour front desk service, fax and secretarial service, and conference facilities for groups of up to 120 people.

 TRAVEL TIP

Once you book your cruise, pay attention to the two-suitcase (plus one carry-on) baggage limitation per person and pack accordingly. Leave space for your souvenirs! Be sure to keep any medications, tickets, your passport, a change of clothes, and toiletries with you in a carry-on.

When traveling on Disney Cruise Lines, satellite telephones are available in every stateroom; however, the price per minute for making calls is extremely high. Public phones are available in Nassau; however, making an international call to the United States, even if you're using a calling card, is both expensive and time-consuming. So, plan on sending postcards rather than calling your friends and family back home.

A somewhat less expensive alternative is to visit the onboard Internet Café and send e-mails home to friends, coworkers, and relatives. There's a charge of seventy-five cents per minute to surf the Web while aboard the ship; however, for a flat fee of $39.99 (for a three- or four-night cruise) or $89.99 (for a seven-night cruise), unlimited Internet access is available.

Disney Cruise Lines truly offers something for everyone. Whether you're looking to schedule activities every minute of the day or night, or you just want to kick back, relax, and enjoy the sunshine, the options are plentiful. With various activities, baby-sitting services, and supervised camplike activities for kids and teens, parents can easily find romantic "alone time" together, in between experiencing quality "family time" aboard the ship.

CHAPTER 14

The Universal Orlando Resort

FOLLOWING IN THE FOOTSTEPS of the WDW Resort, the Universal Orlando Resort has become a vacation destination unto itself, complete with resort hotels, theme parks, and a unique restaurant/shopping area.

Overview of Universal

With not as much land to work with as WDW, Universal Studios Florida had to make every inch count, and they have succeeded. The biggest space saver is a parking garage instead of a giant open parking lot. Their parks also sit side by side and not miles apart. Other features of the Universal Studios include:

- 2 Parks
- 3 Resorts
- 1 Associated water park (Wet 'n Wild)
- 1 Nighlife area
- 1 Character meal
- 60+ Places to dine
- 20+ Bars/lounges
- 1 Movie theater with 20 screens
- 3 Jogging trails

- 3 Fitness centers
- 1 Spa
- 3 Associated golf courses

Universal Orlando Calendar of Events

Like Walt Disney World, Universal has developed many wonderful annual events. All are included with your admission price.

January	
First week of the month	Shake up Your Holidays
February	
Select Saturday nights	Mardi Gras
March	
Select Saturday nights	Mardi Gras
April	
Select Saturday nights	Mardi Gras
End of the month	Universal's Grad Bash
September	
First of the month	Rock the Universe
	The biggest names in Christian rock take the stage
End of the month	Halloween Horror Nights
September	
Entire month	Halloween Horror Nights
November	
End of the month	Shake up Your Holidays
December	
End of the month	Shake up Your Holidays

Once you arrive at the Universal Orlando Resort, plan on spending at least one full day at each of the theme parks, plus your evenings/nights at CityWalk. While both theme parks are family oriented, each offers a totally different overall theme and atmosphere.

The Theme Parks

The two theme parks are Universal Studios Florida and Islands of Adventure. Universal's Nightlife area is called CityWalk and the Universal resorts are Hard Rock Hotel, Portofino Bay Hotel, and the Royal Pacific Resort.

≡FAST FACT

Getting to Universal is much easier than getting to the WDW parks. Simply park in the Universal parking garage and walk (unless you're staying at one of the three resorts). Universal's parking garage provides fast-moving floors (as seen in airports) to get you there quicker. Within minutes you are at the parks.

Universal Studios Florida (like its counterpart in Hollywood, California) offers rides, shows, and attractions based on blockbuster movies like *Twister, E.T.: The Extraterrestrial, The Blues Brothers, Jaws, Shrek, Men in Black, Back to the Future, The Mummy*, and *Terminator 2*. The majority of these aren't traditional thrill rides, yet they offer an interactive and often exciting way to experience the story behind each of these movies in a whole new way. Hence, the overall theme of this park (as well as its advertising slogan) is "Ride the Movies!"

Universal Studios Florida is divided into various themed lands. Woody Woodpecker's KidZone, for example, is a kid-oriented area. Another favorite among the younger crowd is Nickelodeon Studios. This is where some of the most popular shows from the Nickelodeon television network are actually filmed. For families and adults, Production Central, New York, San Francisco/Amity, the World Expo, and Hollywood are the other themed areas of Universal Studios Florida, each of which offers its own rides, shows, attractions, shops, and dining options (all described in Chapter 15).

≡FAST FACT

Universal Studios offers a variety of discounts for members of AARP, HIA, and the Orlando MagiCard. Florida-resident discount offers are also available. For more information, contact the park's Guest Services office at ☎(407) 363-8000.

The second theme park within the Universal Orlando Resort is Islands of Adventure. Also divided into a series of themed areas, this park offers more traditional roller coasters and thrill rides, each with its own story line. Here, Seuss Landing and Toon Lagoon offer an assortment of kid-oriented rides, shows, and attractions (plus shops and dining options), while the Lost Continent, Jurassic Park, and Marvel Super Hero Island will appeal more to teens and adults. Everything that Islands of Adventure has to offer is described within Chapter 16.

CityWalk

Located between these two exciting theme parks is CityWalk, a unique dining and shopping area that by day is family oriented, but by night offers exciting nightlife activities for adults, featuring dance clubs, bars, live entertainment, and an overall party atmosphere. In addition to a state-of-the-art movie theater, CityWalk offers a handful of themed restaurants, plus several fine-dining restaurants, mixed with unique shops. Somewhat similar in concept to Disney's Pleasure Island (and Downtown Disney area), you can learn all about CityWalk in Chapter 17.

Driving Directions

Driving to Universal is very easy and much easier than WDW. All you need to know is that it's located on I-4 at Exit 30A. Don't worry if you miss it; simply drive to the next exit and turn around.

- From the Orlando International Airport take 528 West (the Bee-line Expressway) toward Tampa. Watch for signs to Interstate 4 East (to Orlando). From Interstate 4 East, take Exit 29B (Universal Boulevard). Take a left onto Universal Boulevard and follow the signs to the Universal Orlando Resort.
- Traveling East on I-4 (from the Tampa area): Exit I-4 at Exit 30A (Universal Boulevard). Take a left onto Universal Boulevard and follow the signs to the Universal Orlando Resort.
- Traveling North on the Florida Turnpike (from the Miami/Ft. Lauderdale area): Take Exit 259 (the second of the Orlando exits) and follow the signs to the I-4 Tampa exit. Exit I-4 at Exit 29B. Take a right onto Hollywood Way and follow the signs to the Universal Orlando Resort.
- Traveling South on the Florida Turnpike (from the Wildwood/ Ocala area): Take Exit 259 and follow the signs to the I-4 Tampa exit. Exit I-4 at Exit 29B. Take a right onto Hollywood Way and follow the signs to the Universal Orlando Resort.
- Traveling West on I-4 (from the Daytona/Jacksonville area): Exit I-4 at Exit 29B. Take a right onto Hollywood Way and follow the signs to the Universal Orlando Resort.

When driving from The Walt Disney World Resort to Universal: Take I-4 to Exit 30A (Universal Boulevard). Take a left onto Universal Boulevard and follow the signs to the Universal Orlando Resort. Driving time is about twenty minutes from most areas within The WDW Resort.

Shuttle buses are available from many non-Disney hotels in the Orlando area, especially those along International Drive and surrounding areas. If you're staying at the WDW Resort, however, the cheapest and fastest way to get to the Universal Orlando Resort is by renting a car, although taxi and shuttle bus service is available. If you need shuttle bus service, contact Mears Transportation at (407) 839-1570. The Yellow Cab Company can be reached at (407) 699-9999.

Parking at the Universal Orlando Resort

Most people arrive at Universal Orlando Resort (Universal Studios Florida, Islands of Adventure, and CityWalk) by car. The theme park offers an enclosed parking garage that is equipped with a 200-camera security system, moving sidewalks, escalators and elevators, wheelchair rental, and a kennel. Daily parking for cars, vans, and motorcycles is $9 per vehicle. Daily parking for RVs and trailers is $10 per vehicle.

Vehicles can exit the garage and return the same day by stopping at the toll plaza upon re-entry and presenting their original parking ticket. Valet parking for cars and vans is offered for an additional charge.

Taxis, buses, limos, and shuttles to hotels and other area destinations are available outside the main entrance at the Transportation Center of the parking structure. For schedules, contact Guest Services.

The distance between the Universal Orlando Resort parking complex and the theme parks is considerable. While moving walkways and escalators are used to make the trip to and from your car easier, the commute takes about twenty minutes on foot and involves walking. Much of this commute is outdoors, so if it's raining, you'll get wet.

Universal Studios Florida VIP Tours

If you're short on time and want to ensure that you see and do the best of what Universal Studios Florida has to offer, consider a VIP Tour. This walking tour of the park lasts about five hours, departs at either 10:00 A.M. or noon (daily), and ensures that participants get to experience many of the park's most popular attractions—without waiting in lines.

Reservations for all tours should be made in advance by calling (888) U-ESCAPE or (407) 363-8295. Reservations are accepted between 9:00 A.M. and 6:00 P.M. (EST), Monday through Friday only. The cost of the VIP Tour is $125 per person.

Exclusive VIP Tours

This eight-hour walking tour is private and can accommodate up to fifteen people. These tours are scheduled at your convenience and will ensure that your group has the opportunity to see and do exactly what you want within the Universal Studios Florida park—without waiting in lines. Priority seating is provided at select restaurants and shows. The cost of this exclusive private tour is $1,700 for the group.

 TRAVEL TIP

If you plan to stay at one of the on-property Universal Orlando Resort hotels or resorts, package deals including accommodations and admission to the parks are available. Call Universal Studios Vacations at ✆(800) 711-0080 or ✆(407) 224-7000 or visit ✉*www.usf.com.*

Ultimate Escape Tours

This two-day private tour offers a true insider's perspective of Universal Studios Florida and also brings to life the stories behind Islands of Adventure. This two-day tour gives you unlimited park-to-park priority entrance to rides, shows, and attractions, plus preferred seating for the attractions of your choice. The cost is $2,600 for the entire group (up to fifteen people).

Islands of Adventure VIP Tours

VIP Tours ensure (for an additional fee) that you get to experience all the thrill rides Islands of Adventure has to offer—with little or no waiting. The VIP Tour departs daily at 10:00 A.M. and noon and costs $100 per person. It includes a five-hour walking tour (nonprivate) of the Islands of Adventure theme park. Participants receive priority entrance and preferred seating for approximately eight popular attractions.

Guest Services

Located just inside the main entrance of each of the theme parks is the Guest Services office. Here you can take advantage of special services for guests with disabilities. Printed disability tour guides, TDD assisted-listening devices, and wheelchairs are available. Tour maps are also available in French, German, Japanese, Portuguese, and Spanish. Each park's lost and found, stroller rental desk, wheelchair rental counter, foreign money exchange, ATM, pay lockers, and mail drop-off are all located at or near Guest Services.

Get the Most out of Your Day

It's always a good idea to save the most popular attractions for lunch-time or dinnertime, when many guests take a break to eat. At these times (between 11:30 A.M. and 1:00 P.M., and 5:00 P.M. to 6:00 P.M.), the lines are somewhat shorter. The lines for the popular attractions also tend to be shorter late in the day, since many guests try to experience the hottest rides and attractions as soon as they arrive.

TRAVEL TIP

To find out the television and motion picture production schedule at Universal Studios during the time you'll be visiting, drop by the Studio Audience Center located to the right of the main entrance turnstiles to Universal Studios Florida. You can also call the Studio Audience Center at ☎(407) 224-4233, and choose option 5.

If the weather is bad, you can count on shorter-than-average lines. You'll want to wear lightweight rain gear (such as a poncho, which can be purchased at various shops) and refrain from carrying an umbrella. Navigating through the park in crowds with an open umbrella is dif-ficult, and if it's windy, you won't stay dry. Also, when you enter into a ride or attraction, there's often nowhere to stow the umbrella.

During periods of rain, you have two options. You can get wet and see the rides and attractions that require you to wait outside, or you can follow the crowds to the indoor rides and attractions. During rain, outdoor shows and attractions will be canceled or postponed.

CHAPTER 15

The Universal Studios Florida Theme Park

WHAT STARTED OUT AS a working television and motion picture studio in Orlando has developed into an extremely popular tourist destination. Universal Studios Florida offers guests a chance to see what happens behind the scenes in television and movie production, as well as a chance to "Ride the Movies."

Park Information

Designed to provide at least one full day's worth of entertainment for the entire family, the majority of things to see and do at this park are suitable for people of all ages. Universal Studios Florida opens every day at 9:00 A.M. Closing times vary, based on the season. For the exact hours of operation during your planned visit, call (407) 363-8000.

USEFUL PHONE NUMBERS

General Information: (407) 363-8000

Hard Rock Hotel: (407) 503-ROCK

Hearing Impaired TDD: (407) 224-4414

Islands of Adventure Guest Services: (407) 224-4233

Merchandise Sales and Information: (407) 363-8320

Portofino Bay Hotel: (407) 503-1000

Royal Pacific Resort: ☎(407) 503-3000

Special Event Hotline: ☎(407) 224-5500

Universal Cineplex Movie Schedule: ☎(407) 354-5998

Universal Studios Florida Guest Services: ☎(407) 224-4233

Universal Studios Florida Lost and Found: ☎(407) 224-4244

Vacation Package Information: ☎(800) 711-0080 or ☎(407) 224-7000

Universal Express Passes

Just like the WDW Resort's popular FASTPASS, Universal Orlando Resort offers the Express Pass for the majority of its popular theme park attractions. Unlike the WDW FASTPASS, it is not free, but costs an extra $50 per person. However, it gets you to the front of the line anytime.

Choose a Place to Meet

As soon as you arrive at Universal Studios Florida, choose a place where you'll meet up with the other people in your group if you happen to get separated. Two ideal meeting places are in front of Guest Services (near the entrance) and in front of Back to the Future . . . The Ride. Arrange to meet on the half-hour if you become separated. Cell phones and walkie-talkie radios work well too.

≡FAST FACT

Award-winning producer and director Steven Spielberg is one of this theme park's creative consultants. He's worked hands-on in the development of several of the park's most popular rides, shows, and attractions.

The Rides

The slogan for this theme park is "Ride the Movies," and that's exactly what you'll do when you experience the various rides at Universal Studios Florida. All of the rides and attractions are based on popular motion pictures and television shows produced by Universal Studios. Many of these rides are cutting-edge and can't be experienced anywhere else (except in some cases at Universal Studios Hollywood in California).

Back to the Future . . . The Ride

Ages 2–4:	N.S.
Ages 5–10:	★★★
Ages 11–15:	★★★
Ages 16–Adult:	★★★

For a reminder of the rating system, see page xiv.

This ride is awesome, so expect to wait for up to an hour (or longer) to experience it. About 90 percent of your waiting time will be under a covered awning or inside.

Once inside the ride's building, you'll see the preshow on video monitors. This preshow stars several actors from the *Back to the Future* movie trilogy, including "Doc Brown" and "Biff," although you won't see Michael J. Fox's character. Just before boarding the ride, you'll see a second four-minute preshow, which is shown to you in a small room.

As you climb aboard the actual ride, you'll step into a time-traveling vehicle, which is Doc Brown's latest invention (just like the one in the movie), except this model holds eight passengers. As the ride itself begins, prepare yourself for four minutes of turbulent excitement as you race through time.

Using state-of-the-art flight simulator, audio, and Omnimax movie technology, your vehicle will move and bounce around in a way that's perfectly synchronized with the Omnimax movie shown on a massive 80-foot-tall projection screen in front of you. You'll hear (and feel) the realistic sound effects through the 300 speakers that surround you.

To make the experience even more realistic, smoke and other special effects are used. Back to the Future . . . The Ride was two years in the making and cost over $16 million to create. This ride is as turbulent as a roller coaster, although there are no real drops (but it feels like there are).

✔ This is a must-see attraction.

E.T. Adventure

Ages 2–4:	★
Ages 5–10:	★★★
Ages 11–15:	★★★
Ages 16–Adult:	★★★

Only Steven Spielberg himself (in conjunction with Universal Studios' attraction designers) could have created this ride, which is absolutely charming. Guests sit on moving bicycle-shaped vehicles that roll and eventually fly while being piloted by E.T. himself. The visuals throughout this ride experience are stunning and realistic. As a passenger, guests have the opportunity to visit E.T.'s home planet. At the very end, E.T. even says "goodbye" to each passenger by saying his or her name (something kids absolutely love). E.T. Adventure is loosely based on the movie *E.T.: The Extra-Terrestrial*.

This is one of the most popular attractions within this park, so be prepared for a wait. Virtually all of the waiting, however, is inside, as guests wind around a maze and have a chance to see lifelike Animatronic re-creations of E.T.'s friends and relatives. Sure, E.T. Adventure is somewhat kid-oriented, but just like the movie itself, it'll appeal to everyone and shouldn't be missed.

✔ This is a must-see attraction.

═FAST FACT

John Williams, the composer who created the original soundtrack for the *E.T.* motion picture, also created an original score for this ride. Steven Spielberg created several new characters that appear during the ride.

Earthquake—The Big One

Ages 2–4:	N.S.
Ages 5–10:	★★
Ages 11–15:	★★★
Ages 16–Adult:	★★★

Using highly realistic sets and special effects, guests feel like they're trapped within San Francisco's Embarcadero subway station during an earthquake that measures 8.3 on the Richter scale. In other words, there's a whole lot of shaking going on. Don't worry, though; this ride is perfectly safe, although you will bounce around a bit in the vehicle you're traveling in, while 65,000 gallons of water rush past you (you'll stay dry, however).

The Hollywood-style special effects used in this ride are impressive. This attraction is based on the 1974 movie *Earthquake*, starring Charlton Heston and Ava Gardner. Young children might get frightened by this ride, so you might want to have them sit this one out. The ride itself lasts about six minutes.

≡FAST FACT

If the earthquake visitors experience in this attraction were real, it would register 8.3 on the Richter scale. To make this attraction more realistic, over 65,000 gallons of water are released and recycled every six minutes.

Jaws

Ages 2–4:	N.S.
Ages 5–10:	★★★
Ages 11–15:	★★★
Ages 16–Adult:	★★★

Located in the area of Universal Studios Florida that re-creates the small town of Amity in which the movie *Jaws* took place, there's an exciting and somewhat scary ride/attraction starring Jaws himself. While guests remain dry (for the most part), everyone winds up face-to-face with a very lifelike Animatronic shark. The 32-foot-long creature weighs three tons and is made of steel and fiberglass, but even up close, he looks very real and very hungry. The shark travels at a rate of 20 feet per second around the attraction's man-made 5-million-gallon, 7-acre lagoon. This ride is so realistic, young children may get frightened.

Men in Black: Alien Attack

Ages 2–4:	N.S.
Ages 5–10:	N.S.
Ages 11–15:	★★★
Ages 16–Adult:	★★★

Guests team up to save Earth from alien terrorists. While riding in special vehicles through a simulated New York City, riders directly affect the environment around them as they try to shoot and capture aliens roaming freely. Each rider is equipped with a "Series IV Alienator" device with which to shoot aliens (who will also be shooting at the vehicles guests are traveling in). This exciting ride offers twelve different endings, from a hero's welcome to an embarrassing defeat. It's based on the popular *Men in Black* motion picture.

Curious George Goes to Town

Ages 2–4:	N.S.
Ages 5–10:	★★★
Ages 11–15:	★
Ages 16–Adult:	N.S.

This attraction takes the popular children's books and brings them to life in an area that kids can interact within. Kids can climb, explore, play, and even get a little wet (if they choose to). This area is not suitable for children under age three. Parents should maintain constant supervision over their kids while they play in this innovative playground area.

Woody Woodpecker's Nuthouse Coaster

Ages 2–4:	N.S.
Ages 5–10:	★★★
Ages 11–15:	★★
Ages 16–Adult:	★

This kid-oriented roller coaster offers an 800-foot-long track that travels through a factory filled with gears and gadgets. The coaster is a mild thrill ride that lasts for about ninety seconds. It's for young people, so don't expect any big drops, sharp turns, loops, or other surprises. The highest point on the ride is 28 feet off the ground. Guests must be at least three years old and be able to sit upright to ride this coaster. Kids under 48 inches tall must be accompanied by an adult.

✔ This is a must-see attraction.

A Day in the Park with Barney

Ages 2–4:	★★★
Ages 5–10:	★★★
Ages 11–15:	★
Ages 16–Adult:	★

If you're traveling with kids ages ten and under, one of the stops you'll definitely want to make while visiting this park is to see Barney, who performs in live shows throughout the day. After each show, kids get to meet their favorite purple dinosaur.

The preshow stars one of Barney's human friends, Mr. Peekaboo, but once you enter into the main theater, the main show stars Barney, Baby Bop, and BJ from the PBS television series *Barney and Friends*. Kids are invited to sing and clap along as Barney performs popular songs that kids know and love. This show is presented in a specially built indoor theater that contains a 360-degree stage (that resembles a park) and offers benches for kids (and their parents) to sit on. All of the seats in the theater offer an excellent view.

The theater itself holds 350 people. During the actual performance, no flash photography is permitted; however, during the meet-and-greet session after each performance, you're welcome to take photographs of Barney shaking hands with or hugging your child. While many adults find Barney annoying, this show is actually rather charming. Young kids will absolutely love it, and most parents will find it tolerable.

✔ This is a must-see attraction.

⊕ HOT SPOT

After the show, guests exit the theater into an adjoining gift shop that sells all sorts of Barney merchandise, so be prepared to either spend money or have to explain to your child why he or she can't have whatever Barney toy catches his or her attention. Also near the exit to the theater is a Barney-themed playground that kids will love exploring.

Animal Planet Live!

Ages 2–4:	★★
Ages 5–10:	★★★
Ages 11–15:	★★★
Ages 16–Adult:	★★

Based on programming from the Animal Planet television cable network, as the name suggests, this is a totally live, twenty-minute stage show featuring live animal trainers and a cast of animals you've seen on popular television shows and in movies. Exotic birds, trained monkeys, snakes, and famous dogs are among the animals that perform in a show that can best be described as extremely cute and enjoyable.

This is a highly entertaining and rather humorous show that is suitable for and appealing to people of all ages. The theater in which this show is presented is large, so there's seldom a wait, assuming you arrive about fifteen minutes before a scheduled showtime. Showtimes are posted in front of the theater, on the information board locations throughout the park, and in the printed park schedule available from the ticket booths. The theater itself is covered, so you'll be sheltered from direct sunlight or rain.

After each performance, some of the animals and their trainers remain onstage to meet and greet young audience members. This provides for an excellent photo opportunity.

✔ This is a must-see attraction.

Fievel's Playland

Ages 2–4:	★★★
Ages 5–10:	★★★
Ages 11–15:	N.S.
Ages 16–Adult:	N.S.

This fun-filled playground is for children only. It's based on the animated movie *An American Tail* and features all sorts of activities for young kids to experience, like slides, a water flume, and a massive jungle gym. There's also a shooting fountain that allows kids to get wet and cool off on a hot day. As you make your way to or from A Day in the Park with Barney and/or E.T. Adventure, you might want to drop by this playground with your kids.

✔ This is a must-see attraction.

TRAVEL TIP

For parents, there are nearby benches where you can relax while your kids play. While sitting on a nearby bench, however, keep a constant eye on the young people you're with.

Universal Studios Florida . . . Take 3!

In addition to the awesome rides, you won't want to miss these highly entertaining shows, many of which feature talented live performers (who don't lip-synch). For the majority of these shows, the wait is minimal, especially if you time your arrival to the appropriate theater correctly. On the days when the park isn't totally jammed, arrive at the appropriate theater about fifteen minutes before the posted showtime. Arrive thirty minutes prior to a show if the park is crowded and you want to be assured a good seat.

When you arrive at Universal Studios Florida and purchase your ticket, you'll be given a full-color guide booklet that lists all showtimes and show locations. While some shows are continuous, others are presented only a few times each day, at specific times.

An ideal time to catch popular attractions is during the Dynamite Nights Stuntacular show that's held every evening.

Beetlejuice's Graveyard Revue

Ages 2–4:	★
Ages 5–10:	★★★
Ages 11–15:	★★★
Ages 16–Adult:	★★

Several times throughout the day, a group of Universal Studios' official monsters get together for a fun-filled concert, featuring adaptations of popular rock 'n' roll songs. This twenty-five-minute show is suitable for the entire family, and features a cast of talented performers who perform all of the songs live. Join Dracula, the Phantom of the Opera, the Wolfman, the Bride of Frankenstein, and Frankenstein himself in a lighthearted musical extravaganza.

Dynamite Nights Stuntacular

Ages 2–4:	N.S.
Ages 5–10:	★★
Ages 11–15:	★★
Ages 16–Adult:	★★

In the center of Universal Studios Florida is an eight-acre, man-made lagoon that holds 13,850,000 gallons of water. Every evening, this lagoon is the stage of an awesome show featuring high-speed power-boats, jet skis, and other aquatic vehicles performing a stunt show that's accompanied by a flashy pyrotechnics demonstration (lots of explosions).

This show will appeal to guests of all ages and offers some pretty incredible and rather dangerous stunts. Dynamite Nights Stuntacular is presented once each evening (around 6:00 P.M.) during good weather conditions only.

 TRAVEL TIP

If you don't want to see this show, while it's going on is an excellent time to experience the other popular attractions. If you choose to see this show, there are excellent viewing locations around the perimeter of the lagoon. Some of the best spots to watch this show from are along the Embarcadero, in the Central Park area, or along Exposition Boulevard.

Lucy—A Tribute

Ages 2–4:	N.S.
Ages 5–10:	N.S.
Ages 11–15:	★
Ages 16–Adult:	★★

This museum-like exhibit offers a salute to Lucy. It will appeal to fans of the *I Love Lucy* sitcom. This self-paced, walk-through exhibit features a handful of interactive displays, TV show clips, props from *I Love Lucy*, and other memorabilia.

Horror Make-Up Show

Ages 2–4:	N.S.
Ages 5–10:	N.S.
Ages 11–15:	★★
Ages 16–Adult:	★★

Do you like scary movies? Watch a live demonstration of how an actor is transformed into a monster using makeup and special effects. A scene from *An American Werewolf in London* is used in this demonstration.

Also, discover how decapitations, severed limbs, bullet holes, stab wounds, and other special effects are incorporated into TV shows and movies. This show is both entertaining and educational (especially if you're a horror movie buff).

The show takes place in an air-conditioned theater and utilizes special fog effects. The Horror Make-Up Show is not suitable for kids under the age of thirteen.

⊕ HOT SPOT

Stage 54 is a soundstage that houses actual props, sets, and memorabilia from a popular (current) motion picture. The interactive exhibit changes every few months, but it offers an up-close and behind-the-scenes look at how a movie is made. This is a self-paced walking tour of a soundstage (a large building where movies are actually filmed).

Terminator 2: 3-D

Ages 2–4:	N.S.
Ages 5–10:	★★
Ages 11–15:	★★★
Ages 16–Adult:	★★★

You can experience every single ride, show, and attraction at the Magic Kingdom, Epcot, the Disney-MGM Studios, Universal Studios Florida, and at every other theme park and tourist attraction in the Orlando area, but you won't see anything like *Terminator 2: 3-D* . . . it's that good! This 3-D movie/attraction cost over $60 million to produce, and reunited Arnold Schwarzenegger, Linda Hamilton, Edward Furlong, and director James Cameron in a truly spectacular twelve-minute-and-forty-one-second film that's presented in 3-D.

This attraction is much more than simply a 3-D movie. The theater was custom built just for this presentation, and the entire theater becomes part of the show. Three 23-foot-high by 50-foot-wide movie screens are used to project the 3-D movie, while lasers, smoke, robots, special effects, and moving seats in the theater itself all add to the overall experience. Live actors (stunt doubles) literally go from the stage and leap into the movie screens using effects never used before in a theme park attraction. The story itself takes audience members from the present to the year 2029.

Whatever you do, don't leave Universal Studios Florida without experiencing *Terminator 2: 3-D*, no matter how long the wait is. Young children might find this movie a bit scary. This show/3-D movie is equivalent to a rated PG-13 movie that you'd see in a regular theater in terms of suitability for kids.

✔ This is a must-see attraction.

Revenge of the Mummy—The Ride

Ages 2–4:	N.S.
Ages 5–10:	N.S.
Ages 11–15:	★★★
Ages 16–Adult:	★★★

In May 2004, Universal Studios transformed the motion pictures *The Mummy* and *The Mummy Returns* into one ground-breaking new thrill ride that was ten years in the making. This fast-paced and turbulent ride combines Animitronics, projected CGI computer graphic effects, original motion picture footage (starring Brendan Fraser), and motion simulator technology to create a totally new type of theme park experience. Designed for teens and adults, Revenge of the Mummy is designed to take you on a trip inside an ancient tomb, where you'll experience first-hand many of the horrors seen in the movie. Not only is this ride scary due to its fast and turbulent element (like a high-tech roller coaster), but it also creates the feeling that you're inside a horror film, complete with mummies, scarab beetles, and fireballs. This ride was "directed" by Stephen Summers, who also directed the two popular motion pictures. Just as the movies were rated PG-13, this ride should carry a similar rating.

Twister . . . Ride It Out

Ages 2–4:	N.S.
Ages 5–10:	★★
Ages 11–15:	★★
Ages 16–Adult:	★

The blockbuster movie *Twister* has been developed into another special-effects attraction at Universal Studios Florida. You'll experience a simulated twister from only 20 feet away. In this case, a five-story-tall tornado is created inside this 25,000-square-foot attraction. While a real tornado is actually created, guests remain totally safe as they watch this. Although Universal worked very hard to pull off this illusion, the simple fact is that it just doesn't work. Everything is great except for the simulated tornado. It seems very weak and not believable. However, very young children may find it haunting.

Shrek 4-D

Ages 2–4:	★★★
Ages 5–10:	★★★
Ages 11–15:	★★★
Ages 16–Adult:	★

Shrek and Donkey are back in a totally original 3-D movie with a twist. In this adventure, you'll join Princess Fiona, Shrek, and Donkey as they take you along every step of an all-new honeymoon adventure. Along with the 3-D visual effects are dozens of other visual and audio effects that add excitement and realism to this unique movie experience. Through the miracle of "OgreVision," you will see, hear, and actually feel the action right from your seat. After experiencing other 3-D movies at other parks, adults may find this one not up to par. However the kids will like it.

Jimmy Neutron's Nicktoon Blast

Ages 2–4:	★★★
Ages 5–10:	★★★
Ages 11–15:	★★
Ages 16–Adult:	★★

Replacing the attraction called the FUNtastic World of Hanna-Barbera, this all-new and state-of-the-art attraction allows you to blast off on an adventure with Nickelodeon's Jimmy Neutron. The evil Ooblar (from the planet Yokian) has stolen Jimmy's newest rocket creation, the Mark IV. You'll blast off on a neutronic trip as you board your rocket and follow Jimmy, his best friend Carl, and Jimmy's faithful robotic dog Goddard on a wild chase through your favorite NickToons. Along the way, you'll meet up with familiar faces from *SpongeBob SquarePants*, *The Fairly Odd Parents*, *Hey Arnold!*, and *Rugrats*. It's a colorful, fun, and lighthearted adventure no child will want to miss!

Universal Studios Florida . . . Take 4!

Along with the rides and shows, there are also plenty of interactive entertainment opportunities available throughout this theme park. There's an additional charge to participate in some of these activities. These attractions aren't anywhere near as entertaining or exciting as the rides and shows, but if you have some free time, they're worth checking out.

- **Amity Pitch and Skill Games**—Play an assortment of carnival-like games that require both skill and luck. These games can be found near the entrance of the Jaws ride. The cost to participate is $1 per try. Prizes are awarded to winners.
- **AT&T at the Movies**—Learn about the history and future of moviemaking from this interactive attraction.
- **Caricature Artist**—Located at kiosks throughout the theme park are artists who will create caricatures of guests while they wait. There is a charge to take home this personalized souvenir.
- **Sega's Coney Island Arcade**—Check out some of the hottest new arcade games here. Just as in any arcade, be prepared to pay for each game you want to play.
- **Sega's Space Station Arcade**—This is a second arcade located in the Universal Studios Florida park.

Nickelodeon Studios Florida

The most popular cable network for kids, Nickelodeon, has a full production facility located in the heart of Universal Studios Florida.

Special forty-five-minute, kid-oriented guided tours of this studio complex are given throughout the day. Kids get a chance to see some of their favorite Nickelodeon shows in production.

At the entrance to this studio area is a 17-foot green slime geyser (instead of a fountain). The Nickelodeon Studios Tour is included in the general admission price to Universal Studios Florida. In addition to seeing the sets of popular Nickelodeon shows (and maybe even having the opportunity to see actors and actresses from those shows), free tickets for kids to be in the audience during show tapings are often available.

Kids of all ages will enjoy this fun-filled and informative tour of Nickelodeon Studios, which includes a stop at the gack kitchen, where guests learn how green slime is created. Special Nickelodeon merchandise is sold near the exit of the Nickelodeon Studios. If you're traveling with kids, plan on spending at least two hours exploring the Nickelodeon Studios, experiencing the Game Lab, and taking the guided tour.

Meet the Characters

At Universal Studios Florida, kids have the chance to meet some of their favorite animated idols, who roam around the park continuously and participate in special meet-and-greet sessions held at specific times and locations in the park throughout the day.

Some of the characters you're apt to meet at Universal Studios Florida include Boo Boo Bear, Yogi Bear, Scooby Doo, Fred Flintstone, Frankenstein, Harry Henderson, George Jetson, Fievel Mousekewitz, Rocky and Bullwinkle, Barney Rubble, Winnie Woodpecker, and Woody Woodpecker. Oh, and kids also get a chance to meet and greet that lovable purple dinosaur . . . Barney! As you explore Universal Studios, you'll also meet celebrity look-alikes ranging from Beetlejuice and Charlie Chaplin to Groucho Marx and Marilyn Monroe.

If you're traveling with kids, be sure to take photos of them meeting these characters and celebrity look-alikes. They'll make a perfect addition to your family photo album. You'll also want to bring along an autograph book so that your children can collect the autographs of the "celebrities" they meet. Autograph books are an inexpensive souvenir that kids really appreciate and look forward to taking home to show their friends.

Dining Opportunities

Whether you're looking for a quick bite or a full sit-down lunch or dinner, there are many dining opportunities available in the main Universal Studios Florida theme park area, plus plenty of other restaurants in the CityWalk area. Reservations are accepted at some of the Studios' full-service restaurants. Here is a list of some of your dining options:

- **Animal Crackers**—Hot dogs, chicken fingers, and smoked sausage hoagies are among the fast-food and snack options served here.
- **Beverly Hills Boulangerie**—Sandwiches, pastries, and cappuccino are among the popular menu selections. Counter service and nearby tables are offered.
- **Boardwalk Funnel Cake Company**—Funnel cakes and soft drinks make up the menu here.
- **Brody's Ice Cream Shop**—Ice cream, sundaes, and floats are the dessert and snack items you can purchase here and enjoy on a hot day.
- **Café LaBamba**—Rotisserie chicken, burgers, sandwiches, and barbecue ribs are the popular entrées served here. Counter service and nearby seating are offered.
- **Captain Quint's Seafood and Chowder House Restaurant**—Enjoy a fresh selection of coastal seafood and chowder.
- **Chez Alcatraz**—Hot dogs, shrimp cocktail, clam chowder, and sandwiches are served here. Counter service and nearby seating are offered.
- **Finnegan's Bar & Grill**—This is a full-service restaurant that serves traditional Irish-American food and beverages. Live

entertainment and a fully equipped bar are provided for your pleasure. During mealtimes, be prepared to wait for a table.

- **The Fudge Shop**—The name says it all. Homemade fudge is created here daily.

- **International Food Bazaar**—Everything from pizza to fried chicken, tacos, burgers, sweet-and-sour chicken, and a wide range of desserts is offered here. Counter service with nearby seating is offered.

- **Lombard's Landing**—At this full-service restaurant, you'll find seafood dishes like fresh lobster, as well as steak, pasta, and sandwiches. During lunch and dinner periods, expect to wait for a table.

- **Louie's Italian Restaurant**—Pizza, pasta, Italian desserts, and a full espresso bar are offered here. Counter service and nearby tables are provided.

- **Mel's Drive-In**—This 1950s diner offers burgers, fries, shakes, and other popular diner entrées. Limited indoor table service is offered. While you eat, you'll be entertained by a disc jockey who plays popular 1950s and 1960s music. Outside seating is more readily available. This is one of the better mid-priced eating places within the park.

- **Midway Grill**—Sausage hoagies, Philly cheese steaks, and beer are served here.

- **Schwab's Pharmacy**—In addition to ice cream, the specialty at this eating establishment is hand-carved turkey and ham sandwiches that are really tasty. Limited table service is available.

- **Universal Studios Classic Monster Café**—Salads, pizza, and other lunch items are served here.

CHAPTER 16

Universal's Islands of Adventure

THE ISLANDS OF ADVENTURE theme park offers traditional amusement park thrill rides, spread out over a series of themed areas. These themes encompass every aspect of the park, from the rides, shows, and attractions to the architecture, the landscaping, and the music you'll hear in the background. The result is a truly enthralling adventure.

Park Overview

Islands of Adventure is a 100-acre park designed to be a theme park for the new millennium. Many of the rides and attractions are truly state-of-the-art and offer full entertainment experiences, not just basic rides. For example, even the roller coasters have a story line.

When visiting Islands of Adventure, be prepared for a full day (and evening) of walking, so wear comfortable shoes. If you want to experience the rides that involve getting wet, seriously consider bringing along a change of clothes and storing it in a locker. Ride all of the water-based rides in a row and then change into dry clothes before continuing your day.

For more information about Islands of Adventure, be sure to check out the park's Web site at *www.usf.com* before you leave home. You can also make reservations and purchase admission tickets online in order to save time once you arrive at the park.

Layout of the Park

From the Port of Entry, which is the main entrance to Islands of Adventure (accessed by walking through CityWalk), all of the themed islands surround a large lake. Moving counterclockwise, once you enter into the park is Seuss Landing, a ten-acre area designed specifically for young people (and those who are young at heart). This is really the only kid-oriented area within this park. The other "islands" are more suited to kids over the age of nine, teens, and adults. The Lost Continent is the next island of adventure and features rides, shows, and attractions for teens and adults alike.

As guests continue their island-hopping adventure, Jurassic Park is next. Based on the movies, this area features the Jurassic Park River Adventure along with an assortment of other dinosaur-themed rides and attractions suitable for people of all ages. Comic strips come alive within Toon Lagoon, where characters like Popeye, Dudley Do-Right, and Beetle Bailey are the basis for a handful of whimsical rides, shows, and attractions.

Finally, for comic book fans of all ages, Marvel Super Hero Island is where you'll find two of the park's most popular thrill rides, the Incredible Hulk Coaster and Doctor Doom's Fearfall.

TRAVEL TIP

To avoid the longest lines, the best times to visit Islands of Adventure are during the winter (January through March), the month of May, or in the fall (September through mid-December). These periods offer the mildest weather and allow you to avoid peak tourist traffic.

By combining thrill rides with family-oriented entertainment, shops, restaurants, and attractions, Islands of Adventure offers something for everyone in a not-so-traditional theme park atmosphere. Visiting Islands of Adventure offers a very different (but equally exciting) experience from anything the Walt Disney World Resort has to offer.

Restrictions

Islands of Adventure contains multiple adult-oriented thrill rides, plus separate rides and attractions designed specifically for young kids. Certain rides and attractions have height restrictions. For example, people under 54 inches tall are not permitted to ride Dueling Dragons or the Incredible Hulk Coaster. Those under 52 inches tall cannot ride Doctor Doom's Fearfall, and those under 48 inches tall won't be allowed to experience Popeye and Bluto's Bilge-Rat Barges. Visitors must be over 42 inches tall to experience Dudley Do-Right's Ripsaw Falls and over 40 inches tall to experience Jurassic Park River Ride and the Amazing Adventures of Spider-Man. Finally, children must be at least 36 inches tall to ride the Pteranodon Flyers.

═FAST FACT

The hours of operation for Universal Studios Islands of Adventure vary by season. The park typically opens at 9:00 A.M. and remains open until between 6:00 P.M. and 8:00 P.M. For the hours of operation during your planned visit, call ✆(407) 363-8000.

Due to the turbulent nature of the above-mentioned rides, expectant mothers and people with certain physical disabilities or limitations should not experience these rides either. For additional information about special accommodations for people with physical disabilities, contact the Guest Services office located near the main entrance of the park.

Port of Entry

Upon passing through CityWalk, you'll find yourself at Port of Entry, the main entrance to Islands of Adventure. This area contains a handful of shops, a package pickup station, plus a few snack areas. Port of Entry is an ideal meeting spot if you and the people you're traveling with happen to become separated. In the Port of Entry, you'll also find restrooms, lockers, ATMs, public telephones, the lost and found, and Guest Services. Stroller and wheelchair rentals are also available here.

Shopping

The shops you'll find in the Port of Entry area include:

- **De Foto's Expedition Photography**—Film, camera supplies, batteries, and anything else you'll need to take vacation pictures can be found here. As you enter into Islands of Adventure, professional photographers will be on hand, snapping pictures and welcoming guests. If you choose to purchase the picture taken of you and your family, you can pick it up at this location.
- **Island Market and Export**—Candy, gourmet foods, and gift baskets are among the edible offerings sold here.
- **Ocean Trader Market**—Carver and loom artists sell their crafts here.
- **Port Provisions**—T-shirts, caps, rain ponchos, and souvenirs are sold here.
- **Silk Road Clothiers**—Travel wear, leather bags, jewelry, gifts, and souvenirs are sold at this shop. Any of your purchases made within the park can also be delivered to this location (near the entrance/exit of Islands of Adventure).

 TRAVEL TIP

Once you've explored some of the shops located within the Port of Entry, it's time to travel toward the various islands. You'll probably want to travel to the right if you're with young kids, or to the left if you're traveling with teens and/or adults. You can also climb aboard the Island Skipper Tour boat and experience a sea voyage that takes you directly to Jurassic Park.

Dining

Throughout the park, you'll find a wide range of dining options, including several full-service restaurants, many snack shops, and countless food kiosks. Pizza, burgers, hot dogs, and chicken dishes are among the main entrées offered.

Confisco Grille (and Backwater Bar) is a full-service restaurant featuring personal pizzas, pasta, fresh seafood, grilled meats, specialty burgers, and fresh desserts. Reservations are accepted. Get autographs and photos with some of your favorite Universal Studios Islands of Adventure characters during the Confisco Grille Character Lunch. There's no extra charge—just the normal cost of your menu selections. The Confisco Grille is open every Monday through Friday from noon until 2:00 A.M.

Other dining options within the Port of Entry area include: Arctic Express (featuring fruit-topped funnel cakes, Belgian waffles, waffle-cone sundaes), Croissant Moon Baker (fresh-baked pastries and desserts, coffee, cappuccino, espresso, latte, beer, wine, and soda), and Spice Island Sausages (grilled Italian sausage sandwiches, jumbo hot dogs, corn dogs, fresh-cut French fries, beer, wine, and soda).

Seuss Landing

For kids (and those who are young at heart), there's Seuss Landing. This colorful area offers rides, shows, and attractions based on some of Dr. Seuss's famous and beloved characters and children's books. This entire area is designed to make visitors feel as if they've stepped into the pages of a Dr. Seuss story. All of the buildings and surroundings are painted in pastel colors.

Costumed characters taken from the pages of Dr. Seuss's popular books can be seen roaming around this area of the park and are available for pictures and autographs. Weather permitting, there's also the "Seuss Street Show," a live music show presented several times daily. This show is suitable for children ages twelve and under. Shows typically begin midmorning and continue every hour or two throughout the afternoon. For exact showtimes, refer to the free Adventure Guide.

⊕ HOT SPOT

The Green Eggs & Ham Café serves an array of meals and snack items, but the specialty of the house is green eggs and ham. This is a fun place for a family with young children to eat breakfast, lunch, or an early dinner. It's also ideal for a midday snack. Hamburgers and chicken fingers are among the other main entrées available.

The High in the Sky Suess Trolley Train Ride

Ages 2–4:	★★★
Ages 5–10:	★★★
Ages 11–15:	★★★
Ages 16–Adult:	★★★

For a reminder of the rating system, see page XX.

Ride gently in the sky to get a bird's-eye view of Seuss Landing. The train also travels through the Circus McGurkus Café Stoo-pendous restaurant! This is great fun for the whole family.

Caro-Seuss-el

Ages 2–4:	★★★
Ages 5–10:	★★★
Ages 11–15:	★★
Ages 16–Adult:	★★

This is no ordinary merry-go-round. It features the colors, characters, and music that Dr. Seuss made famous. Ride around in circles on the back of a popular character. Some of the characters move up and down, while other are stationary on the turning merry-go-round.

The Once-Ler's House

This interactive area comes straight from the pages of one of Dr. Seuss's popular stories. Listen on the Whisper-ma-phone as the Once-ler tells you the story of the Lorax. Guests can also stand on the stone podium where, by the seat of his pants, the Lorax lifted himself through a hole in the clouds.

One Fish, Two Fish, Red Fish, Blue Fish

Ages 2–4:	★★★
Ages 5–10:	★★★
Ages 11–15:	★★
Ages 16–Adult:	★

Steer your flying fish up, down, and around and around as you avoid shooting water. This ride has its own catchy theme song that will certainly put even the most serious adults in a lighthearted, childlike mood. If you're traveling with young kids, this is one ride that shouldn't be missed. Riders can fly 15 feet into the air as they travel in the Seussian fish vehicle. Topping off the center pedestal of the ride is an 18-foot-tall sculpture of the star-belly fish featured in the Dr. Seuss book *One Fish, Two Fish, Red Fish, Blue Fish*.

✔ This is a must-see attraction.

⊕ HOT SPOT

At the Hop on Pop food kiosk, guests can create their own sundae on a stick. Banana splits and ice cream served in waffle cones are also available. If you're really thirsty and don't want soda, check out Moose Juice Goose Juice, a drink kiosk that serves juices, fruit cups, and other beverages.

The Cat in the Hat

Ages 2–4:	★★★
Ages 5–10:	★★★
Ages 11–15:	★★★
Ages 16–Adult:	★★★

Thanks to Animatronics, the pages of Dr. Seuss's most famous book, *The Cat in the Hat*, come to life. Visitors ride in moving vehicles that take them through scenes lifted directly from the storybook. The scenes, however, are depicted in 3-D using life-size characters and colorful sets. This ride is lighthearted and recommended for people of all ages. Although it's not a thrill ride, it's definitely one of the most impressive, original, and imaginative attractions within Islands of Adventure.

✔ This is a must-see attraction.

⊕ HOT SPOT

For a more elaborate, sit-down meal in a theme-oriented dining area, kids will enjoy chowing down on fried chicken, lasagna, spaghetti, and pizza at Circus McGurkus Café Stoo-pendous. Special kids' meals are available.

If I Ran the Zoo

Ages 2–4:	★★
Ages 5–10:	★★★
Ages 11–15:	★★
Ages 16–Adult:	N.S.

This is an interactive play area that tells the story of Gerald McGrew and his quest to create a totally different zoo of strange and unusual animals. This attraction is divided into three distinct areas: Hedges, Water, and New Zoo.

✔ This is a must-see attraction.

Shopping with Seuss

The shops within Seuss Landing include:

- **Cats, Hats & Things**—All kinds of clothing, gifts, and toys based on *The Cat in the Hat* can be purchased here. As you exit the Cat in the Hat ride, you'll find yourself within this colorful shop.
- **Dr. Seuss's All the Books You Can Read**—This bookshop offers a complete library of Dr. Seuss books, videocassettes, CDs, and computer software.
- **Mulberry Street Store**—Merchandise featuring all of your favorite Dr. Seuss characters can be found here.
- **Picture This!**—Purchase a unique photo of yourself (or your children) within the pages of a popular Dr. Seuss story.
- **Snookers & Snookers Sweet Candy Cookers**—A large selection of candy will satisfy your sweet tooth, while the gifts sold here make excellent souvenirs.

The Lost Continent

This area of Islands of Adventure houses one of the most thrilling roller coasters in Orlando—the Dueling Dragons. Out of all the areas within Islands of Adventure, the Lost Continent is the smallest. It'll appeal mainly to people in their teens or early-adult years looking for the thrill of a roller coaster ride they won't soon forget.

Poseidon's Fury: Escape from the Lost City

Ages 2–4:	N.S.
Ages 5–10:	★
Ages 11–15:	★★
Ages 16–Adult:	★★

Explore the relics of a once-glorious civilization as you tour the ruins of a mysterious lost city. This city isn't totally dead, however. After eons, something may have survived. You'll find out what it is when Poseidon himself opens a portal to the underseas through a 42-foot swirling vortex of water. This is the gateway to Atlantis! During your adventure, Zeus suddenly appears and challenges Poseidon on your behalf. Watch out, or you could get caught in the deadly battle between the gods! This is a walk-through attraction that features live actors and many stunning special effects. Young children might find it scary.

Dueling Dragons

Ages 2–4:	N.S.
Ages 5–10:	N.S.
Ages 11–15:	★★★
Ages 16–Adult:	★★★

You'll soar up to 125 feet in the air and travel at speeds of 55 miles per hour on one of two distinct, yet simultaneously running tracks that put you perilously close to collision. At one point, the two tracks bring riders within a foot of each other. No matter which track you experience, this is an inverted coaster, so your legs will be dangling freely.

Dueling Dragons is a thrill ride in every sense of the term, so if you don't like high-speed and turbulent roller coasters, you'd best skip it. Since this is one of the most popular attractions within the park, expect a long line. It's best to check out this coaster first thing in the morning or during peak mealtimes. The coaster has a capacity of 3,264 riders per hour, so while the line may seem long, it moves constantly. It's a favorite among thrill seekers!

✔ This is a must-see attraction.

≡FAST FACT

According to the coaster's designers, the tracks of Dueling Dragons feature one Immelmann, a 70-degree inclined loop, two vertical loops, one cobra roll, one 45-degree inclined loop, one "zero g" roll, a flat spin, and two interlocked flat rolls. This is the world's first inverted dueling coaster.

The Eighth Voyage of Sinbad

Ages 2–4:	N.S.
Ages 5–10:	★
Ages 11–15:	★★
Ages 16–Adult:	★★

This is a live-action stunt show presented several times throughout each day, typically every two hours in the afternoon. During peak vacation times, the show is presented more frequently. Check the Adventure Guide (available free of charge at the ticket window) for exact showtimes. The show itself features fifty pyrotechnic effects, including a 10-foot-tall circle of flames.

The Flying Unicorn

Ages 2–4:	N.S.
Ages 5–10:	★★★
Ages 11–15:	★★★
Ages 16–Adult:	★

This ride offers a gentle, yet exciting ride through an enchanted forest. The ride simulates flying on a unicorn and is cute and rather kid-oriented.

Dine with the Gods

Within the Lost Continent, you'll find several places to grab a bite to eat. Several of these places offer indoor seating, which provides an excellent opportunity to get out of the sun, sit down, and take a break.

- **The Enchanted Oak Tavern (and Alchemy Bar)**—Within this "buffeteria," hickory-smoked barbecue chicken and ribs, roasted corn on the cob, chicken salad, kids' meals, and soda are served. The adjoining bar features fifty brands of bottled beers.

- **Fire-Eater's Grill**—Sausages are served in a roll or on a stick. Grab an order of fresh fries to round out the meal. Soda, beer, and wine are also served.

- **Frozen Desert**—Soft-serve ice cream and sundaes are guaranteed to cool you down on a hot day. Fresh fruit cups, cookies, and an assortment of candy items are also available.

- **Mythos Restaurant**—This is a full-service restaurant. Menu items include appetizers, fresh seafood, grilled meats, entrée salads, gourmet wood-oven pizzas, pasta, and desserts. There's also a full bar and an extensive wine menu. Reservations are accepted.

- **Oasis Coolers**—If you're in the mood for a snack or refreshing drink while on the go, check out this food kiosk for lemonade, soda, nachos, pretzels, and fruit cups.

≡FAST FACT

If you return home and wish you had purchased an item you saw at any of the shops within Islands of Adventure, you can order merchandise by phone. Call ✆(407) 363-8320.

Shopping for Treasures

Souvenirs are plentiful within the Lost Continent. Here's a sampling of what treasures you'll encounter:

- **The Coin Mint**—Choose from one of several dozen designs and watch as your selected design gets minted on a metal coin right before your eyes. This is a personalized and rather unique souvenir you can actually watch being made.

- **The Dragon's Keep**—If you survive the coaster, you might want to pick up a Dueling Dragons T-shirt or souvenir. Dragons are the theme behind the merchandise sold here.
- **Garlands**—Handmade silk garlands and satin garters will make any woman feel like a princess.
- **Metal Smith**—Bronze and copper items are available here. There's also a selection of handcrafted pottery.
- **Shop of Wonders**—Silks, copper, brass, woven rugs, travel bags, leather, and cotton goods are among the offerings at this shop. There's also an extensive jewelry selection.
- **Treasures of Poseidon**—Themed merchandise from the Poseidon's Fury: Escape from the Lost City attraction is sold here.

Jurassic Park

Steven Spielberg's motion pictures come to life within this area of Islands of Adventure. If you thought dinosaurs were extinct, think again! This area offers activities and attractions for young kids, and more thrill-oriented rides for teens and adults—all with a dinosaur theme. The state-of-the-art Animatronic creatures look and act extremely real, which adds to the overall ambiance of this area. This is the largest of the areas within the Islands of Adventure theme park.

Camp Jurassic

Ages 2–4:	★
Ages 5–10:	★★★
Ages 11–15:	★★★
Ages 16–Adult:	N.S.

Kids can make their way through this prehistoric playground/maze that offers volcanoes and cascading waterfalls. The play area is filled with secret caves and an amber mine to explore. Visitors can also climb along dinosaur capture-nets, ride down slides, and cross suspension bridges. This play area is a self-paced attraction for kids only. Parents can watch from nearby, but will be too large to fit in some parts of this play area.

⊕ HOT SPOT

If you want to know what your future holds, visit with the psychic who's on duty within the Shop of Wonders area.

As a parent, if you're looking to rest your feet, let your kids roam freely in this area while you park yourself at a nearby bench and act as a spectator. Needless to say, never leave your child unattended within this or any other area of a theme park.

Pteranodon Flyers

Ages 2–4:	N.S.
Ages 5–10:	★★
Ages 11–15:	★★
Ages 16–Adult:	★

Riders will feel like they've been grabbed by a flying pteranodon as they soar through the air and take an all-too-quick tour of the Jurassic Park area. This ride is most suitable for kids.

TRAVEL TIP

While kids will enjoy this swing ride around Jurassic Park, the wait is typically extremely long, but the ride itself is rather short. Unless you happen to be visiting Jurassic Park on an unusually quiet day, you probably don't want to spend too much time waiting to experience Pteranodon Flyers.

Jurassic Park River Adventure

Ages 2–4:	N.S.
Ages 5–10:	★★
Ages 11–15:	★★★
Ages 16–Adult:	★★★

Pass through the grand gates of this prehistoric theme park (just like in the movie) and travel within a riverboat as you see firsthand the scientific marvels that brought dinosaurs back to roam the earth.

While the initial part of your river journey will be quiet, peaceful, and rather beautiful, things don't always go as planned. In fact, you'll soon discover deadly raptors and venomous spitters that don't appreciate your visiting their territory. As if that weren't bad enough, a raging T-Rex has gotten loose, and this creature is hungry.

Just when you think you're safe, grab on to your personal belongings and prepare for an 85-foot plunge into total darkness for the conclusion of your adventure. This exciting and somewhat scary ride ultimately ends with a splash, so be prepared to get wet. (Also, be sure to protect your valuables, such as cameras and camcorders, from the water.)

✔ This is a must-see attraction.

═FAST FACT

Over 1.5 million gallons of water are used to create this man-made river ride that ends with a splash!

Jurassic Park Discovery Center

Ages 2–4:	N.S.
Ages 5–10:	★★
Ages 11–15:	★★★
Ages 16–Adult:	★★

Within the hands-on interactive exhibits and displays that make up this attraction, you can examine the massive fossilized remains of a T-Rex. Visitors can also join the activity in the nursery, where you might see a velociraptor hatching from its egg. Visitors along this self-paced walking tour can see how dinosaurs were brought back to life and how they're being raised within Jurassic Park.

Triceratops Encounter

Ages 2–4:	N.S.
Ages 5–10:	★★
Ages 11–15:	★★
Ages 16–Adult:	★★

Thanks to the latest in Audio-Animatronic technology, an extremely life-like (not to mention life-size) triceratops is part of this unique interactive attraction. This 24-foot-long and 10-foot-tall beast is friendly and outgoing. As guests visit, this creature will snort, blink, flinch, and even make sounds. Visitors are allowed to pet the triceratops and take pictures. (If this creature were really alive, it would weigh more than two full-size elephants.)

TRAVEL TIP

While Triceratops Encounter is somewhat entertaining, if you're pressed for time or there's a long wait, skip it in favor of the more popular and exciting rides and attractions that Islands of Adventure has to offer.

Dining with the Dinos

If encountering dinosaurs makes you hungry, there are several snack shops and dining areas within Jurassic Park that will help you quench your hunger or thirst.

- **The Burger Digs**—The name says it all. Burgers and chicken sandwiches are among this dining area's primary offerings.
- **Pizza Predattoria**—Personal pan pizzas, sandwiches, salads, dessert items, along with soda, beer, and wine are served here.
- **Thunder Falls Terrace**—Rotisserie chicken, baby back ribs, beef kabobs, and roasted corn are among the entrées available here.
- **The Watering Hole**—For adult visitors, an assortment of alcoholic beverages is served, including coolers, margaritas, and rum runners.

Bring Home a Dino-Size Souvenir

Dinosaurs don't make the best pets, but you can pick up a wide range of dinosaur-themed gifts and souvenirs at these shops located within Jurassic Park:

- Camp Jurassic Outpost—Youth survival gear and Jurassic Park–themed merchandise are among the offerings.
- Dinostore—If it has to do with dinos, you'll find it here. Toys, books, plush toys, and plenty of educational (and not so educational) souvenirs are available—all with a dinosaur theme.
- Jurassic Outfitters—After experiencing Jurassic Park River Adventure, you can see the look on your own face (and take it home with you), because your photo gets taken as you experience that massive drop at the end of the ride. This personalized souvenir is available for purchase at this shop. Here, you'll also find a wide range of Jurassic Park and Islands of Adventure souvenirs.

Toon Lagoon

Take your favorite comic strip characters, add some water, and you have the makings of some lighthearted fun that's suitable for the entire family. All of the rides in this area are family oriented and aren't really considered thrill rides (with the possible exception of Dudley Do-Right's Ripsaw Falls, which ends in a mighty splash).

Keep in mind, many of the rides and attractions within Toon Lagoon are waterbased, so be prepared to get wet (and possibly soaked).

Dudley Do-Right's Ripsaw Falls

Ages 2–4:	N.S.
Ages 5–10:	★★
Ages 11–15:	★★★
Ages 16–Adult:	★★★

Based on Rocky and Bullwinkle, the popular cartoon from the 1960s, this water-flume ride takes guests on a wild and wet adventure around a 400,000 gallon lagoon. This ride ends with a major splash, so be prepared to get wet. Also, be sure to protect your camera, camcorder, and other valuables from the water when you experience this ride.

⊕ HOT SPOT

On the bridge that overlooks Dudley Do-Right's Ripsaw Falls, passersby have a chance to squirt water at those brave enough to experience this water flume firsthand.

Popeye & Bluto's Bilge-Rat Barges

Ages 2–4:	N.S.
Ages 5–10:	★★★
Ages 11–15:	★★★
Ages 16–Adult:	★★★

This wet and wild water raft ride has its turbulent moments, but overall it's suitable for people of all ages who don't mind getting wet. Twelve people at a time ride in specially designed rafts that travel along the man-made river at about 16 feet per second. If you're carrying valuables or other items you want to keep dry, consider putting them in lockers or within the center (watertight) compartment of the raft before the ride begins.

While this is a fun-filled and rather exciting ride, if the weather is chilly or you don't want to get drenched, consider skipping this attraction. It does, however, offer an awesome way to cool off on a hot and sunny day. As if the water along the ride weren't enough, people on land (exploring Popeye's boat) have a chance to squirt water at those aboard the rafts.

Me Ship, The Olive

Ages 2–4:	N.S.
Ages 5–10:	★★★
Ages 11–15:	★★★
Ages 16–Adult:	★

Popeye the Sailor Man invites guests (primarily younger ones) to climb aboard his three-story boat and partake in a fun-filled exploration. From bow to stern, the boat is loaded with interactive activities and things to do. There are water cannons to shoot, whistles to blow, organs to play, bells to clang, and plenty of things to crawl and climb through. If you're traveling with young kids, this will be a fun-filled stop.

Pandemonium Cartoon Circus

Within this amphitheater, live shows and special events are held throughout the day. To find out what live shows are being presented during your visit, check the Adventure Guide booklet offered at all ticket windows.

 TRAVEL TIP

Along the street that winds through Toon Lagoon, be on the lookout for comic strip captions hanging overhead. Find an appropriate message and have the person or people you're traveling with stand under these signs for a funny photo opportunity.

Dine with Your Favorite Toons

Kick back, relax, read a comic strip, and have some food. The following are the dining options available within Toon Lagoon. If you're looking for a more formal, sit-down meal, consider one of the full-service restaurants located within CityWalk.

- **Blondie's Home of the Dagwood**—This kitchen-style deli offers a 3-foot-long Dagwood sandwich, chicken noodle soup, jumbo smoked turkey sandwiches, kosher deli dogs, veggie sandwiches, kids' meals, chef salads, hi-top apple pie, soda, beer, and wine.
- **Cathy's Ice Cream**—Hot fudge sundaes, waffle-cone sundaes, and soda are what's served here. If you're looking for a cool snack, this is the place to visit.
- **Comic Strip Café**—This buffeteria offers American, Mexican, Italian, and Chinese fast food. Soda, beer, and wine are available for toon-loving adults.
- **Wimpy's**—If you're looking for a place to break for lunch, Wimpy's offers charbroiled burgers and cheeseburgers,

jumbo hot dogs, spinach salad, kids' meals, fries, soda, beer, and wine.

Shopping in Toon Lagoon

For those who love reading the Sunday comics or have a special affinity for a specific comic strip character, chances are you'll find a souvenir at one of these shops located within Toon Lagoon:

- **Gasoline Alley**—Comic strip and Islands of Adventure–themed souvenirs are sold here.
- **Photo Funnies**—One-of-a-kind, personalized souvenirs are created while you wait. Photo Funnies allows guests to have their picture taken and then incorporated into a comic strip that costars some of their favorite characters.
- **Toon Extra**—A selection of clothing, accessories, gifts, and souvenirs, all with a toon theme are sold here. You can also pick up personalized gifts and limited-edition collectibles featuring Betty Boop, Popeye, and Beetle Bailey. Some of these items will appeal more to adults and collectors than to kids.
- **Toon Toys**—Nostalgic toys and novelty gifts from sipper straws to plush toys, costumes to candy, activity sets to stationery are what you'll find at this shop. Adults more than kids will find Toon Toys a fun place to visit.
- **WossaMotta U**—Fans of Dudley Do-Right and Rocky and Bullwinkle will find a selection of merchandise including clothing, accessories, watches, backpacks, totes, activity sets, rubber stamps, glassware, and collectibles featuring these and other popular characters.

Marvel Super Hero Island

Rounding out Islands of Adventure is an area designed for teens, young adults, and Marvel comic book fans of all ages. This entire area focuses on characters and themes from Marvel comics, so don't be surprised if you run into the X-Men, Spider-Man, the Incredible Hulk, or other characters as you explore this area.

The main rides within Marvel Super Hero Island are considered thrill rides and aren't suitable for young kids or many senior citizens. If there's a comic book collector in your family, you'll definitely want to check out some of the shops within this area and take a look at the collectibles offered.

The Amazing Adventures of Spider-Man

Ages 2–4:	N.S.
Ages 5–10:	★★★
Ages 11–15:	★★★
Ages 16–Adult:	★★★

The Amazing Adventures of Spider-Man combines moving vehicles with filmed 3-D action and special effects, resulting in a visually stunning attraction/ride that most visitors want to experience multiple times. Upon boarding, guests get a tour of the *Daily Bugle* (the newspaper where Peter Parker, a.k.a. Spider-Man, works). It's a typical day for Peter until he discovers that evil villains, including Doctor Octopus, are using an antigravity gun to steal the Statue of Liberty. This is where the action heats up. You, along with Spider-Man, experience an action-packed adventure worthy of any superhero.

✔ This is a must-see attraction.

≡ FAST FACT

While this ride is somewhat turbulent, most of the thrill-ride elements are created using visual special effects. This ride isn't suitable for toddlers, but everyone else will enjoy it. Expect a wait to experience this ride, but it's well worth it.

Doctor Doom's Fearfall

Ages 2–4:	N.S.
Ages 5–10:	N.S.
Ages 11–15:	★★★
Ages 16–Adult:	★★★

What goes up, must come down. That's the premise behind this free-fall ride that takes guests up a 200-foot tower and then drops them.

✔ This is a must-see attraction.

Incredible Hulk Coaster

Ages 2–4:	N.S.
Ages 5–10:	N.S.
Ages 11–15:	★★★
Ages 16–Adult:	★★★

Perhaps the most popular ride in all of the Islands of Adventure, this roller coaster allows riders to experience the same thrust as the pilot of a real-life U.S. Air Force F-16 fighter attack jet experiences. The ride starts with a blast (from zero to 40 miles per hour in less than two seconds) and continues with a series of loops, twists, turns, and flips. The ride lasts only two minutes and fifteen seconds, but is one that won't soon be forgotten.

As with any thrill ride, this one isn't suitable for young children. Be prepared for a long wait because this ride is so popular, but if you're a roller coaster fanatic, it's well worth the wait.

✔ This is a must-see attraction.

═FAST FACT

The Incredible Hulk Coaster features one cobra roll, one weightless roll, one 360-degree carousel, two loops, one inclined loop, one high-speed carousel, and two flat spins. According to the ride's designers, the track measures 3,800 feet in length and includes two subterranean enclosures, one under water and one under land.

Storm Force Accelatron

Ages 2–4:	N.S.
Ages 5–10:	★
Ages 11–15:	★★★
Ages 16–Adult:	★★★

If you thought the Mad Tea Party (Tea Cups) ride at the Magic Kingdom took you for a spin, just wait until you experience this faster-spinning thrill ride. Here, Storm faces Magneto in a ride that features sound and visual effects, plus a whole lot of spinning. It's certainly not for young kids or those who have just eaten.

⊕ HOT SPOT

A selection of the most popular video arcade games is offered at Kingpin's Arcade. Your admission ticket to Islands of Adventure does not include the cost of these arcade games.

Recharge Your Super Powers

You don't have to be a superhero or a notorious villain trying to take over the world to work up an appetite. The following are your dining options within Marvel Super Hero Island:

- **Café 4**—This Italian buffeteria's menu includes minestrone soup, Caesar salads, pizza by the slice, spaghetti, fettuccini, Italian hoagies, sausage sub sandwiches, kids' meals, desserts, soda, beer, wine, espresso, and cappuccino.
- **Captain America Diner**—Charbroiled burgers and cheeseburgers, chicken sandwiches, kids' meals, onion rings, apple pie à la mode, shakes, and soda are among the offerings served here.
- **Chill**—Soft-serve ice cream, sundaes, and other treats are available here.
- **Cotton Candy**—Freshly made cotton candy, snacks, soda, and other items that will satisfy your sweet tooth are available here.

- **Freeze**—Snow cones, snacks, and soda are available from this kiosk located in the heart of Marvel Super Hero Island.
- **Fruit**—Whole fruit, fresh fruit cups, snacks, and juice are served here and give health-conscious visitors an alternative to junk food when they're ready for a snack.

Take the Comics Home with You

Marvel Super Hero Island offers the following shops. Here, you can purchase a wide range of toys, comic books, clothing, and other themed merchandise based on Marvel comic book characters.

- **Arcade News**—Here you'll find Dr. Doom merchandise, much of which isn't available anywhere else.
- **Comics Shop**—As the name suggests, comic books and trading cards, plus other comic book–related items for the casual and serious collector, are available here.
- **Hulk Photo**—For those who experience the Incredible Hulk Coaster and don't think they'll remember the experience without a photo, personalized photos can be purchased near the ride's exit. (Photos of every rider are taken.)
- **The Marvel Alterniverse Store**—Higher-priced collectibles, clothing, jewelry, and other items (all based on Marvel comics) are available at this shop.
- **Spider-Man Shop**—Fans of this popular Marvel superhero will find toys, clothing, and other merchandise all based on Spider-Man.

CHAPTER 17

Universal CityWalk

BY DAY, CITYWALK CONTAINS an array of themed, family-oriented dining and shopping experiences, while at night, this area transforms into an adult-oriented party scene, complete with restaurants, cafés, shops, nightclubs, movie theaters, bars, and plenty of live entertainment.

An Overview of CityWalk

Even if you've been to CityWalk at Universal Studios Hollywood, this CityWalk offers a very different nighttime entertainment experience, primarily targeted to adults. During the day, however, people of all ages are invited to experience one of several theme-oriented restaurants located within CityWalk, plus explore the unique shops within this area. During the days, street performers are often on hand (weather permitting), entertaining passersby. CityWalk is a 30-acre entertainment complex unto itself. After 6:00 P.M. there is no charge for parking.

Admission to CityWalk is free; however, there may be a cover or admission charge for the nightclubs and/or for special events. A separate admission is required to see a movie at the Universal Cineplex (a twenty-screen movie theater).

The Restaurants

The restaurants within CityWalk typically serve both lunch and dinner; however, many are open late and are ideal for late-night snacks or meals (after visiting a club or seeing a movie). If you're traveling with children or underaged teens, arrange for baby-sitting services at your hotel so that the adults you're traveling with can enjoy the nightlife offered at CityWalk.

The Hard Rock Café

This is the world's largest Hard Rock Café. It offers seating for 2,200 people and often features live entertainment by top-name artists. Of course, this Hard Rock Café also offers an extensive rock memorabilia collection. The dining room is open from 11:00 A.M. to midnight daily. Don't forget to drop into the gift shop for official Hard Rock Café Orlando merchandise.

≡FAST FACT

For a flat fee of $9.95 per person, unlimited access to all of CityWalk's clubs and bars is available. For $15, admission to the clubs and bars is included along with one Universal Cineplex movie ticket.

The Hard Rock Café Live arena offers seating for 2,500 and live entertainment nightly. There is a cover charge to see the Hard Rock Live house band. The ticket prices vary for national acts that perform at this venue (primarily on the weekends).

While dining, be sure to explore the multilevel dining room and check out the over 1,000 pieces of music memorabilia. For more information, visit the Hard Rock Café Web site at *www.hardrock.com*. For dining reservations at this or any CityWalk restaurant, call (407) 363-8000.

Jimmy Buffett's Margaritaville

This is a family-oriented restaurant by day, but at night, adults will enjoy the three full-service bars. The menu offers a combination of Key West and Caribbean-style foods, known as Floribbean cuisine. Fruits, vegetables, and seafood are the various entrées' main ingredients. The restaurant is open from 11:00 A.M. to 2:00 A.M. daily. There's a $3.25 cover charge after 10:00 P.M. Live musical performances begin at 10:00 P.M. For reservations and live entertainment information, call (407) 224-2155.

Emeril's Restaurant Orlando

You've seen Emeril Lagasse on TV's Food Network as the host of *Emeril Live*. Now, this world-renowned chef has a permanent home in Orlando, where New Orleans Creole-based cuisine is served. The wine cellar houses over 12,000 selections. Lunch is served daily from 11:30 A.M. to 2:00 P.M. Dinner begins at 5:30 P.M. and is served until 10:00 P.M. (Sunday through Thursday) and until 11:00 P.M. (Fridays and Saturdays). Within the restaurant is a gift shop that sells *Emeril's New Orleans Cooking* and *Louisiana Real & Rustic* cookbooks, plus his own line of spices and plates.

The restaurant also houses a cigar bar containing a wall-sized humidor. The dining room seats 250 people. This restaurant appeals mainly to adults.

 TRAVEL TIP

While the food is top-notch, the prices at this award-winning restaurant are rather steep. Due to the restaurant's popularity (and Emeril's huge fan base), reservations are an absolute must to avoid a several-hour wait. Call ✆(407) 224-2424.

The Bubba Gump Shrimp Co.

This restaurant gets its name from the movie *Forrest Gump*. "Run Forrest, Run!" It's a family fun restaurant that features shrimp, shrimp, and more shrimp. The restaurant serves other foods items as well and is decorated with *Forrest Gump* memorabilia. Open for lunch and dinner every day.

Bob Marley—A Tribute to Freedom

Set in a Jamaican atmosphere, this one-of-a-kind restaurant celebrates the music, style, and philosophy of Bob Marley. The venue is part museum (featuring over 100 photographs and portraits of Marley), part restaurant, and part nightclub.

On the menu, you'll find Jamaican jerk chicken and roasted plantains. Live reggae music is presented nightly. The full-service bar offers island drinks and Red Stripe beer. Dinner is served nightly (Mondays through Fridays), between 5:00 P.M. and 1:30 A.M. On weekends, the restaurant is open 11:00 A.M. to 1:30 A.M. There's a $4.25 cover charge after 8:00 P.M. to enter the bar. Live musical performances begin at 8:00 P.M. This restaurant/bar will appeal mainly to adults. To learn more about this restaurant, visit its Web site at *www.bobmarley.com*. The dining room offers an adult-oriented atmosphere.

NBA City

NBA City is a colorful, basketball-themed restaurant endorsed and licensed by the National Basketball Association. This is a joint venture between the Hard Rock Café and the NBA/WNBA, so you know it offers a hip place to eat for basketball fans of all ages. The menu offers a wide range of entrées from burgers to sandwiches. Open from 11:00 A.M. to 2:00 A.M., this is definitely a family-oriented restaurant that also contains a gift shop that sells official NBA and WNBA merchandise.

Patamoré

This open-air marketplace café environment offers authentic Italian cuisine served à la carte or family style. Open from 8:00 A.M. to midnight (marketplace area) and 5:00 P.M. to midnight (restaurant area), pizzas, grilled chicken, and steaks, plus pasta, pastries, and sandwiches are served. Full bar service is available.

The Motown Café

Music and memorabilia from top Motown artists are what you'll hear and see throughout this unique restaurant. Get a behind-the-scenes look at the Supremes, the Temptations, and other music legends as you enjoy slow-cooked American cuisine and live entertainment. An in-house singing group performs many of Motown's classic hits live onstage every twenty minutes.

This restaurant will definitely appeal more to adults with an appreciation for Motown's music and history. It is open Sundays through Thursdays between 5:00 P.M. and midnight, and Fridays and Saturdays between 5:00 P.M. and 2:00 A.M. There's a $5.25 per-person cover charge to visit the bar after 9:00 P.M.

⊕ HOT SPOT

To learn more about this restaurant, visit the official Motown Web site at ✍www.motown.com.

The NASCAR Café

No matter how old you are, if you're a NASCAR racing fan, you'll appreciate this themed restaurant. It's jam-packed with NASCAR memorabilia that's displayed throughout the dining room and all public areas. In addition, there are full-size stock cars on display, plus video monitors showing NASCAR racing highlights.

Open from 10:00 A.M. to 10:00 P.M., in addition to the dining room, this restaurant offers an arcade area and a gift shop. Like the Hard Rock Café and NBA City, this is a fun, family-oriented restaurant that tends to get crowded during lunchtime and early evenings (for dinner).

Pat O'Brien's

Modeled after the famous New Orleans watering hole, Pat O'Brien's is suitable for adults, over the legal drinking age. Every evening, guests are entertained by dueling pianos and sing-alongs. A full-service bar is offered. Dining hours are between 11:00 A.M. and 1:00 A.M. daily in the main bar and courtyard. Guests must be over the age of twenty-one to enter after 7:00 P.M. There's a small cover charge to enter the dueling piano bar, which is open (and features live music) between 6:00 P.M. and 2:00 A.M.

≡FAST FACT

In addition to the themed restaurants, CityWalk contains a unique assortment of shops. Whether you're looking for something to do for an hour or an entire evening, chances are you'll be pleased with what's offered at CityWalk.

The Latin Quarter

This area offers food and entertainment inspired by twenty-one Latin American nations. Dining and dancing are offered late into the night as guests are entertained by music from Central America, South America, Mexico, and the Caribbean. It is open from 11:00 A.M. to 1:30 A.M. There's a small cover charge after 10:00 P.M.

The Universal Cineplex

After a day of roller coasters, rides, and shows, perhaps you'll want to kick back and enjoy one of Hollywood's latest blockbuster films. The Universal Cineplex within CityWalk features twenty screens, all offering stadium seating, cutting-edge projection equipment, state-of-the-art sound systems, and air conditioning. For showtimes and movie listings, call (407) 354-3374.

On bad-weather days and evenings, or when a hit movie first opens, expect larger-than-normal crowds here. The good news is that when a blockbuster film first opens, it'll typically be shown on multiple screens to accommodate the larger crowds.

CityJazz

This jazz center features ongoing live performances (nightly) in a nightclub setting. It's also the home of the Down Beat Jazz Hall of Fame, which was established in 1952 and features such distinguished jazz luminaries as Louis Armstrong, Ella Fitzgerald, and Dave Brubeck.

Over 500 pieces of memorabilia are on display. A light menu is served daily between 8:30 P.M. and 1:00 A.M. The Down Beat Jazz Hall of Fame museum is open from 3:00 P.M. to 6:00 P.M. There's a small cover charge after 8:30 P.M. (which includes the live entertainment).

The Groove

This dance club offers state-of-the art lighting and sound, plus a full-service bar. If you're an adult looking to dance the night away, this should be your destination for the evening. The dancing begins nightly at 9:00 P.M. and goes until 2:00 A.M. There's a small per-person cover charge. All guests must be twenty-one or older.

TRAVEL TIP

The Groove hosts "The Quest for the Best" every October. The very best flair bartenders from around the world are invited to compete in this competition. It's definitely a show not to be missed or forgotten.

The Red Coconut Club

This ultra-lounge has a balcony so that you can party under the stars. It features hip and sexy décor and a live band. The party begins nightly at 9:00 P.M. and goes until 2:00 A.M. There's a small per-person cover charge. All guests must be twenty-one or older.

Blue Man Group

Downtown Disney has Cirque du Soleil but Citywalk has Blue Man Group. This extraordinary theatrical show appeals to all ages, but is not recommended for children under the age of five. Their unique form of entertainment combines music, comedy, and multimedia theatrics to create a blissful party atmosphere that people of all ages agree is a totally outrageous experience. If your seats are close to the stage its encouraged to bring a plastic poncho. Ticket prices range from $60 to $80.

CityWalk Shopping

Throughout the day and into the night, a handful of unique shops are available within CityWalk. Shop here for souvenirs, collectibles, and a wide range of unusual merchandise. Shops include:

- **All-Star Collectibles**—Autographed sports memorabilia and other collectibles are on display and can be purchased.
- **Cartooniversal**—Check out the wide assortment of character apparel and souvenirs.
- **Cigarz at CityWalk**—Here, cigar aficionados can find an unparalleled assortment of cigars and accessories, plus a knowledgeable staff.
- **Dapy**—Novelty items for kids and adults are available. This is a chain store found in many malls.
- **Elegant Illusions**—Inexpensive replicas of fine jewelry are sold here.
- **Endangered Species Store**—A wide range of merchandise, toys, and clothing based on wild animals and the rain forest are sold here. This is a fun place to shop, especially with children.

- **Fossil**—Fine leather goods, watches, apparel, and sunglasses are what's ticking at this shop.
- **Fresh Produce**—Men's, women's, and children's apparel, all in festive colors, can be found here.
- **Glow!**—This shop sells items that glow in the dark, reflect, and/or illuminate.
- **Quiet Flight Surf Shop**—Surf and beach wear from well-known labels and designers is sold here.
- **Silver**—This jewelry shop offers a wide range of merchandise created from sterling silver. The prices are reasonable and the selection is impressive for this type of shop.
- **Starbucks**—That's right, you can get that all-important caffeine boost at a full-service Starbucks, located in the heart of CityWalk. It's a great place to stop in the morning, or anytime throughout the day or night when you want a cup of gourmet coffee.
- **The Universal Studios Store**—If you didn't pick up a souvenir at Universal Studios Florida or Islands of Adventure, you'll find a large selection of merchandise, clothing, and toys here.

CHAPTER 18

SeaWorld and Discovery Cove

LOCATED JUST A FEW miles in between the WDW Resort and the Universal Orlando Resort is another extremely popular, family-oriented theme park—SeaWorld Orlando and it's additional interactive park, Discovery Cove.

SeaWorld Overview

SeaWorld owns the least amount of land when compared to WDW and Universal, so they only have two parks; however, they provide more adventure programs (over 200!) than any park in the world. Here is an overview of SeaWorld:

- 2 Parks
- 1 Water park (coming in 2008)
- 30+ Places to dine
- 4+ Bars/lounges
- 1 Character meal
- 2 Live-animal dining experiences
- 1 Dinner show
- 9 Tours
- 200+ Adventure Camps

While Disney's Animal Kingdom offers guests an up-close look at land-based animals living in their natural habitats, SeaWorld offers a look at sea creatures and combines that experience with rides, shows, and other attractions. In addition, a second theme park, called Discovery Cove, offers an even more personalized look at some of the ocean's most amazing creatures, including dolphins.

SeaWorld is a 200-acre park that's open year-round, from 9:00 A.M. to 7:00 P.M. (with extended hours during the summer months and holiday periods). To truly see the majority of what SeaWorld has to offer, you'll need at least eight hours. If you haven't visited this park in a while and you have an extra day in your travel itinerary, it's well worth experiencing, especially if you're traveling with kids and teens.

Both SeaWorld and Discovery Cove are owned and operated by Anheuser-Busch. For more information about these two theme parks, call (800) 4-ADVENTURE or (407) 351-3600. You can also visit the SeaWorld Web site at *www.seaworld.com*.

≡FAST FACT

Like any theme park or tourist attraction, gift shops, snack shops, and restaurants are all in abundance throughout the SeaWorld park. Guest services such as wheelchair rentals, locker rentals, kennels, first aid, ATMs, and a foreign currency exchange are all available within the park.

Getting to SeaWorld

SeaWorld is located at the intersection of Interstate 4 (I-4) and the Beeline Expressway (approximately ten minutes south of downtown Orlando and fifteen minutes from the Orlando International Airport).

The easiest way to reach SeaWorld (from the airport, the WDW Resort, or Universal Orlando Resort) is via car; however, taxi service and shuttle buses are available.

Special Tours

In addition to the exciting rides, shows, and attractions that bring guests closer to understanding the mysteries of the ocean and the exotic creatures that live within the sea, SeaWorld offers a series of highly educational tours and programs, including the following.

Marine Mammal Keeper Experience

This eight-hour program allows guests to experience the thrill of working alongside marine mammal experts at SeaWorld. Guests will bottle-feed orphaned manatees, interact with seals and walrus, plus get a close-up look at other creatures of the sea. Priced at $399 per person, this experience is not open to people under the age of fourteen, or expectant mothers. The program begins at 6:30 A.M. and includes lunch, a T-shirt, a career book, souvenir photograph, wetsuit during the interaction, and a seven-day pass to SeaWorld. The program is limited to only three participants per day. Sunglasses and all jewelry are not permitted, cell phones or pagers may not be worn during the program, and no underwater cameras are allowed. Smoking is not permitted. It's suggested that you wear a swimsuit with shorts, nonskid shoes or sandals, and a hat. You must also assume that you will get very wet.

Sharks Deep Dive

This unique experience takes place within the Shark Encounter attraction. Participants don SeaWorld wetsuits and either snorkel or scuba dive in an authentic shark cage during their close encounter. The cage traverses through a 125-foot-long underwater habitat teeming with an array of more than fifty sharks. This is a two-hour program that's priced at $150 per person (for scuba diving) and $125 per person (for snorkeling). This price does not include park admission.

Trainer for a Day

This seven-hour program allows guests to work with SeaWorld's expert animal trainers as they interact with a wide range of animals, including killer whales, sea lions, and dolphins. Priced at $389 per person, this experience is open to people over the age of thirteen. It includes lunch, T-shirt, waterproof disposable camera, and a seven-day pass to SeaWorld.

Whale Swim Adventure

Come face-to-face with killer whales and interact with these unique creatures. Four guests at a time suit up in SeaWorld wetsuits and enter the water with the whales during this two-hour program. The program includes lunch, and a T-shirt, and is priced at $200 per person. Park admission is not included.

SeaWorld Orlando's Beluga Interaction Program

The Beluga Interaction Program (BIP) at SeaWorld Orlando puts animal enthusiasts up-close and hands-on with beluga white whales. The Program focuses on education and personal animal interaction. Interactions include touching and feeding the belugas, and helping trainers communicate with the animals through hand signals. Participants must be thirteen years or older and be comfortable in 55-degree water. There is no smoking, jewelry, sunglasses, or underwater cameras allowed. This program is not for expectant mothers. Park admission is required in addition to the $175 per person.

Sharks Deep Dive

Come face-to-face with over thirty sharks of more than five different species in this two-hour experience. You will be immersed in a shark cage for a fascinating underwater experience with these predators of the deep. The shark cage takes up to two guests at a time through a 125-foot-long underwater habitat teeming with sand tiger sharks, nurse sharks, sawfish, and hundreds of schooling fish. The cost per person is $150 and includes a T-shirt, shark information booklet, and a souvenir photo. This program requires park admission and participants must be at least ten years of age. Sunglasses, jewelry, cell phones, pagers, smoking, and underwater cameras are not allowed. This program is not for expectant mothers.

Adventure Express Tour

This first-class six-hour tour gets you front-of-the-line access to Kraken, Journey to Atlantis, and Wild Arctic. You also get reserved seating at two select shows; get to touch a penguin; and feed dolphins, sea lions, and stingrays. The cost is $89 for adults and $79 for children (ages three to nine) and includes lunch, but does not include admission to the park.

Polar Expedition

Spend an hour exploring the backstage areas of Wild Artic with the penguins. The cost is $16 for adults and $12 for children ages three to nine, which does not include admission into the park.

Saving a Species

For one hour, visit SeaWorld's rescue and rehabilitation facilities where endangered manatees and sea turtles receive state-of-the-art medical treatment. You'll get to hand-feed exotic birds as well. The cost is $16 for adults and $12 for children (ages three to nine). The price does not include admission to the park.

Predators

Spend an hour peering down into the 600,000-gallon shark encounter, visit the backstage of Shamu Stadium, and even touch a small shark. The cost is $16 for adults and $12 for children ages three to nine. The price does not include admission to the park.

Dolphin Nursery Close-Up

Visit the dolphin nursery for one hour and discover fascinating facts about Atlantic bottlenose dolphin reproduction and calf rearing. You also get to interact poolside with SeaWorld's dolphin family, which may include mothers and calves, while talking to the Animal Care Specialists. Price per person (ten years old and up) is $40 and park admission is not included.

Shamu's Birthday Bash

Enjoy five and a half hours of fun. You and your guests will enjoy SeaWorld invitations, reserved seats at a Shamu Show, a penguin touch, birthday cake, decorated room with party supplies and favors, a character visit, free parking, a birthday gift, and a pizza snack as well as have the opportunity to feed animals at two SeaWorld venues. Make reservations in advance. Prices for a party of up to twenty people (children and adults) is $795. Add $25 for each additional guest up to a maximum of thirty guests.

For more information about these tours and special programs, call (800) 406-2244 and choose option 5, or (407) 363-2380.

SeaWorld Highlights

Ages 2–4:	★★
Ages 5–10:	★★★
Ages 11–15:	★★★
Ages 16–Adult:	★★★

For a reminder of the rating system, see page xiv.

SeaWorld offers a wide range of rides, shows, and attractions, most of which cater to a family audience. Perhaps the most popular show at this theme park is the Shamu Adventure, a fun-filled live show starring killer whales interacting with their trainers. The nighttime version of this show, Shamu Rocks America, features SeaWorld's trainers and whales performing with rock music in the background.

 TRAVEL TIP

The Shamu Rocks America show is typically presented right before the park closes every evening. This exiting show can take up to forty minutes, plus you'll have to deal with heavy crowds. The show, however, is fabulous.

Check with the park's ticket office or customer relations desk for daily showtimes. Shows are presented on a weather-permitting basis. Be sure to arrive at least fifteen to thirty minutes early to the show in order to ensure admission and good seats, especially during peak vacation periods. For kids especially, there's a section of seats within Shamu Stadium that guarantees audience members will get splashed by the performing whales. To learn more about Shamu and SeaWorld's killer whales, visit the Shamu Web site at *www .shamu.com*.

✔ This is a must-see attraction.

Kraken

Ages 2–4:	★★
Ages 5–10:	★★★
Ages 11–15:	★★★
Ages 16–Adult:	★★★

This is the tallest, fastest, longest, and only floorless roller coaster in Orlando. It will take you to the height of a fifteen-story building and turn you upside down seven times, all at speeds reaching 65 miles per hour.

Kraken is named after a legendary sea monster—a massive, mythological underwater beast. As you experience this coaster, your feet will dangle as you sit on open-air, pedestal-like seats with nothing around you except shoulder restraints. There's no one to hold on to, nothing in front of you, and nothing below you. There's only sky above and the wind in your face.

✔ This is a must-see attraction.

Believe

Ages 2–4:	★★★
Ages 5–10:	★★★
Ages 11–15:	★★★
Ages 16–Adult:	★★★

This is a stunning Shamu show that no one should miss. Underwater cameras show what is happening under the surface as Shamu swims up and then rises high above the surface. The musical score combined with the majestic presence of Shamu will move and inspire you.

✔ This is a must-see attraction.

Blue Horizons

Ages 2–4:	★★★
Ages 5–10:	★★★
Ages 11–15:	★★★
Ages 16–Adult:	★★★

Experience acrobatic dolphins, whales, and soaring birds in this huge theatrical performance, which is all about where the sea meets the sky. Great for all ages.

✔ This is a must-see attraction.

Shamu Express

Ages 2–4:	★
Ages 5–10:	★★★
Ages 11–15:	★★★
Ages 16–Adult:	★★★

This family-oriented roller coaster gently thrills the entire family as they ride in a Shamu-themed car.

✔ This is a must-see attraction.

Clyde and Seamore Take Pirate Island

Ages 2–4:	★
Ages 5–10:	★★
Ages 11–15:	★★★
Ages 16–Adult:	★★

Sea lions, otters, and walrus perform with trainers in this rather lighthearted "adventure" designed for kids and teens. While the story line is a bit childish, this show features a cast of well-trained sea lions interacting with their trainers and the audience.

Journey to Atlantis

Ages 2–4:	N.S.
Ages 5–10:	N.S.
Ages 11–15:	★★★
Ages 16–Adult:	★★★

As you kick off your adventure to the lost city of Atlantis, you'll be traveling on water and high-speed rails. Evil spirits will try to keep you from your destination, but your bravery and sheer guts will keep you one step ahead. Along your journey, you never know what's around the next corner or the next drop. Oh, and there are drops. In fact, one drop is 60 feet long and goes nearly straight down. Journey to Atlantis is a thrill ride that nicely combines special effects, the excitement of a roller coaster, and the thrills of a turbulent water ride.

Shamu's Happy Harbor

Ages 2–4:	★★★
Ages 5–10:	★★★
Ages 11–15:	N.S.
Ages 16–Adult:	N.S.

For young kids, this is a freestyle play area filled with giant pink flamingos and palm trees. Young guests are encouraged to run, jump, and climb as they explore four stories of nets, shoot through tunnels, cool down in a splashy water maze, and slip down nine slippery slides.

Pets Ahoy!

Ages 2–4:	★★★
Ages 5–10:	★★★
Ages 11–15:	★★
Ages 16–Adult:	★★

This is a fun-filled and funny live show starring a cast of trained dogs, cats, birds, rats, potbellied pigs, and other animals performing a series of entertaining skits. Nearly all of the cast members were rescued from local animal shelters. Kids in particular will enjoy this show; however, it's definitely suitable for the entire family.

Odyssea

Ages 2–4:	N.S.
Ages 5–10:	★
Ages 11–15:	★★★
Ages 16–Adult:	★★★

Acrobatics, athleticism, modern dance, and special effects are used to create a fun-filled but nontraditional circus (sort of like Cirque du Soleil). The thirty-minute show comprises several specialty circus acts, featuring performers from around the world.

Shark Encounter

Ages 2–4:	★★
Ages 5–10:	★★
Ages 11–15:	★★
Ages 16–Adult:	★★

Travel through the world's largest underwater acrylic tunnel and find yourself just inches away from dangerous predators like eels, barracuda, venomous fish, and more than fifty sharks. This is a large and beautiful coral reef habitat.

Key West Dolphin Fest

Ages 2–4:	N.S.
Ages 5–10:	★★★
Ages 11–15:	★★★
Ages 16–Adult:	★★★

Guests have a chance to see Atlantic bottlenose dolphins perform live with their trainers in an entertaining, family-oriented show. SeaWorld also offers a pool area where guests can see, feed, and pet dolphins. In addition, be sure to check out the Dolphin Nursery, a chance to see newborn dolphins with their moms.

✔ This is a must-see attraction.

≡FAST FACT

At SeaWorld, more than 200 programs designed for various age groups are offered year-round and include day camps, resident camps, sleepovers, family camps, teacher camps, and group programs. To learn more about the various SeaWorld Adventure Camp programs, call ☎(866) GO-TO-CAMP or ☎(800) 406-2244.

Wild Arctic

This motion-simulator-based thrill ride takes guests on a helicopter journey to the frozen north for an Arctic exploration that's filled with surprises. The photography and overall realism is highly impressive. You're about to preview a part of the world that few see firsthand.

Manatees: The Last Generation?

Ages 2–4:	N.S.
Ages 5–10:	★
Ages 11–15:	★★★
Ages 16–Adult:	★★★

This exhibit allows guests to see Florida manatees up close and learn about the dangers this species is currently facing. It's both educational and entertaining, like all of the shows and exhibits at SeaWorld that involve live animals.

Pacific Point Preserve

Ages 2–4:	★★
Ages 5–10:	★★
Ages 11–15:	★★★
Ages 16–Adult:	★★★

Sea lions and fur seals living in a 2.5-acre naturalistic environment that replicates the rocky northern Pacific coast are the stars of this exhibit. Young people, in particular, will enjoy this zoolike attraction.

Getting Hungry?

Ages 2–4:	N.S.
Ages 5–10:	★★★
Ages 11–15:	★★★
Ages 16–Adult:	★★

SeaWorld offers many restaurants, ranging from full-service to cafeteria style to fast service.

Makahiki Luau Dinner and Show

The Makahiki Luau Dinner and Show features traditional music, song, dance, and food from the islands of Hawaii. Sadly, the other two luaus in Orlando (WDW and Universal) are better than this one mainly because it is indoors and most people think of a luau as being outdoors. Park admission is not required. Reservations are required. Call (800) 327-2420. The luau is performed nightly at the Seafire Inn and is priced at $37.95 (adults) and $27.95 (kids).

 TRAVEL TIP

If you decide to attend the luau during peak seasons you can experience a little bit of SeaWorld for free because the entrance to the luau is through the main gate. Around 6:00 P.M. at the main gate you simply say that you are going to the luau and they let you in the park. There is no charge for parking.

Rise and Shine with Shamu and Crew

This breakfast buffet costs $14.95 for adults and $9.95 for children ages three to nine, plus tax. Children under three get in free but also need to be mentioned when making the reservation so arrangements can be made. Costumed characters like Shamu give cuddly hugs, pose for photos, and give autographs while walking around to each table. Reservations are available by calling 1-800-327-2420. Park admission is required and not included.

Dine with Shamu!

This is exclusive, intimate, and up-close buffet-style dining right next to Shamu. Backstage passes are $37 for adults and $19 for children three to nine. Park admission is required. Reservations are required. Call (800) 327-2420.

Shark's Underwater Grill

For world-class entrées from SeaWorld's best chefs, the Shark's Underwater Grill fits the bill. This restaurant is underwater and more than fifty sharks swim all around you. Don't worry, though; they are behind glass. There is a children's menu and adult entrée's start around $15. Guests wanting to make reservations to Shark's Underwater Grill can do so by visiting the host/hostess stand in front of the restaurant on the day of their visit.

When it comes to dining and shopping, one of the newest areas of SeaWorld is the Waterfront. This 5-acre nautical neighborhood (located in the heart of SeaWorld) offers a selection of dining and shopping options, plus live music and street performers throughout the day.

Kids and SeaWorld

Since SeaWorld combines fun with wildlife education, the theme park's animal trainers offer these suggestions to parents regarding how to enhance a child's experience while visiting this theme park:

- At the end of each day, encourage your kids to draw pictures or write short stories about the favorite parts of their day at SeaWorld.
- Take lots of pictures, with a focus on your kids interacting with the various animals. Later, spend time reviewing the photos (or video) with your kids.
- Throughout your vacation, keep a "memory bag" close by. A "memory bag" can be a purse, pocket, or a backpack pouch reserved for holding fun keepsakes that your kids collect (or purchase).
- While the trip is still fresh in their minds, ask your children what they learned during their trip and what they would like to do next time.

There are a handful of other activities and exhibits at SeaWorld. For example, the Penguin Encounter is an exhibit featuring penguins, while the Rico and Roza's Musical Feast offers a twenty-five-minute musical revue celebrating food, family, and fun. The Clydesdale Hamlet is the home to SeaWorld's famous Budweiser Clydesdale horses. Guests can pet the horses and have photos taken with them.

Discovery Cove

Located adjacent to SeaWorld is Discovery Cove, which opened in summer 2000. This truly unique theme park re-creates an exotic tropical island, complete with sandy beaches. Unlike most theme parks, however, only a limited number of visitors are granted admission each day to Discovery Cove. Advanced reservations are definitely required.

Instead of rides, shows, and attractions, Discovery Cove offers a one-on-one, up-close, and hands-on look at marine wildlife, including dolphins.

The park is staffed by a team of highly trained and knowledgeable animal trainers and caregivers who work directly with guests to provide an extremely personalized experience that includes interacting one-on-one with dolphins and other sea creatures. This park is designed for guests over the age of six. Younger children will be limited in terms of what activities they can participate in.

Discovery Cove offers snorkeling in a man-made coral reef, lagoon, and tropical river; the chance to swim and interact with dolphins; and a lovely man-made beach. Best of all, this park is open to only 800 to 1,000 people per day, so there are never any long lines or crowds.

Visiting Discovery Cove is an all-day experience (with lunch included). The package includes:

- A reserved dolphin swim experience
- Unlimited access to snorkeling in the coral reef
- Unlimited access to wade and swim in the ray pool
- Unlimited access to the free-flight bird aviary, the resort pool, and the tropical river
- A freshly prepared meal for lunch
- Use of a mask, snorkel, swim vest, towels, lockers, and other amenities
- All-day self-parking
- A seven-day pass to SeaWorld Orlando

Anyone who has ever thought about swimming or interacting with dolphins, or who wants to try snorkeling in a 100 percent safe and supervised environment, will definitely enjoy this experience.

The only drawback to this park is that the souvenir photographs taken of guests by the on-staff professional photographer are rather expensive, yet this is a special personalized keepsake that virtually all guests wind up purchasing. For more information about Discovery Cove, call (877) 4-DISCOVERY or visit the park's Web site at *www .discoverycove.com*.

CHAPTER 19

Exploring Greater Orlando

IF YOU CHOOSE TO explore some of the nearby greater Orlando area, you'll find literally hundreds of family-orientated activities. This chapter will highlight some of the non-theme-park activities you'll find throughout Orlando.

Introduction to Orlando

Orlando is only around 150 years old. In the 1800s the primary industry in Orlando was cattle. When the railroad was built it connected Orlando with the rest of the country, turning this cow town into one of the biggest citrus industries in the nation—it was known as "the city built on a peel of an orange." By 1960, the population of Orlando was over 60,000 due to military bases, NASA, and the relocation of the Glenn Martin Company (Martin Marietta/Lockheed Martin).

In 1965, Walt Disney realized he needed a place with room to grow. So he secretly came to Orlando and spent almost $6 million on land in someone else's name.

Walt finally announced at a press conference, "Here in Florida, we have something special we never enjoyed at Disneyland—the blessing of size. There's enough land here to hold all the ideas and plans we can possibly imagine." He died one year later and his brother, Roy, took over and changed the name of the resort from Disney World to Walt Disney World. Roy died in 1971, and the rest is history.

⊕ HOT SPOT

While purchasing land in Orlando, Walt lived on the fifth floor of the Cherry Plaza Hotel, which was turned into apartments in the 1980s and renamed the Plaza. Today they have been converted to condos and renamed Post Parkside. If you're a real Disney buff, then check them out on Lake Eola in downtown Orlando. The address is 425 East Central Blvd.

The Magic Kingdom Park opened in 1971 and WDW has never stopped growing since. In time, SeaWorld, Universal Studios, hotels, restaurants, and every attraction imaginable packed their bags and moved to Orlando as well. Orlando is now the number one vacation destination in the world and is home to 1.5 million residents. This city has no intention of slowing down.

≡ FAST FACT

Today Disney owns land and parks all over the world, ESPN, ABC, and nine other TV stations, sixty-six radio stations, six film companies, NASCAR.com, NBA.com, five record companies, one sports team, and an additional list five pages long.

Orlando Overview

In the immediate Orlando area there are basically three hot spots, and they are all located on the same Interstate (I-4).

- Lake Buena Vista/Kissimmee area (near WDW)
- SeaWorld/Universal/International Drive area (three to five miles from WDW)
- Downtown Orlando area (fifteen miles from WDW)

Other areas outside of Orlando include the beach destinations such as Daytona, Cocoa Beach, Clearwater Beach, and any other attractions within a 100-mile radius of Orlando.

The Top Things to Know about Orlando

Key information is always helpful when trying to wrap your brain around a destination. The following will catch you up to speed.

The main state highway/freeway that runs from the east coast to the west coast of Florida is I-4. However, in the Orlando area it curves many times, which will seem confusing to your sense of direction. Ninety percent of all Orlando attractions can be found directly off this highway. Some of the main roads in Orlando require a toll. When coming up to the toll station, stay near the right because the locals use an E-PASS on the left. Also, a lot of the main roads in Orlando are given a name and a number, so it can be confusing at times. The major roadways and their numbers are:

- 528 = Beeline (toll)
- 426 = Semoran
- 192 = Irlo Bronson Memorial Highway
- 535 = Apopka Vineland Road
- 408 = East West Expressway (toll)
- 522 = Osceola Parkway (toll)
- 17/92 = Orange Blossom Trail (also called OBT or 441)
- 417 = Central Florida Greenway (toll)
- 50 = Colonial

The Turnpike (the superhighway in Florida) also runs through Orlando straight to Miami. From Orlando to Miami it will cost around $20.

When driving, keep in mind that you are driving next to other tourists, truckers, college students, retirees, and aggressive locals. When traveling on the major freeways simply dial 511 on your cell phone to hear visitor information and current traffic reports.

The minimum drinking age in Florida is twenty-one. Many of the resorts and entertainment centers allow you to travel with alcohol in nonbreakable containers. It's against Florida state law to bring your own alcohol into a public area; however you may have your own alcohol in private areas such as your room.

The Wal-Mart stores in Orlando dedicate around 2,000 square feet to Disney products at a fraction of what they cost at WDW. If you plan to bring back souvenirs to friends and family, then the savings will be worth the trip.

Wal-Mart Supercenter Store #5420   ✆(407) 397-1125
3250 Vineland Road, Kissimmee, FL 34746.
Wal-Mart Supercenter Store #908   ✆(407) 354-5665
8101 South John Young Parkway, Orlando, FL 32819.
Wal-Mart Supercenter Store #1220   ✆(407) 290-6977
2500 South Kirkman Rd, Orlando, FL 32811.

In 2003, Florida passed an indoor no-smoking law. The law is based on whether food is sold or not, so many of the nightclubs allow indoor smoking; however, it is a policy decided by the proprietor.

What to Do in the Lake Buena Vista/Kissimmee Area

Contrary to popular opinion, the pronunciation of Kissimmee is "kuh-SEM-me" not "KISS-uh-me." The word is a modern spelling of the sixteenth- and seventeenth-century tribal words Atissimi, Jizimi, and Cacema. The town of Lake Buena Vista was named and is controlled by Walt Disney Company.

Celebration, Florida
Walt Disney dreamed of one day creating an actual town. Well, in 1996, Walt's dream became a reality when the town of Celebration, Florida, was officially founded. This town of yesterday has charm and family appeal. The community even has its own schools and

hospital with a focus on technology. While Celebration is a private residential community, tourists are invited to explore the unique shops and restaurants, and to take in the atmosphere of this storybook-like community.

TRAVEL TIP

If you're interested in possibly purchasing some real estate in Celebration and making this town your home, be sure to visit the Celebration Preview Center (open 10:00 A.M. to 6:00 P.M. daily). It's located in the heart of downtown Celebration. To reach Celebration Realty, call ✆(407) 566-4663.

Air Florida Charter, Inc.

Air Florida Charter ((407) 888-4114)—Aerial sightseeing flights that include a bird's-eye viewing of the WDW Resort, SeaWorld, and Universal Studios Florida are offered. All tours are narrated and provide excellent photo opportunities.

Arabian Nights

This family-oriented dinner show features a cast of over fifty of the world's most famous horses in an indoor, twenty-five-act equestrian show. In the preshow area there is a twenty-five-minute magic show. There is a choice of five entrées and all the beer and wine you can drink. The best seats are the center stadium seats. Prices are around $50 for adults and $30 for children. True lovers of horses and those with knowledge of the difficulty of riding horses will appreciate this show to the fullest. Reservations are required. (800) 553-6116.

⊕ HOT SPOT

If you're looking for a place to rejuvenate yourself in the Kissimme/ Lake Buena Vista area, try the Canyon Ranch Spa Club ✆(407) 586-4772, Wyndham Palace Spa ✆(407) 827-2727, or the Marriott World Center ✆(407) 238-8705.

Belz Factory Outlet World

This shopping center features 170 outlet shops in one location. Save up to 75 percent off of retail prices. (407) 354-0126.

Bob's Balloon Charters

Take a hot-air balloon ride! It's the ride of a lifetime. Everyone should ride at least once in their lives! The cost is $175 per adult and $90 per child (under 90 pounds). The price includes the flight, Champagne toast, all you can eat brunch, and a certificate. (407) 466-6380, *www.bobsballoons.com*.

Boggy Creek Airboat Rides

Explore some of Florida's wetlands with a professional guide, while traveling at speeds of up to 45 miles per hour. You might even see alligators in their natural habitat. (407) 344-9550, *www.bcairboats.com*.

Buena Vista Watersports

Buena Vista Watersports is a privately owned tropical recreational water sports facility located on Lake Bryan, in the Lake Buena Vista area of Orlando. You can rent jet skis, water skis, wakeboards, and boats. (407) 239-6939, *www.bvwatersports.com*.

Capone's Dinner and Show

Experience a speakeasy from the 1920s as you journey back in time to Al Capone's time. Check online for printable discount coupons. (800) 220-8428, *www.alcapones.com*.

Congo River Golf

This is a fun miniature golf course for the whole family. There's also an arcade and live alligator feeding. (407) 396-6900, *www .congoriver.com*.

Dolly Parton's Dixie Stampede Dinner and Show

Of all the dinner shows, Dolly serves the most food. You are even given a doggie bag! As you walk up to the building you hear Dolly singing over the many speakers as you look at horses in open-air stables. The preshow area is designed to replicate the old carriage houses from the past. There is plenty of seating and overflow seating in the balcony with its own bar. The preshow is an entertaining juggling act. You'll enjoy a delicious rotisserie chicken dinner as you watch this fun-filled musical extravaganza and relive the splendor of the Old South as you watch cowboys on horses perform stunts and see a stampede of buffalos. You'll also see ostrich races and during the Christmas show you'll see saddled camels for a special nativity scene show. A small ice-skating rink drops from the ceiling during the Christmas show as well. This $28 million production is colorful, action-packed, patriotic, and fun for the whole family. Shows are presented nightly at 6:30 P.M. and 8:30 P.M. Admission: $43.99 (adults) and $28.99 (kids). (866) 443-4943, (407) 238-4455, *www.dixiestampede.com*.

Gatorland

See live alligator wrestling, along with many alligators up close. This zoolike attraction also features all sorts of exotic snakes and a special kids' area/petting zoo. (407) 855-5496, (800) 393-JAWS, *www .gatorland.com*.

First Strike Bass

Captain Brent Sloan is an Orlando fishing guide with a lifetime of experience and knowledge gathered as a second generation central Florida fishing guide. He offers freshwater and saltwater fishing, alligator hunts, and airboat rides. (888) 937-6843, *www.firststrikebass.com*.

Green Meadows Petting Farm

Designed with kids in mind, this petting zoo allows young people to get close to the animals. Visitors can interact with ostriches, ducks, potbellied pigs, peacocks, sheep, cows, donkeys, an American bison, and other farm animals. (407) 846-0770, *www.greenmeadowsfarm .com.*

Horse World

These stables have hundreds of acres to explore with a good horse beneath you and blue sky above you. They offer lessons and three types of trail rides and are open seven days a week. (407) 847-4343, *www.horseworldstables.com.*

ICE!

Using 2 million pounds of ice, this special-ticket exhibit at the Gaylord Palms Hotel is transformed into a shimmering Santa's Toyland, an unforgettable Life-sized Nativity, a glistening Church in the Woods, and new this year, a walk-through train depot with a locomotive that you can climb aboard. ICE! also features a Victorian house complete with life-size horse-drawn carriage that you can sit in. Frozen within these unique sculptures are twinkling lights that create an ever-changing luminescence. This is real ice and is kept at 9 degrees. Parkas are provided; however, it's best to wear long pants and closed-toed shoes. Prices are $21 for adults and $10 for children ages four to twelve. There's also ice skating for an additional $5. (407) 586-0000, *www.gaylordhotels.com/gaylordpalms.*

Jungleland Zoo

See hundreds of rare and exotic animals (over 500 in all). Several live animal shows are also presented throughout the day. This outdoor zoo is located at 4580 West Irlo Bronson Highway in Kissimmee (192). (407) 396-1012, *www.thejunglelandzoo.com.*

Kissimmee Billie Swamp Safari

The Seminole Tribe of Florida invites guests to their reservation for a fun-filled day of air-boat rides, swamp buggy eco-tours, reptile and alligator exhibits, hiking tours, and other family-oriented activities. (800) 949-6101.

Medieval Times Dinner and Tournament

This dinner show transports guests back to the medieval era, a time when knights were revered as heroes. After parking, you walk through a medieval village full of interesting relics from Europe actually used during the Middle Ages. You then pick up your tickets and can upgrade for only $10 per person, which will get you the best seats in the house, banners to root for your knight, a DVD, and a souvenir program. If you decide not to upgrade, just know that the best seats in the house (center of the arena) are yellow and red, and black and white. The other color choices are red, yellow, green, and blue. You then trade your tickets for a crown of the same color. As you enter the preshow area there are many gift shops, bars, photo opportunities, and knightings performed by the king. At showtime all the Sirs and Ladies are called into the arena by color. Your seat is accompanied with pewter tableware and no utensils of any kind. Dinner includes all the beer you can drink, and a cocktail server walks around taking cocktail orders for an additional price. The show includes authentic jousting matches, hand-to-hand combat, and a rather lighthearted story line. Overall, the ambiance and experience is worth the price. Kids love this dinner show! There are many Medieval Times around America, but this was the very first one built. (407) 396-4888, *www .old-town.com*. Price (including dinner): $44.95 (adults) and $29.95 (kids). Gratuity is not included. The standard tip to the server is $5 per adult and $3 per child. (800) 229-8300, (407) 396-1518, *www .medievaltimes.com*.

Old Town

Old Town is built to look like an old-fashioned town full of charming shops, restaurants, and bars. There are many permanent carnival rides including a Ferris wheel and merry-go-round. Every night there is free live entertainment on the main stage. Thursdays through Saturdays locals drive their antique cars and motorcycles around Old Town, putting on a show (Thursday, motorcycles; Friday, muscle cars; and Saturday, antique cars). Security is low at Old Town, so if you choose to visit just pay extra attention by watching your children at all times. Admission is free, but it costs to ride the carnival rides.

Orange Blossom Balloons

Looking for a very special treat for yourself or someone else? This is something that you will remember for the rest of your life. Orange Blossom Balloons offers spectacular sunrise hot-air balloon rides. It includes a Champagne toast and a breakfast buffet after the ride. They are very family oriented and offer discount prices for families. Adults cost around $175 and children $90. Look on their Web site for discount coupons. (407) 239-7677, *www.orangeblossomballoons .com.*

Osceola Flea and Farmers Market

This large, covered flea market and farmers market is filled with aisles and aisles of everything imaginable. Admission and parking is free. (407) 846-2811, *www.fleaamerica.com/osceola.html.*

Skycoaster

Most people have heard of bungee jumping and skydiving; Skycoaster is a spinoff of these sports. It allows brave riders to soar through the air at speeds of up to 70 miles per hour while strapped into a harness that's held by a giant rubber band that swings freely from a tall tower. This attraction is located in nearby Kissimmee, Florida. Prices start at $37 per flight. Visit the Web site for a $5-off discount coupon. (407) 397-2509, *www.adventuresinflorida.net/Skycoaster.htm.*

Wallaby Ranch

Wallaby Ranch is the first and largest aerotow hang-gliding flight park in the world. Experience the thrill of hang-gliding from 2,000 feet with the world's most experienced instructor with more than 30,000 incident-free tandem flights under his belt. It is open daily, and no experience is necessary. Tent and RV camping as well as a few rustic cabins are offered. There is also a bathhouse with indoor and outdoor showers, game room, satellite TV, swimming pool, hot tub, playground, tree house, trampoline, climbing wall, hiking and bike trails, and wireless Internet access. 1-800-WALLABY *www .wallaby.com.*

Warbird Adventures

Wow! Looking for adventure? Take in a smooth sightseeing flight or a thrilling aerobatic adventure in military aircraft. It's the real thing folks, and it's worth every penny! (407) 870-7366, *www .warbirdadventures.com.*

Water Mania

Fans of water parks will enjoy the various fun-filled water slides and water-based attractions at this park. (407) 396-2626, *www .watermania-florida.com.*

What to Do in the SeaWorld/Universal/ International Drive Area

There is so much to see and do in this area of Orlando. Currently, the International Drive (I-Drive) area is host to five parks, over 100 hotels, 200-plus restaurants, three entertainment complexes with three stadium-style movie cinemas, over 500 stores, and the home of the second-largest convention center, which will soon be the number one largest convention center. Future plans include adding more glitz to make this a strip like the one found in Las Vegas. I-Drive also has an I-Ride trolley service *www.iridetrolley.com* that operates from 8:00 A.M. to 10:30 P.M. You can buy a one-day to a fourteen-day pass ranging between $3 to $16 per person. Look on the Internet for more information about International Drive at *www.international driveorlando.com.*

Bass Pro Shops Outdoor World

The World's Leading Supplier of Premium Outdoor Gear, this fishing and hunting superstore is located at the Festival Bay Mall. (407) 563-5200, *www.basspro.com.*

Café Tu Tu Tango

This café offers a dining experience unlike any other. The décor makes you feel like you are in an artist's loft. Lots of spontaneous entertainment includes dancers, artists, and a restaurant full of artwork. The starving artist menu is filled with bite-sized appetizers from around the world. It's all about sharing here. (407) 248-2222, *www .cafetututango.com.*

Dottie's Orlando Comedy Theater

Dottie spent eighteen years as a cruise ship director and now brings an early comedy show suitable for families and a late-night comedy show suitable for adults. Popcorn, sandwiches, pizza, soft drinks, and beer and wine are available. There is not table service in the theater; however, you can bring your purchased snacks in with you. (407) 226-3680, *www.dottiesorlando.com.*

⊕ HOT SPOT

Are you looking for a place to get married or renew your vows? Here are the most popular places in the International Drive area: Discovery Cove (407) 370-1280, Portofino Bay Hotel ✆(407) 503-1000, Titanic—The Experience ✆(407) 248-1166, and the DoubleTree Castle Hotel ✆(407) 345-1511.

Festival Bay Mall

This unique shopping area on International Drive features over sixty specialty stores, eleven dining destinations, and exciting entertainment venues. This is where you'll find Bass Pro Shops, Ron Jon

Surfpark, Sheplers Western Wear, indoor glow-in-the-dark miniature golf, a skate park, and the Cinemark theater. (407) 351-7718, *www .shopfestivalbaymall.com.*

Florida Mall

Features more than 250 specialty stores and connected to an Adam's Mark Hotel. (407) 851-6255, *www.shopsimon.com.*

Hard Rock Café

This is the largest Hard Rock Café in the world. It's shaped like a guitar! It's located at Universal Studios Orlando in the CityWalk entertainment complex. (407) 351-ROCK, *www.hardrock.com.*

Holy Land Experience

Go 2,000 years back in time to the biblical world. This museum is filled with exhibits, venues, and entertainment. It is across I-4 from the Millenia Mall at Conroy Exit 78. (407) 367-2065, *www.holylandex perience.com.*

⊕ HOT SPOT

Looking to pamper yourself around the International Drive area? You have a choice of many spas: The L'Espirit Day Spa at the Sheraton World ✆(407) 355-0505, the Innervision Salon and Spa at the Renaissance Orlando Resort at SeaWorld ✆(407) 248-7428, the Mandara Spa at the Portofino Bay Hotel ✆(407) 503-1000, Body & Sol Spa at the Rosen Centre Hotel ✆(407) 996-9840, The Ritz-Carlton Spa ✆(407) 206-2400, and Spa Sensations ✆(407) 345-0343.

Magical Midway

Filled with go-carts, bumper cars, bumper boats, thrill rides, and classic midway rides, they also have the only StarFlyer ride of its kind in the nation. The StarFlyer is a chair that reaches heights of over 230 feet in the air at 54 mph. (407) 370-5353, *www.magicalmidway.com.*

Makahiki Luau at SeaWorld

SeaWorld's Seafire Inn celebrates with a Polynesian festival filled with exotic tastes and entertainment. 1-800-327-2424.

McDonald's

Okay, you're probably wondering why McDonald's is in this book. Well, this isn't just any old McDonald's. This is the World's Largest McDonald's! This huge three-story building has an elevator, over fifty arcade games, a puppet show, gift shop, 25,000 feet of twisty tubes to play in, a 60-foot slide, games, and prizes. Just take the Sand Lake/International Drive Exit off I-4 (75A) and you can't miss it!

⊕ HOT SPOT

Another extraordinary two-story McDonald's is just a half a mile west of the World's Largest McDonald's. It offers unique cuisine from gourmet sandwiches to pasta dishes, granite countertops, artwork, and silver condiment containers. Simply drive under I-4 a half a mile from the World's Largest McDonald's and it's on your left.

Mall at Millenia

This is the newest and most prestigious indoor mall located in between downtown Orlando and International Drive. It features state-of-the-art technology with a focus on airy natural surroundings. Anchor stores are Bloomingdales, Macy's, and Neiman Marcus. The mall is open Monday through Saturday, between 10:00 A.M. and 9:30 P.M., and on Sundays, between 11:00 A.M. and 7:00 P.M. It's located right off of Exit 78 of I-4 at 4200 Conroy Road in Orlando. (407) 363-3555, *www.mallatmillenia.com.*

Peabody Ducks

One of the things that the Peabody hotel is known for is its traditional and world-famous duck march on the red carpet. The duck march can be seen at 11:00 A.M. and 5:00 P.M. daily. Between 11:00 A.M. and 5:00 P.M. the ducks splash around in a marble fountain, then at 5:00 P.M. they march to their penthouse via the elevator. (407) 352-4000, *www.peabodyorlando.com.*

Pirate's Dinner Adventure

Pirate's Dinner Adventure dinner show puts you and your family right in the middle of all of the swashbuckling action. If you are attending with children, the absolute best way to experience the Pirate's Dinner Adventure is to purchase the $20 upgrade for each person in your group. With the prices being $55 per adult and $34 per child (ages three to eleven), the $20 upgrade can seem like the cost of a WDW park admission, but you and your group will have front-row seats. Your child or children will have guaranteed participation in the show and all will be given extra items like a pirate hat, flags, beads, and so much more. There is also a $10 upgrade that gives the possibility of show participation, but does not guarantee it. This upgrade gets you a seat in the second to third rows and headbands. As you enter the pre-show area there are complimentary appetizer stations all around the room. There are many gift shops, face–painting stations, three bars, and a fortune-telling gypsy. If you decide not to purchase the upgrade, the best color tickets/seats to buy are orange or red; however, if you have children with you, you will still hear them complain and ask why do those kids "down there" (front row) have hats and get to be in the show? Reservations are recommended. (407) 248-0590, *www.pirates dinneradventure.com.*

Pointe Orlando

Pointe Orlando features an open-air unique mix of shops, eateries, and entertainment venues with a tropical flair. They offer a "Food and Flick" ticket that allows patrons to enjoy dinner at select restaurants and enjoy a movie at Muvico Pointe 21 Theaters all for $20. Visit them online to obtain a discount booklet. (407) 248-2838, *www.pointeo rlandofl.com.*

Putting Edge

Wow! This miniature golf course is glow-in-the-dark! Great fun for all ages. (407) 248-0700, *www.putting-edge.com.*

Race Rock

A full-service motor sports–themed restaurant packed with rare racing memorabilia from all forms of motor sports! Race Rock is a sight and sound experience with over thirty video monitors and interactive simulators depicting the world of racing while you dine on monster-size portions of fantastic food. You never know what racing legend might be making a pit stop at Race Rock! (407) 248-9876, *www .racerock.com.*

Ripley's Believe It or Not! Museum

See, hear, and experience a museum full of the strange, wacky, and totally outrageous. Make sure that you use the restroom before entering the maze or you will have to return to the beginning. Admission: $15.95 (adults) and $10.95 (kids). (407) 363-4418, *www.ripleysor lando.com.*

Ron Jon Surfpark

This is the first Surfpark in the world. There's a Pro Surf Pool, a Training Pool, and a Bodyboarding Pool. It also has many food, drink, shopping, and entertainment venues in a one-of-a-kind setting. Look for it at the Festival Bay Mall on International Drive. *www.ronjonsurf park.com.*

Sheplers Western Wear

This store has the largest selection of Western wear in the world. This also happens to be the only Sheplers in the state of Florida. (407) 563-1063, *www.sheplers.com.*

⊕ HOT SPOT

Are you a roller coaster fanatic? The top roller coasters in the greater Orlando area are: The Hulk and Dueling Dragons Fire and Ice (Universal's Island's of Adventure); Rock 'n' Roller Coaster (Disney-MGM Studios); Space Mountain and Big Thunder Mountain Railroad (Magic Kingdom); Kumba, Montu, and SheiKra (Busch Gardens); and Kraken (SeaWorld).

Skull Kingdom

This "haunted family attraction" is a fun-filled haunted mansion, complete with live actors and special effects. A magic dinner show is presented nightly for an additional admission fee. They offer day and night shows as well. The night show offers "The Chamber of Magic Show" with complimentary pizza, soda, beer, and wine. The day show is $9 per person and the night magic dinner show is $20 per adult and $16 for children seven and under. (407) 354-1564, *www.skullkingdom.com.*

Skyventure

This is an awesome skydiving wind tunnel that allows nonexperienced and experienced skydivers alike to experience the thrill of skydiving without jumping out of a plane. Instead, riders fly on a 120-mile-per-hour column of air. It is an experience that you will never forget! Appropriate for ages three and up. The cost is around $30 per person. The extra $20 purchase of a DVD of you in flight is worth the price! (407) 903-1150, (800) SKY-FUN1, *www.skyventure.com.*

Sleuth's Mystery Dinner Shows

You'll be kept on the edge of your seat as you enjoy a delicious dinner and dessert with unlimited beer, wine, and soft drinks. All shows are two to two and a half hours of scripted mystery, improvisation, and audience participation. Watch for anything suspicious, interrogate the suspects, and help solve the crime! (407) 363-1985, *www.sleuths.com.*

Titanic: Ship of Dreams

This museum is designed primarily for teens and adults. Guests are given real Titanic passenger names and actors tour you through a replica of the ship. At the end you find out if you've survived or not. The exhibit features over 200 priceless artifacts from the Titanic as well as multimedia documentaries and interactive exhibits that retell the story of this ill-fated cruise ship. Highly recommended for Titanic lovers. (407) 248-1166 ext: 3103, *www.titanicshipofdreams.com.*

Wet 'n Wild

This water park features all sorts of water slides, pools, and fun-filled activities for the entire family. Filled with thrill rides, multiperson rides, kids rides, and relaxing water rides. Don't miss the Black Hole, Disco H2o, the Storm, or Bomb Bay. Wet 'n Wild also offers a huge video arcade. In the summer, this water park stays open until midnight and provides a band. Prices are around $30 per child and $35 per adult. Wet 'n Wild is in association with Universal Studios, so if you plan to visit Universal ask about special tickets that may include Wet 'n Wild and Universal Studios to save the most money. (407) 351-1800, *www.wetnwild.com.*

WonderWorks

This high-tech arcade and entertainment center offers a variety of cutting-edge arcade games, virtual reality attractions, and motion-simulator rides. Also featured is what WonderWorks calls the world's largest Laser Tag Arena and a virtual reality attraction that allows guests to "create" their own virtual roller coaster and then ride it. Look for the upside-down building on International Drive and you've found it! A magic dinner show is presented nightly (for an additional admission fee). (407) 351-8800, *www.wonderworksonline.com.*

What to Do in the Downtown Orlando Area

Downtown Orlando has an exciting nightlife with many bars, restaurants, and nightclubs. The main route through downtown is Orange Street, which is known for its nightlife and its many skyscrapers. Downtown Orlando is also home to the Amway Arena, which hosts the Orlando Magic NBA team.

Antique Row

Antique Row and Ivanhoe Row on North Orange Avenue (stretching from Colonial Dr./Hwy. 50 to Lake Ivanhoe) in downtown Orlando is filled with many shops showcasing an interesting assortment of the old, the new, and the unusual.

Lake Eola Park

Lake Eola is the most popular place downtown. There's a lake with a sidewalk that circles it, a beautiful fountain that lights up at night, large swan paddle boats, romantic Gondola cruises, a Chinese gazebo, an amphitheater for plays and concerts, a state-of-the-art playground, a snack bar and other lakeside dining, beautiful landscaping, swans, ducks, birds, and squirrels. They have a yearly calendar of events, weekly farmer's market, free movie nights, and more. It's located at Rosalind Ave and Washington St. Parking is metered all around the lake. (407) 246-2827, *www.cityoforlando.net.*

Orlando Improv

The new Orlando Improv is the premier comedy nightclub and café. Located on Orlando's historic Church Street, the Improv is surrounded by excitement, culture, and a great atmosphere. This comedy theater offers dinner during the show if you desire. You can choose from salmon, pasta, chicken, or steak. The Improv raises money for local children's charities; however the shows are meant for adults. (352) 281-8000, *www.orlandoimprov.com.*

Orlando Science Center

If you're looking for an educational and fun indoor activity to experience with your kids, visit Orlando's Science Center, which offers many fully interactive exhibits, plus a planetarium and laser shows. (407) 514-2000, (888) OSC-4FUN, *www.osc.org*.

SAK Comedy Lab

SAK Comedy Lab is the place to go if you like live improv comedy. The theater has 200 seats and an improv comedy theater in downtown Orlando. (407) 648-0001, *www.sak.com*.

The Charles Hosmer Morse Museum of American Art

This museum houses the world's most comprehensive collection of the works of Louis Comfort Tiffany (1848–1933), including Tiffany jewelry, pottery, paintings, art glass, leaded-glass windows, lamps, and the chapel interior he designed for the 1893 World's Columbian Exposition in Chicago. The Museum's holdings include a major collection of American art pottery and representative collections of late nineteenth- and early-twentieth-century-American paintings, graphics, and decorative arts. (407) 645-5311, *www.morsemuseum.org*.

The Mennello Museum of American Art

This museum exhibits the most complete collection of works by American folk artist Earl Cunningham. (407) 246-4278, *www .mennellomuseum.org*.

The Orlando Museum of Art

One of the South's best museums, it houses a permanent home for collections of American art from the eighteenth, nineteenth, and twentieth centuries, including works by world-renowned artist Georgia O'Keefe and photographer Ansel Adams. The museum also holds an impressive collection of Art of the Ancient Americas, including artifacts from the Aztecs and many other cultures, as well as an extensive collection of ceremonial and utilitarian African art. (407) 896-4231, *www.omart.org*.

Winter Park

Winter park is an upscale artsy community. It was once the winter playground for the northern snowbirds. It's nestled around three beautiful lakes connected by canals. There are fine old homes, museums, parks, and gardens. Park Avenue, the heart of the city, boasts galleries, unique boutiques, and fine restaurants. The annual sidewalk art festival in March is not to missed. *www.ci.winter-park.fl.us*.

What to Do in the Greater Orlando Area

The greater Orlando area covers anything outside of Orlando within a 100-mile radius.

Big Tree

This park is home to a 3,500-year-old tree named "The Senator." The tree stands 118 feet tall with a girth of 425 inches and its crown spread is 57 feet. The 11-acre park is located on General Hutchinson Parkway between U.S. 17-92 and State Road 427 north of Longwood. Picnic tables and restroom facilities are available in the front of the park and it is open from 8:00 A.M. to sunset daily. (407) 788-0405.

Blue Spring State Park

Blue Springs State Park is a picturesque getaway along the Saint Johns River near Orange City in central Florida. Temperatures in the spring remain a constant 72 degrees, creating a safe haven for the manatee during the cooler months and a cooling swim for humans during the long hot days of summer. Air-conditioned cabins or primitive campsites are available. Simply take Exit 114 off Interstate 4 and follow the signs. Go south on 17-92 to Orange City, about 2.5 miles. Make a right onto West French Avenue. (386) 917-0724, *www .floridastateparks.org/bluespring*.

Busch Gardens

Located in Tampa, Florida (about a sixty-minute drive from the WDW Resort), this is an entirely different theme park experience that features some of the best thrill rides you'll find anywhere on the East Coast. Busch Gardens also features a world-famous wildlife animal park and a water park. (888) 800-5447, *www.buschgardens.com*.

Cassadaga

Known as "The Psychic Center of the World," Cassadaga continues today as the premiere psychic community and is home to some of America's finest psychics. To find this little sleepy-looking town take Exit 114 off of I-4. At the first traffic light turn left, at the second traffic light go straight, and at the third traffic light turn right onto Dr. Martin Luther King Beltway. Go to Cassadaga Road, turn right, and it's approximately 1.5 miles on the left. *www.cassadaga.com*.

Cypress Gardens

Cypress Gardens opened in 1936 as a botanical garden. It then became popular because of its water-ski shows. When Disney opened in 1971 business declined. Today it is alive and well, offering rides and concerts. It's located between Orlando and Tampa. Simply take Exit 55 (U.S. Hwy 27 south) off I-4, then continue south on U.S. Hwy. 27. Turn right off U.S. Highway 27 at State Road 540/Cypress Gardens Boulevard. The park is four miles on the left. (863) 324-2111, *www .cypressgardens.com*.

Daytona International Speedway

Home of the Daytona 500! Call or check online for events at this popular speedway. (386) 253-7223, *www.daytonainternationalspeed way.com*.

Daytona USA

This is the official and ultimate motor sports attraction of NAS-CAR located in Daytona Beach, Florida. It offers Richard Petty driving experiences, shotgun lap experiences, IMAX theater experiences, motion simulator rides, and more. (386) 947-6800, *www.daytonausa .com.*

TRAVEL TIP

Want to spend the day at a Florida beach? The closest beaches are located on the east coast: Cocoa Beach, New Smyrna Beach, and Daytona Beach. Cocoa and New Smyrna are only forty-five minutes away once you're on the Beeline (528) off I-4. Have some change with you to pay tolls. To reach Daytona Beach in about an hour and a half, simply head east on I-4. The closest beach on the west coast (gulf side) is Clearwater Beach. Simply head west on I-4 to Tampa and follow the signs. It will take two hours, but the white sand and blue water is worth it.

Fantasy of Flight

Located midway between Tampa and Orlando in Polk City, Florida, Fantasy of Flight is an aviation-themed attraction that takes visitors back to Early Flight, World War I, World War II, and beyond. They also offer planes and hot-air balloon rides. (863) 984-3500, *www .fantasyofflight.com.*

⊕ HOT SPOT

In addition to the lovely beaches and the Kennedy Space Center, some of the awesome family-oriented activities and attractions available within the Space Coast area include: Cocoa Beach Pier ✆(3210783-7549), Ron Jon Surf Shop ✆(321-799-8888), the Brevard Zoo ✆(321-254-WILD), the Air Force Space and Missile Museum ✆(321-499-4444), The U.S. Space Camp Florida (S800-63-SPACE), the U.S. Astronaut Hall of Fame ✆(321-269-6100), and Island Boat Rides ✆(321-544-3490).

Historic Bok Santuary Gardens, Belltower, and Estate

These gardens located in Lakes Wales, Florida, were created in 1921 by Pulitzer Prize–winning author, Edward W. Bok. The centerpiece is a singing bell tower that stands 205 feet. The estate includes a koi pond, carillon library, 100-year-old trees and vegetation, a twenty-room Mediterranean mansion, a nature trail, café, gift shop, and more. Adult prices are $10 and children five to twelve are $3. (863) 676-1408, *www.boksanctuary.org.*

Kennedy Space Center

The Kennedy Space Center offers about a day's worth of activities, tours, and fun for all ages. There's also an IMAX theater showing the 3-D movie *Space Station*, which takes viewers on a visually stunning journey to the space station located 220 miles above Earth.

The Kennedy Space Center is very different from your typical museum, and it offers an experience that's far different from what you'd get at nearby theme parks. You'll find many hands-on exhibits that are designed to be inspirational, educational, and fun at the same time. There's also a Spaceflight Simulator that guests can experience firsthand, and special programs like the Astronaut Training Experience. Another special treat offered here is the Lunch with an Astronaut program. For an additional fee, kids and teens can experience a once-in-a-lifetime chance to have a three-course lunch with a real-life astronaut. Guests have the opportunity to ask questions and have their photo taken with the astronaut. It costs $29.95 (adults) and $19.95 (kids). Reservations are required.

For additional information about Kennedy Space Center, call (321) 499-4444 or visit *www.kennedyspacecenter.com.* The visitor's center is open daily from 9:00 A.M. until dusk. Admission prices vary, based on the tours, exhibits, live shows, and activities you'd like to experience. The Maximum Access Admission Ticket is priced at $33 (adults) and $23 (kids) and includes the Kennedy Space Center Tour, IMAX films, admission to the Astronaut Hall of Fame, and all attractions and exhibits.

TRAVEL TIP

Looking for some out-of-this-world gifts and souvenirs? Be sure to visit the Space Shop at Kennedy Space Center. It's the largest retail store in the world that's devoted to space-themed merchandise, such as space ice cream. You can also order merchandise by phone at ✆(800) 621-9826.

Silver Springs

No matter what your age, there are plenty of rides and attractions at Silver Springs that will make you laugh, fill you with wonder, and provide a glimpse into what life was like here more than 10,000 years ago. Call or check online to see what live country entertainment will be offered. Many artists such as Willy Nelson, Trisha Yearwood, Kenny Rogers, and more frequent often. It is located just east of Ocala, Florida, and northwest of Orlando on S.R. 40. Take Exit 352 east off I-75 or Exit 268 west off I-95. (352) 236-2121, *www.silversprings.com.*

The Jesus Film Project

The Jesus film has been shown in every country of the world and translated into over 900 languages. It's a two-hour docudrama about the life of Christ. There are five daily tours. It is located only about fifteen minutes from the Orlando International Airport. (407) 826-2300, *www.jesusfilm.org.*

Weeki Wachee Springs

Weeki Wachee Springs—the City of Live Mermaids—is more than just mermaids; it's a truly original piece of Florida's rich heritage. Weeki Wachee's heyday began in 1959, when the spring was purchased by the American Broadcasting Company (ABC) and was heavily promoted. In the 1960s, girls came from as far away as Tokyo to try out for the privilege of becoming an underwater performing mermaid. The mermaids perform with Florida's wildlife as a variety of fish, turtles, manatees, and an occasional alligator frequent the spring and the show! Weeki Wachee Springs has mermaid camps, lifeguard camps, scuba diving, boat rides, an underwater theater, and an adjoining water park. It's located in Weeki Wachee, Florida, which is about fort-five minutes north of Tampa. (407) 596-2062, *www.weekiwachee.com.*

Wekiwa Springs State Park

Wekiwa Springs offers a glimpse of what Florida looked like when the first Indian settlers arrived 12,000 years ago. The springs discharge 43 million gallons of fresh water a day into a lagoon that has a constant year-round temperature of 72 degrees. The park is open daily from 8:00 A.M. to sundown. (407) 884-2008, *www.floridastateparks.org.*

Orlando-Area Category Breakdown

Let's face it; everyone has his or her own interests, so this next section makes it easy for you to organize your visit. Do you love animals or anything nature related? Then look under that category and you'll find everything around Orlando that caters to this. Love to be in the sky or a roller coaster fanatic? It's all here and more!

Animals and Nature
- Animal Kingdom (WDW)
- Big Tree Park
- Blue Spring State Park
- Boggy Creek Airboat and Swamp Buggy Rides
- Busch Gardens
- Discovery Cove
- Dolly Parton's Dixie Stampede Dinner and Show
- First Strike Bass
- Gatorland
- Green Meadows Petting Farm
- Historic Bok Santuary Gardens, Belltower, and Estate
- Jungleland Zoo
- Kissimmee Billie Swamp Safari
- Lake Eola
- Medieval Times Dinner and Tournament
- Peabody Ducks
- Seaworld
- The Living Seas (Epcot at WDW)
- Wekiwa Springs State Park

Arcades and Games
- DisneyQuest
- Wonderworks

Art
- Café Tu Tu Tango

- The Charles Hosmer Morse Museum of American Art
- The Mennello Museum of American Art
- The Orlando Museum of Art

Comedy

- Dottie's Orlando Comedy Theater
- Orlando Improv
- SAK Comedy Lab

Dinner Shows

- Arabian Nights
- Capone's Dinner and Show
- Dolly Parton's Dixie Stampede Dinner and Show
- Hoop-Dee-Doo Musical Revue (Fort Wilderness Campground at WDW)
- House of Blues Gospel Brunch (Downtown Disney)
- Makahiki Luau Dinner and Show (Seaworld)
- Medieval Times Dinner and Tournament
- Mickey's Backyard BBQ (Fort Wilderness Campground at WDW)
- Murder Mystery Watch (Grosvenor Resort)
- Orlando Improv
- Pirate's Dinner Adventure
- Sleuth's Mystery Dinner Show
- Spirit of Aloha Dinner Show (Polynesian Resort at WDW)
- The Chamber of Magic Show (at Skull Kingdom Haunted Attraction)
- The Outta Control Magic Show at Wonderworks
- Wantilan Luau (Royal Pacific Resort at Universal)

Down Home Country

- Bass Pro Shops
- Cracker Barrel Old Country Store and Restaurant
- Dolly Parton's Dixie Stampede Dinner and Show
- Hoop-Dee-Doo Musical Revue (Fort Wilderness Campground at WDW)
- Horse World Riding Stables
- Mickey's Backyard BBQ (Fort Wilderness Campground at WDW)
- Sheplers Western Wear
- Silver Springs

Flight

- Air Florida Charter
- Bob's Balloons
- Fantasy of Flight
- Orange Blossom Balloons
- Slingshot (Old Town)
- Sky Venture
- StarFlyer (Magical Midway)
- Wallaby Ranch Hang Gliding Flight Park
- Warbird Adventures

Ice

- Blizzard Beach
- ICE! (Gaylord Palms Resort)
- Dolly Parton's Dixie Stampede Dinner Christmas Show
- Titanic Ship of Dreams

Water

- Adventure Island (Busch Gardens)
- Blizzard Beach
- Boggy Creek Airboat and Swamp Buggy Rides
- Buena Vista Watersports

- First Strike Bass Airboat Rides
- Lake Eola
- Ron Jon Surfpark
- Typoon Lagoon (WDW)
- Water Mania
- Wet 'n Wild

Roller Coasters
- Big Thunder Mountain (Magic Kingdom)
- Dueling Dragons (Islands of Adventure at Universal)
- Gwazi (Busch Gardens)
- Kraken (Seaworld)
- Kumba (Busch Gardens)
- Rock 'n' Roller Coaster (Disney's MGM)
- Sheikra (Busch Gardens)
- Space Mountain (Magic Kingdom)
- The Hulk (Islands of Adventure at Universal)

Science
- Orlando Science Center
- Kennedy Space Center

Spiritual
- Cassadaga Spiritual Community
- The Holy Land Experience
- The Jesus Film Projects

Sports
- Race Rock (I-Drive)
- Daytona USA
- Tom Petty Driving Experience (WDW)
- Old Town
- ESPN (Boardwalk Resort at WDW)
- NBA Café (City Walk at Universal)
- Wide World of Sports (WDW)

- NASCAR Café (City Walk at Universal)
- First Strike Bass
- Putting Edge Glow-in-the-Dark Mini Golf (I-Drive)
- Ron Jon Surfpark
- TGI Friday's Front Row Sports Grill (I-Drive)

CHAPTER 20

Planning Your Itinerary

IT'S A WISE IDEA to do a bit of preplanning in order to help ensure you make the most of your vacation and stay within your allocated budget. After all, unless you'll be staying in Orlando for a long period of time, it's impossible to see and do everything. Thus, you need to make decisions about how you'll spend your time.

Plan Accordingly

As you plan your itinerary, make sure to obtain input from everyone you'll be traveling with. Also, leave plenty of flexibility in each day's schedule. Allow ample time to explore and enjoy experiences as they happen, without worrying too much about staying on a timetable and getting to the next preplanned activity. In most cases, creating an itinerary with plans down to the hour or minute might make you more organized, but it will also create a tremendous level of stress during your vacation as you run around trying to stick to your schedule. Be sure to leave time in your schedule for travel between destinations, meals, and rest/relaxation.

For the purposes of preplanning your itinerary and visiting theme parks, it's best to divide your day into three chunks of time: morning, afternoon, and evening/nighttime. Use the following Travel Itinerary worksheets to help preplan your itinerary, keeping in mind that you'll most likely be altering this itinerary once you arrive in Orlando and start actually experiencing your vacation. Use these worksheets to guide you in scheduling the things you believe you (and your family) will most enjoy based on the time you have available.

Airline Information

Departing date:

Departing time:

Airline:

Flight number(s)/connecting cities:

Departing airport:

Arriving airport:

Arrival time:

Seating assignment(s):

Returning date (to go home):

Departing time:

Airline:

Flight number(s)/connecting cities:

Departing airport:

Arrival time (to home city):

Seating assignment(s):

Travel agency used:

Travel agent/airline phone number(s):

Parking lot name/number at airport:

Location/aisle:

Airport Ground Transportation Information

Getting to the airport:

Taxi/limo service name:
Phone number:
Reservation number:
Pickup date/time:
Pickup location:

Getting home from the airport:

Taxi/limo service name:
Phone number:
Reservation number:
Pickup date/time:
Pickup location:

Rental Car Information

Rental car company:
Confirmation number:
Daily rate:
Pickup location:
Rental car company phone number:
Type of car reserved:

Accommodation Information

Hotel/resort name:
Phone number:
Reservation number:
Check-in date:

Check-out date:

Type of accommodations reserved:

Itinerary Worksheets

DAY 1

Date:

Day of week:

Morning Activities

Time	Location	Activity	Description

Breakfast restaurant:

Reservation time:

Restaurant phone number:

Afternoon Activities

Time	Location	Activity	Description

Lunch restaurant:

Reservation time:

Restaurant phone number:

Evening/Nighttime Activities

Time	Location	Activity	Description

Dinner restaurant:

Reservation time:

Restaurant phone number:

Notes

_____

_____

_____

_____

_____

_____

_____

DAY 2
Date:
Day of week:

Morning Activities

Time	Location	Activity	Description

Breakfast restaurant:
Reservation time:
Restaurant phone number:

Afternoon Activities

Time	Location	Activity	Description

Lunch restaurant:

Reservation time:

Restaurant phone number:

Evening/Nighttime Activities

Time	Location	Activity	Description

Dinner restaurant:

Reservation time:

Restaurant phone number:

Notes

_____

_____

_____

_____

_____

_____

_____

_____

_____

_____

_____

DAY 3
Date:
Day of week:

Morning Activities

Time	Location	Activity	Description

Breakfast restaurant:
Reservation time:
Restaurant phone number:

Afternoon Activities

Time	Location	Activity	Description

Lunch restaurant:

Reservation time:

Restaurant phone number:

Evening/Nighttime Activities

Time	Location	Activity	Description

Dinner restaurant:

Reservation time:

Restaurant phone number:

Notes

_____

_____

_____

_____

_____

_____

_____

_____

_____

_____

Important Phone Numbers

THE FOLLOWING ARE MANY of the phone numbers listed within this book that will help you learn more about the various theme parks and other activities within the Greater Orlando area.

AAA Travel Department: ☎(800) 222-7448

AARP: ☎(800) 424-3410

AeroMexico: ☎(800) 237-6639

Air Canada: ☎(800) 247-2262

Air Florida Charter, Inc.: ☎(407) 888-4114

Air Force Space and Missile Museum: ☎(321) 499-4444

AirJamaica: ☎(800) 523-5585

AirTran Airways: ☎(800) AIR-TRAN

AirTransat:☎(877) 872-6728

Alamo Car Rental: ☎(800) 327-9633

Alaska Airlines: ☎(800) 252-7522

American Airlines: ☎(800) 433-7300

American Eagle: ☎(800) 422-7300

American Express Travel: ☎(800) 346-3607

AmericaWest Airlines: ☎(800) 235-9292

Amtrak: ☎(800) USA-RAIL

ANA Airlines: ☎(800) 235-9262

Arabian Nights: ☎(800) 553-6116

ATA Airlines: ☎(800) 225-2995

Avis Car Rental: ☎(800) 831-2847

Bahamasair: ☎(800) 222-4262

Bass Pro Shops Outdoor World: ☎(407) 563-5200

Belz Factory Outlet World: ☎(407) 354-0126

Big Tree: ☎(407) 788-0405

Blue Spring State Park: ☎(386) 917-0724

Bob's Balloons: ☎(407) 466-6380

Boggy Creek Airboat Rides: ☎(407) 344-9550

Brevard Zoo: ☎(321) 254-WILD

British Airways: ☎(800) AIR-WAYS

Buena Vista Watersports: ☎(407) 239-6939

Budget Car Rental: ☎(800) 527-0700

Busch Gardens: (888) 800-5447

Café Tu Tu Tango: ☎(407) 248-2222

Cap'N Jack's Marina: ☎(407) 828-2204

Capone's Dinner and Show: ☎(800) 220-8428

Caribe Royale Resort Suites and Villas: ☎(800) 823-8300

Celebration Health Hospital: ☎(407) 303-4000

Celebration Hotel: ☎(888) 499-3800

Celebration Realty: ☎(407) 566-4663

Centra Care (Walk-In Medical Facility): ☎(407) 239-7777

Central Reservation Service: ☎(800) 548-3311

Champion Air: ☎(800) 225-5658

Check-In Reservation Services: ☎(800) 237-1033

Cirque du Soleil Show and Ticket Info: ☎(407) 939-7600

CityWalk Special Event Hotline: ☎(407) 224-5500

Cocoa Beach Pier: ☎(321) 783-7549

Congo River Golf: ☎(407) 396-6900

ConJet Airlines: ☎(800) 809-7777

Continental Airlines: ☎(800) 523-3273

Copa Airlines: ☎(800) 359-2672

Cypress Gardens: ☎(863) 324-2111

Daytona International Speedway: ☎(386) 253-7223

Daytona USA: ☎(386) 947-6800

Delta Airlines/Delta Express: ☎(800) 221-1212

Destinations Travel Service: ☎(407) 859-3501

Dottie's Orlando Comedy Theater: ☎(407) 226-3680

Discovery Cove (SeaWorld): ☎(800) 4-ADVENTURE

Disney Catalog (Mail Order): ☎(800) 237-5751

Disney Credit Card: ☎(877) 252-6576

Disney Cruise Lines: ☎(888) DCL-2500

Disney Restaurant Advance "Priority Seating" Reservations: ☎(800) WDW-DINE

Disney Souvenir Merchandise: ☎(407) 363-6200

Disney Special Activities / VIP Tours: ☎(407) 560-4033

Disney Theme Park Operating Hours: ☎(407) 824-4321

Disney Tour Information: ☎(407) 939-8687

Disney World Reservations and Information: ☎(407) W-DISNEY

Disney's All-Star Movies Resort: ☎(407) 939-7000

Disney's All-Star Music Resort: ☎(407) 939-6000

Disney's All-Star Sports Resort: ☎(407) 939-5000

Disney's Animal Kingdom Lodge: ☎(407) 934-7639

Disney's Beach Club Resort: ☎(407) 934-8000

Disney's BoardWalk Information: ☎(407) 939-5100

Disney's BoardWalk Resort: ☎(407) 939-5100

Disney's BoardWalk Villas: ☎(407) 939-6200

Disney's Caribbean Beach Resort: ☎(407) 934-3400

Disney's Contemporary Resort: ☎(407) 824-1000

Disney's Coronado Springs Resort: ☎(407) 939-1000

Disney's Fort Wilderness Resort & Campground: ☎(407) 824-2900

Disney's Grand Floridian Resort and Spa: ☎(407) 824-3000

Disney's Kids' Nite Out (Baby-sitting): ☎(407) 828-0920

Disney's Old Key West Resort: ☎(407) 827-7700

Disney's Polynesian Resort: ☎(407) 824-2000

Disney's Pop Culture Resort ☎(407) W-DISNEY

Disney's Port Orleans Resort—French Quarter Resort: ☎(407) 934-5000

Disney's Port Orleans Riverside Resort: ☎(407) 934-6000

Disney's Racquet Club (Tennis): ☎(407) 824-3578

Disney's Saratoga Springs Resort & Spa: ☎(407) W-DISNEY

Disney's Swan / Dolphin Resort: ☎(407) 934-4000

Disney's Vacation Club (Time-Share): ☎(800) 500-3990

Disney's Wilderness Lodge: ☎(407) 824-3200

Disney's Yacht Club Resort: ☎(407) 934-7000

Doctors-On-Call: ☎(407) 399-3627

Dollar Car Rental: ☎(800) 800-4000

Dolly Parton's Dixie Stampede Dinner and Show: ☎(866) 443-4943

Dolphins in Depth / DiveQuest Info: ☎(407) WDW-TOUR

Downtown Disney/Pleasure Island Info: ☎(407) 934-7781

Dream Cars Unlimited Car Rental: ☎(866) 624-6396

Econo Car: ☎(800) 665-9001

El Al Airlines: ☎(800) 223-6700

Enterprise Car Rental: ☎(800) RENT-A-CAR

Entertainment Books: ☎(800) 933-2605

Eventures Unlimited, Inc.: ☎(800) 356-7891

E-Z Car Rental: ☎(407) 352-3131

Fantasy of Flight: ☎(863) 984-3500

Festival Bay Mall: ☎(407) 351-7718

First Strike Bass: ☎(888) 937-6843

Florida Mall: ☎(407) 851-6255

Florida's Space Coast Office of Tourism: ☎(800) 93-OCEAN

Frontier Airlines: ☎(800) 432-1359

Gatorland: ☎(407) 855-5496

Green Meadows Petting Farm: ☎(407) 846-0770

Greyhound: ☎(800) 229-9424

Hard Rock Hotel: (888) 322-5541

Hertz Car Rental: ☎(800) 654-3131

Hertz Gold Club Reservations: ☎(800) CAR-GOLD

Hilton Grand Vacations Club: ☎(407) 238-2600

Holy Land Experience: ☎(407) 367-2065

Horse World: ☎(407) 847-4343

Hotel Reservations Network: ☎(800) 511-5321

House of Blues Concert Info: ☎(407) 934-2222

Ibera Airlines: ☎(800) 772-4642

ICE: ☎(407) 586-0000

Icelander Airlines: ☎(800) 223-5500

Island Boat Rides: ☎(321) 544-3490

Islands of Adventure Guest Services: ☎(407) 224-4233

JetBlue Airlines: ☎(800) 538-2583

Jungleland Zoo: ☎(407) 396-1012

Kennedy Space Center: ☎(321) 499-4444

Kissimmee Billie Swamp Safari: ☎(800) 949-6101

Kissimmee–St. Cloud Convention and Visitors Bureau: ☎(407) 847-5000

LTU Airlines: ☎(800) 888-0200

Magical Midway: ☎(407) 370-5353

Mall at Millenia: ☎(407) 363-3555

Martinair Airlines: ☎(800) 627-8462

Mears Transportation: ☎(407) 423-5566

Medieval Times Dinner and Tournament: ☎(800) 229-8300

Mexicana Airlines: ☎(800) 531-7921

Midwest Airlines: ☎(800) 452-2022

National Car Rental: ☎(800) 227-7368

Northwest Airlines/KLM: ☎(800) 225-2525

Official Visitor Center: ☎(407) 363-5872

Old Town: ☎(407) 396-4888

Orange Blossom Balloons: ☎(407) 239-7677

Orlando Improv: ☎(352) 281-8000

Orlando Science Center: ☎(407) 514-2000

Orlando/Orange County Convention and Visitors Bureau: ☎(407) 363-5871

Osceola Flea and Farmers Market: ☎(407) 846-2811

Payless Car Rental: ☎(800) PAY-LESS

Peabody Ducks: ☎(407) 352-4000

Pirate's Dinner Adventure: ☎(407) 248-0590

Pointe Orlando: ☎(407) 248-2838

Portofino Bay Hotel: ☎(888) 322-5541

Putting Edge Glow-in-the-Dark mini Golf: ☎(407) 248-0700

Race Rock: ☎9407) 248-9876

Ripley's Believe It or Not! Museum: ☎(407) 363-4418

Ron Jon Surf Shop: ☎(321) 799-8888

Royal Pacific Resort: ☎(407) 503-3000

SAK Comedy Lab: ☎(407) 648-0001

Sandlake Hospital: ☎(407) 351-8500

Saudia Airlines: ☎(800) 472-8342

SeaWorld Adventure Camp: ☎(866) GO-TO-CAMP

SeaWorld Tours and Programs: ☎(407) 363-2380

SeaWorld General Information: ☎(800) 4-ADVENTURE

Shades of Green on Walt Disney World Resort: ☎(407) 824-3600

Sheraton/Vistana Resort: ☎(407) 239-3100

Silver Springs: ☎(352) 236-2121

Skull Kingdom: ☎(407) 354-1564

Skycoaster: ☎(407) 397-2509

Skyventure: ☎(407) 903-1150

Sleuth's Mystery Dinner Shows: ☎(407) 363-1985

Song Airlines: ☎(800) 359-7664

Southwest Airlines: ☎(800) 435-9792

Spirit Airlines: ☎(800) 772-7117

Summerfield Suites: ☎(800) 830-4964

SunTrust Bank: ☎(407) 237-4141

The Charles Hosmer Morse Museum of American Art: ☎(407) 645-5311

The Florida Mall: ☎(407) 851-6255

The Jesus Film Project: ☎(407) 826-2300

The Mennello Museum of American Art: ☎(407) 246-4278

Thrifty Car Rental: ☎(800) 367-2277

TicketMaster: ☎(407) 839-3900

Titanic: Ship of Dreams: ☎(407) 248-1166 ext: 3103

U.S. Astronaut Hall of Fame: ☎(321) 269-6100

U.S. Space Camp Florida: ☎(800) 63-SPACE

United Airlines: ☎(800) 241-6522

Universal Cineplex Movie Listings: ☎(407) 354-5998

Universal Orlando Resort Guest Services: ☎(407) 363-8000

Universal Orlando Resort Reservations: ☎(888) U-ESCAPE

Universal Orlando Resort Vacation Package Information: ☎(800) 711-0080

Universal Studios Florida Lost and Found: ☎(407) 224-4244

Universal Studios Merchandise Sales and Information: ☎(407) 363-8320

Universal Studios Studio Audience Info: ☎(407) 224-4233 Option #5

Universal Studios Vacations: ☎(800) 711-0080

Universal Studios VIP Tours: ☎(407) 363-8295

US Airways: ☎(800) 428-4322

US Airways Vacation Packages: ☎(800) 455-0123

Vanguard Airlines: ☎(800) 826-4827

Varig Brazil Airlines: ☎(800) 468-2744

Virgin Atlantic Airlines: ☎(800) 862-8621

Walgreens Pharmacy: ☎(800) 289-2273

Wallaby Ranch: ☎1-800-WALLABY

Walt Disney Travel Company: ☎(407) 939-7675

Walt Disney World Guest Information: ✆(407) 824-4321

Warbird Adventures, Inc.: ✆(407) 870-7366

Water Mania: ✆(407) 396-2626

Weeki Wachee Springs: ✆(407) 596-2062

WDW Golf Info and Reservations: ✆(407) WDW-GOLF

WDW Speedway: ✆(800) BE-PETTY

Weather Forecast Info (Orlando Area): ✆(407) 824-4104

Wet 'n Wild: ✆(407) 351-1800

WonderWorks: ✆(407) 351-8800

Yellow Cab Co. (Taxi): ✆(407) 699-9999

Zoom Airlines: ✆(866) 359-9666

WDW Attraction Selection Worksheet

THE FOLLOWING IS A worksheet that will help you choose which rides, shows, and attractions you and the people you're traveling with will want to experience once you arrive at each of the Disney theme parks. Place a check mark in the appropriate column next to each listed ride, show, and attraction.

The Magic Kingdom

Rides, shows, and attractions listed in alphabetical order.

1=Must see   2=Experience if time permits
3=Already experienced   4=No interest

Attraction Name	1	2	3	4
Astro Orbiter	☐	☐	☐	☐
Barnstormer at Goofy's Wiseacre Farm, The	☐	☐	☐	☐
Big Thunder Mountain Railroad	☐	☐	☐	☐
Buzz Lightyear's Space Ranger Spin	☐	☐	☐	☐
Cinderella's Castle	☐	☐	☐	☐
Cinderella's Golden Carrousel	☐	☐	☐	☐
Country Bear Jamboree	☐	☐	☐	☐
Davy Crockett Keel Boats	☐	☐	☐	☐

Attraction Name	1	2	3	4
Disney Railroad	☐	☐	☐	☐
Donald's Boat	☐	☐	☐	☐
Dumbo the Flying Elephant	☐	☐	☐	☐
Enchanted Tiki Room	☐	☐	☐	☐
Frontierland Shootin' Arcade	☐	☐	☐	☐
Goofy's Country Dancin' Jamboree	☐	☐	☐	☐
Hall of Presidents, The	☐	☐	☐	☐
Haunted Mansion, The	☐	☐	☐	☐
It's a Small World	☐	☐	☐	☐
Jungle Cruise, The	☐	☐	☐	☐
Liberty Square Riverboat	☐	☐	☐	☐
Mad Tea Party (a.k.a. the Teacups)	☐	☐	☐	☐
Main Street Cinema	☐	☐	☐	☐
Many Adventures of Winnie the Pooh, The	☐	☐	☐	☐
Mickey's Country House and Judge's Tent	☐	☐	☐	☐
Mickey's PhilharMagic	☐	☐	☐	☐
Mickey's Toontown Fair	☐	☐	☐	☐
Minnie's Country House	☐	☐	☐	☐
Peter Pan's Flight	☐	☐	☐	☐
Pirates of the Caribbean	☐	☐	☐	☐
Share a Dream Come True Parade	☐	☐	☐	☐
(Afternoon Character Parade)	☐	☐	☐	☐
Snow White's Scary Adventures	☐	☐	☐	☐
Space Mountain	☐	☐	☐	☐
SpectroMagic Parade	☐	☐	☐	☐
Splash Mountain	☐	☐	☐	☐
Stitch's Great Escape	☐	☐	☐	☐
Swiss Family Treehouse	☐	☐	☐	☐
The Magic Carpets of Aladdin	☐	☐	☐	☐
The Laugh Floor Comedy Club	☐	☐	☐	☐
Tom Sawyer Island	☐	☐	☐	☐
Tomorrowland Indy Speedway	☐	☐	☐	☐
Tomorrowland Transit Authority	☐	☐	☐	☐

Attraction Name	1	2	3	4
Toon Park	☐	☐	☐	☐
Toontown Fair Hall of Fame	☐	☐	☐	☐
Walt Disney's Carousel of Progress	☐	☐	☐	☐
Wishes (Evening Fireworks Show)	☐	☐	☐	☐
Other:	☐	☐	☐	☐
Other:	☐	☐	☐	☐
Other:	☐	☐	☐	☐
Other:	☐	☐	☐	☐
Other:	☐	☐	☐	☐
Other:	☐	☐	☐	☐
Other:	☐	☐	☐	☐
Other:	☐	☐	☐	☐
Other:	☐	☐	☐	☐
Other:	☐	☐	☐	☐
Other:	☐	☐	☐	☐
Other:	☐	☐	☐	☐
Other:	☐	☐	☐	☐
Other:	☐	☐	☐	☐

Epcot

Rides, shows, and attractions listed in alphabetical order.

1=Must see	2=Experience if time permits
3=Already experienced	4=No interest

Attraction Name	1	2	3	4
Honey, I Shrunk the Audience	☐	☐	☐	☐
Imagination!	☐	☐	☐	☐
Innoventions	☐	☐	☐	☐
Leave a Legacy	☐	☐	☐	☐
Mission: SPACE	☐	☐	☐	☐

	1	2	3	4
Soarin' over California	☐	☐	☐	☐
Spaceship Earth	☐	☐	☐	☐
Test Track	☐	☐	☐	☐
The Land	☐	☐	☐	☐
The Living Seas	☐	☐	☐	☐
Universe of Energy	☐	☐	☐	☐
Other	☐	☐	☐	☐
Other	☐	☐	☐	☐
Other	☐	☐	☐	☐
Other	☐	☐	☐	☐

The World Showcase at Epcot

Rides, shows, and attractions listed in alphabetical order.

1=Must see

2=Experience if time permits

3=Already experienced

4=No interest

Attraction Name	1	2	3	4
Canada	☐	☐	☐	☐
China	☐	☐	☐	☐
France	☐	☐	☐	☐
Germany	☐	☐	☐	☐
IllumiNations: Reflections of Earth	☐	☐	☐	☐
Italy	☐	☐	☐	☐
Japan	☐	☐	☐	☐
Mexico	☐	☐	☐	☐
Morocco	☐	☐	☐	☐
Norway	☐	☐	☐	☐
Tapestry of Dreams Parade	☐	☐	☐	☐
United Kingdom	☐	☐	☐	☐
Other	☐	☐	☐	☐
Other	☐	☐	☐	☐

| Other | ☐ | ☐ | ☐ | ☐ |
| Other | ☐ | ☐ | ☐ | ☐ |

The Disney-MGM Studios

Rides, shows, and attractions listed in alphabetical order.

| 1=Must see | 2=Experience if time permits |
| 3=Already experienced | 4=No interest |

Attraction Name	1	2	3	4
Beauty and the Beast	☐	☐	☐	☐
Disney Stars and Motor Cars Parade	☐	☐	☐	☐
Disney-MGM Studios Backlot Tour, The	☐	☐	☐	☐
Fantasmic!	☐	☐	☐	☐
Great Movie Ride, The	☐	☐	☐	☐
Honey, I Shrunk the Kids Movie Set Adventure	☐	☐	☐	☐
Indiana Jones Epic Stunt Spectacular	☐	☐	☐	☐
Jim Henson's Muppet Vision 3-D	☐	☐	☐	☐
Lights, Motors, and Action! Extreme Stunt Show	☐	☐	☐	☐
Mickey's Sorcerer's Hat	☐	☐	☐	☐
Osborne Family Spectacle of Lights, The	☐	☐	☐	☐
Playhouse Disney—Live on Stage!	☐	☐	☐	☐
Radio Disney Studios	☐	☐	☐	☐
Rock 'n' Roller Coaster Starring Aerosmith	☐	☐	☐	☐
Sorcery in the Sky Fireworks Spectacular	☐	☐	☐	☐
Sounds Dangerous: Starring Drew Carey	☐	☐	☐	☐
Star Tours	☐	☐	☐	☐
Twilight Zone: Tower of Terror 4, The	☐	☐	☐	☐
Voyage of the Little Mermaid	☐	☐	☐	☐
Walt Disney: One Man's Dream	☐	☐	☐	☐
Other	☐	☐	☐	☐

Disney's Animal Kingdom

Rides, shows, and attractions listed in alphabetical order.

1=Must see   2=Experience if time permits

3=Already experienced   4=No interest

Attraction Name	1	2	3	4
Affection Section	☐	☐	☐	☐
Boneyard, The	☐	☐	☐	☐
Conservation Station, The	☐	☐	☐	☐
Cretaceous Trail	☐	☐	☐	☐
DINOSAUR	☐	☐	☐	☐
Discovery Island	☐	☐	☐	☐
Expedition EVEREST	☐	☐	☐	☐
Festival of the Lion King	☐	☐	☐	☐
Finding Nemo-The Musical	☐	☐	☐	☐
Flights of Wonder at Caravan Stage	☐	☐	☐	☐
Fossil Fun Games	☐	☐	☐	☐
It's Tough to Be a Bug!	☐	☐	☐	☐
Kali River Rapids: A Whitewater Adventure	☐	☐	☐	☐
Kilimanjaro Safaris	☐	☐	☐	☐
Look Backstage!	☐	☐	☐	☐
Maharajah Jungle Trek	☐	☐	☐	☐
Mickey's Jammin' Jungle Parade	☐	☐	☐	☐
Oasis, The	☐	☐	☐	☐
Pangani Forest Exploration Trail	☐	☐	☐	☐
Pocahontas and Her Forest Friends	☐	☐	☐	☐
Primeval Whirl	☐	☐	☐	☐
Rafiki's Planet Watch	☐	☐	☐	☐
Tree of Life, The	☐	☐	☐	☐
Tricera Top Spin	☐	☐	☐	☐
Wildlife Express to Conservation Station	☐	☐	☐	☐

Height Restrictions for Orlando Theme Park Rides

Disney's Animal Kingdom
40" – Dinosaur
44" – Expedition Everest
38" – Kali River Rapids

Epcot
44" – Mission: SPACE
40" – Soarin'
40" – Test Track

The Magic Kingdom
40" – Big Thunder Mountain
44" – Space Mountain
40" – Splash Mountain
52" – Speedway
40" – Stitch

Disney-MGM Studios
48" – Rock 'n' Roller Coaster
40" – Star Tours
40" – Tower of Terror 4

Seaworld
42" – Journey to Atlantis
54" – Kraken
42" – Wild Arctic

Universal Studios
36" – Spiderman
40" – Back to the Future
40" – Bluto's Bilge Rat Barges
44" – Dr. Doom's Fear Fall
42" – Dudley Do-Right's Ripsaw Falls
54" – Dueling Dragons
52" – Incredible Hulk
40" – Jurassic Park

Index

Everything® You Need for a Family Vacation to Remember

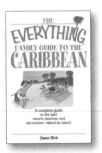

The Everything® Family Guide to the Caribbean
ISBN 10: 1-59337-427-5
ISBN 13: 978-1-59337-427-3
$14.95

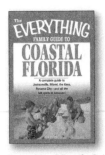

The Everything® Family Guide to Coastal Florida
ISBN 10: 1-59869-157-0
ISBN 13: 978-1-59869-157-3
$14.95

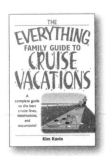

The Everything® Family Guide to Cruise Vacations
ISBN 10: 1-59337-428-3
ISBN 13: 978-1-59337-428-0
$14.95

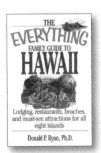

The Everything® Family Guide to Hawaii
ISBN 10: 1-59337-054-7
ISBN 13: 978-1-59337-054-1
$14.95

The Everything® Family Guide to Las Vegas, 2nd Ed.
ISBN 10: 1-59337-359-7
ISBN 13: 978-1-59337-359-7
$14.95

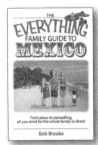

The Everything® Family Guide to Mexico
ISBN 10: 1-59337-658-8
ISBN 13: 978-1-59337-658-1
$14.95